The Nine Eyes of Light

Other books by Padma Aon Prakasha

*The Christ Blueprint: 13 Keys to Christ Consciousness*

*The Power of Shakti: 18 Pathways to Ignite the Energy of the Divine Woman*

# The
# Nine Eyes of Light

## ASCENSION KEYS
## FROM EGYPT

**PADMA AON PRAKASHA**

North Atlantic Books
Berkeley, California

Published by
North Atlantic Books
P.O. Box 12327
Berkeley, California 94712

Cover art by David Andor
Cover and book design by Brad Greene

Printed in the United States of America

*The Nine Eyes of Light: Ascension Keys from Egypt* is sponsored by the Society for the Study of Native Arts and Sciences, a nonprofit educational corporation whose goals are to develop an educational and cross-cultural perspective linking various scientific, social, and artistic fields; to nurture a holistic view of arts, sciences, humanities, and healing; and to publish and distribute literature on the relationship of mind, body, and nature.

North Atlantic Books' publications are available through most bookstores. For further information, visit our website at www.northatlanticbooks.com or call 800-733-3000.

Library of Congress Cataloging-in-Publication Data

Prakasha, Padma Aon.
  The nine eyes of light : ascension keys from Egypt / by Padma Aon Prakasha.
      p. cm.
  Includes bibliographical references and index.
  Summary: "This is the light-body guide book for the spiritual traveler. Deeply relevant to what we are experiencing in our tumultuous times today, and leading into 2012, are the ascension keys hidden in the Egyptian tradition, which served as the foundation for Egypt's awakened civilization. Author Padma Prakasha brings these nine levels of consciousness into easy and experiential language relevant to our times"—Provided by publisher.
    ISBN 978-1-55643-890-5
  1. Egypt—Religion. 2. Consciousness—Religious aspects. 3. Mind and body. I. Title.
  BL2443.P73 2010
  299'.3144—dc22
                                                                    2009033825

2 3 4 5 6 7 8 9 VERSA 17 16 15 14 13 12

# CONTENTS

Preface . . . xi

Introduction . . . 1

## 1. The Physical Bodies . . . 17

The Khat . . . 17

The Khat Scan: Scanning the Body for Healing . . . 20

Aufu: The Fleshy Body . . . 23

The Seven Elements of the Body: Flesh and Light . . . 25

Ascension Symptoms of the Second Stage . . . 29

The Third Stage: Earth Body, Human Body . . . 32

The Technosphere . . . 34

Babble: The Inner Technospheric Mind . . . 43

The Technosphere: Its Present and Its Future? . . . 45

The Technosphere Is Watching . . . 49

## 2. Ren: Name and Form—Sound, Vibration, and Creation . . . 55

Finding your Ren: Making the Mantra for Your Name . . . 57

Sound and Consciousness . . . 60

The Four Stages of Sound . . . 63

The Architecture of Ren . . . 67

The True Nature of Sound . . . 71

Portals to Innocence . . . 75

## 3. Shew: The Shadow . . . 79

The Ghost . . . 83

The Golden Shadow . . . 84

Shadow, Power, and Soul . . . 88

The Power of Aloneness . . . 90

Protector and Separator . . . 93

Remedies for Reconciling the Shadow and Physical Body . . . 96

The Djed Pillar of the Spine . . . 100

The Djed Pillar of the Spine: Gold and Green . . . 114

Shadow Myths . . . 120

Meeting Your Shew Firsthand . . . 125

The Collective Shadow . . . 130

The Mystical Shadow: Hell Realms . . . 137

Five Guidelines to Working with the Shadow . . . 142

The Essence of the Shew . . . 146


## 4. Sekhem: Power, Life Force, Bliss . . . 151

Power . . . 155

Life and Death . . . 158

Destroyer . . . 159

The Four Locks . . . 161

Ruthless Compassion . . . 163

Tantra . . . 167

## 5. Ka: Your Double . . . 173

Your Crystalline Double . . . 175

The Biophotonic Field . . . 180

The Ten Ka Memories . . . 183

Coloring the Ka . . . 189

Ka Dependency and Sexuality . . . 191

Ka Clearing Practice . . . 194

The Ka Clock: 13:20 . . . 199

Meeting the Ka . . . 202

The Divine Ka of the Egyptians . . . 203

The Ka of Asar Osiris . . . 204

Driving Your Ka . . . 208

The Cube . . . 211

The Octahedron . . . 211

The Sphere . . . 214

The Sphere of Ma'at: The Forty-two Notes on the Scale of Creation . . . 216

Spheres of Sound . . . 219

Driving your Ka: The Practice . . . 222

The Five Faces of Anubis . . . 228

## 6. Ab: The Human Heart . . . 247

Purifying the Heart . . . 249

Space . . . 253

Holy Desire . . . 255

Giving . . . 256

The Open Heart of Harmony: Ma'at . . . 258

The Hall of Two Truths . . . 260

The Journey of Balancing the Heart . . . 263

Judgment . . . 268

Embrace . . . 277

The Dance of Ma'at . . . 280

The Forty-two Doorways to the Open Heart . . . 284

## 7. Ba: The Soul . . . 293

Your Soul Purpose . . . 297

Soul Form . . . 300

Appreciation . . . 303

Gratitude . . . 303

The Divine Child . . . 308

Ba: Vehicle for Ascension . . . 311

## 8. Sahu: The Immortal Body—Light in Form . . . 317

Sahu and the Physical Body . . . 321

Sahu and Akhu . . . 325

Hu . . . 326

Black Light . . . 329

Sahu Tantra: Merging Form and Formless . . . 330

Sahu and Galactic Center . . . 333

Sahu: The Hymn to the Great Heart . . . 339

## 9. Akhu: The Shining One . . . 345

The Sound of Surrender . . . 349

The Indestructible . . . 351

The Khat-Akh . . . 354

Light Body and DNA . . . 356

## 10. The Holographic Interface . . . 359

Looking through the Khat/Aufu: The Physical Body . . . 360

Looking through the Ka: Holographic Interface . . . 361

Looking through the Shew: The Shadow . . . 363

Looking through the Ab: The Heart . . . 364

Looking through the Ba: The Soul . . . 366

Looking through the Ren: Name and Form . . . 367

Looking through Sekhem: Power . . . 368

Looking through Sahu: Universal Body . . . 369

Looking through Akhu: The Shining One . . . 370

Acknowledgments . . . 373

Resources . . . 375

Further Reading . . . 377

About the Author . . . 379

# PREFACE

*The Nine Eyes of Light: Ascension Keys from Egypt* is nothing new; rather it is a resurfacing of wisdom that has been guarded throughout the ages, precisely timed to resurface when humanity is responsible and ready enough to receive it and work with it practically rather than just intellectually. When the time is ripe for the revelation of these hidden teachings, people appear to reveal them for the benefit of others and to continue the lineage. These treasures of wisdom are accessible when someone has reached that level of consciousness in order to decode it. To decode it requires that you listen and see in innocence, without your own filters, which is to "see" without your own thoughts, thus entering the holographic universe.

This book is written from experience of the Nine, deep meditation, study, and teaching. In India this experiential education technique is known as *smriti* and *sruti:* learning through traditional initiation and wisdom, and then receiving experiential wisdom through direct revelation once one has mastered a certain aspect of the tradition. Authentic revelation in meditation becomes the mainstay of any mystical tradition once the initiate is clear and starts to teach the tradition. The more one teaches, the more that is given by the lineage to share. Additional research and reading from both modern and ancient experts on the Egyptian lineages came from many sources, which are listed in the Further Reading section at the end of the book.

Before I could teach others, I had to fully experience. My experiences in the mystic arts began with my initiation at age two into the Brahmin lineage, then reading the Bhagavad Gita at age four, followed by the Koran, the Bible, and the European philosophers by age seven. At age twenty-one an experience of God Consciousness changed my life forever. Shortly after this, I was initiated by the Divine Mother in India, which opened the doorways to becoming initiated into Saivite Tantra through the head priests of Kedarnath, Badrinath, and Pashupatinath, and into the Sama Veda through the Arunachala Sampradaya, among others. Perhaps the most powerful initiations came through Sri Om, an awakened teacher in the Lineage of Tsongkhapa and Maitreya in London, after which I sat in *samadhi,* the highest form of meditation, and the goal of meditation, for two months.

In 2006 I completed several initiations into the Order of Melchizedek and the Gnostic Christian Lineage, the successor to the ancient Egyptian Lineage, in the south of France, and I wrote my first book, *The Christ Blueprint* (North Atlantic Books, 2010), shortly followed by *The Power of Shakti* (Inner Traditions, 2009). This was followed by the culmination of a ten-year-long process of Egyptian initiation, marked by a successful departure from the Duat, or underworld, in Egypt. This is the requirement in Egypt for teaching the Nine Eyes of Light, so after the initiation I was able to write this book.

Writing about the subject required years of immersing myself in and becoming each of the Nine Eyes. Before I could write a word to accurately express what these states of being are and provide a map for you to effectively immerse yourself in the Nine Eyes, I went on sojourns to over sixty countries, allied with much journeying in the inner worlds. These journeys involved the deepest forms of sitting meditation and shamanic ritual in sacred sites, delving deep into the light and shadow of tantric relationships and living in the contrasts of nature and the city, exploring the depths of the body, shadow, and the power of the life force, light force, and holographic communication, all combined with immersing myself in sacred geometry and sound aligned to the healing of the heart and soul.

The revelation of this information to humanity is urgently needed, for as we race headlong into 2012 and beyond, more and more of us are experiencing strange and unknown "ascension symptoms," or evolutionary changes in our biology and consciousness as we change rapidly and as the earth also changes rapidly. The tools to navigate through these strange and "new" phenomena that modern science and many sacred traditions cannot explain are found in holographic tools and ways of being that are gradually being reintroduced again to us all. Humanity is maturing in these last days before 2012 and beyond, and as enough people reach the emotional and spiritual status of an adult rather than a teenager, more and more of this timeless wisdom can emerge.

Today, all the mystical traditions are opening the doors to their secrets in order to accelerate transformation in those who genuinely desire it and are committed to doing the deep inner work required to accomplish this noble goal. To become initiated into a genuine mystical tradition over time means one's life changes drastically, and one can receive, through the four stages of the science of Ren, or vibration, all the accumulated wisdom of that lineage from thousands of years.

Many Egyptologists may wonder why there is little reference to the afterlife in this book. Truly, this wisdom is a guide for the living rather than the dead, as this is how it was originally used. In the accelerated times we are living in, the realms of life and death are becoming more readily available to everyone in the collective consciousness. These steps in the journey of the soul, known as the rungs of Jacob's Ladder or the states of the *bardo* mentioned in both the Egyptian *Book of the Dead* and the *Tibetan Book of the Dead,* are stages we can experience and move through while living. Hence this book is about embodiment of the Nine, here and now.

There are many teachings and techniques from the Egyptian tradition that are being used without being understood, and only as pieces of a larger whole. This not only lessens the effect of these tools but sometimes may even lead to harm for the people practicing them. This misuse of power and tools is a legacy of the latter part of the Egyptian tradition, when it became corrupted by those seeking power for power's sake and for selfish ends and means. These people lived to get rather than to give, practicing the darker arts to acquire more wealth, power, prestige, and status. This part of the Egyptian legacy is one that dogs all those who seek higher wisdom on this path. The key to complete this learning is contained in the body of light known as the shadow, or Shew.

The Nine Eyes, while being a source of great wisdom and spirited philosophy, are very experiential means to immerse oneself in higher consciousness. Most Egyptologists have done a lot of useful research without going really deep within themselves, which is where the deepest research occurs in the sacred wisdom lineages. Thus some of the wisdom contained within these pages is already known in the world, and some of it is not. In reading this book, I invite you to explore the missing pieces found through the experiential connection with the Nine Eyes of Light, so that you can properly use the Ascension Keys from Egypt.

Padma Aon Prakasha
Hawaii, January 19, 2009

# INTRODUCTION

Have you ever considered why the Egyptians have had such an impact on humanity? Egypt is the heart and soul of the Western world, culture, and civilization. Its wisdom has been covered over and forgotten, lost in the dust of history and power, consigned to ancient memories of wonder and awe at their achievements, intense scholarly debate about how and why they did what they did, and superstition among spiritualists and magicians.

It is by following the lead of Egyptian genius that many of Europe's greatest cathedrals were built, with entire cities like Paris, Washington, London, Philadelphia, and even Nashville, Tennessee, built on Egyptian guidelines. Much of the mathematics, alchemy, astronomy, astrology, and philosophy that were revered in Greece came from Egypt, and even the American dollar bill has the Egyptian eye and pyramid emblazoned on it. In a more spiritual vein, Christ and many of his disciples were taught in Egypt, blending these teachings to create Gnostic Christianity and the basis of the Knights Templar. Much of the goddess culture was last established on a large scale in Egypt as well, before the downfall of the matriarchy there. One could say that the Egyptians have connected to, shared common wisdom with, and impacted our culture on almost every level.

The basis of the Egyptian art and science of the soul are the Nine Bodies of Light, also known as the Nine Eyes of Light. These Nine are the ruling principles that form the basis of Egyptian spirituality, culture, art, and their worldview: how the Egyptian culture navigated through life. To the Egyptians, just as we have our physical body, so too do we have eight other bodies that are just as real in other dimensions or wavebands of vibration. These additional nonphysical bodies allowed them to sense, feel, navigate, and create the many astounding feats of technology, science, and spirituality that still baffle us today.

These Nine are interpenetrating subtle bodies—layers of light, thought, feeling, color, and vibration emanating out from the physical body into our planet, our solar system, and into the galaxy, back to the Source of where the Egyptians felt their home was: Sirius, Orion, and the Galactic Center. According to Egyptian legend, there are nine crystal spheres underneath the Sphinx that map out the Nine Bodies, or nine lenses of consciousness. This can be readily seen by simply drawing nine different concentric circles, with each lens of consciousness having its own specific formation within these circles. Each circle can be accessed to provide a way of interpreting reality, a way of navigating through life.

In practice, many of us are naturally using some of these lenses, but not all of them. Many other traditions hint at the workings of these light bodies, however the Egyptians were perhaps the clearest and most precise in applying how they worked in order to build an awakened civilization, something that is particularly pressing at this point in history as we race into 2012 and beyond. This basis for an awakened civilization arises from a holographic understanding of how life operates, and how we function as part of much larger holograms, such as our planet, solar system, and beyond.

The Nine effectively create and operate a holographic reality. Source uses all of the Nine at different times to experience and create reality. This is also how we are designed to operate: as a cocreative part of Source here on earth, understanding that we are each composed of the Nine. You come to "know thyself" by experiencing and becoming the Nine in physical form, with this journey leading into every facet of human and divine experience so that you may become "A Shining One," a temple for Hu, or spirit, to live in.

Each one of us is composed of the Nine different bodies or eyes.

Each of the Nine is in relationship to the others, and when all Nine become known to each other through the lens of the conscious soul, they create a fully conscious human being. In this full communication of all bodies, one could become enlightened, embodying spirit or light in matter, thus ending the cycle of reincarnation. This was the crux of the Egyptian mysteries: for the soul to become fully embodied and realized while on earth in the physical form.

Egyptian alchemy is the root of Gnostic Christian wisdom and practices. It is an alchemy in which the baser, grosser elements of mind, body, and spirit are refined to realize and embody conscious, empowered, loving wisdom. As this alchemy progresses through the Nine Bodies, a soul body, an immortal body, is created that carries individual consciousness beyond physical mortality into the immortal bodies of light.

This realization of subtler and subtler layers of refined conscious expression and unconditioned love was the basis of Egyptian civilization at its height. This alchemy of consciousness harmonized the physical bodies with the psychic and spiritual bodies to allow the full descent of light into physical form. Igniting these Nine within you was the journey of life and death: uniting them all was to enter into eternal life.

The Egyptians interacted with nature in a more precise and advanced way than we do today based on the understanding of how the Nine apply to all life, from the most esoteric to the most mundane. Universal laws are simply that, universal laws, and the Egyptians lived in harmony with these laws as a living language or key. This language was used to establish two-way communication with the archetypal forces of creation, all of which were observed and seen in nature, and then applied to human affairs. In our forgetting of these natural laws that underpin our planet, our bodies, and our energy fields, we have forgotten the essential nature of who we are.

In gaining deeper knowledge about anything or anyone, it is wisest to access information about its principles on the causal level, from which the form is derived. Once this is understood and harnessed, we are able to influence and work harmoniously with the principles that underlie both nature and ourselves. Within all Nine lie our DNA codes, mapped by the forms of the sixty-four DNA codons, known in Egypt as the families of the sixty-four Neters, or Egyptian gods and goddesses. These Neters are the principles and powers of nature, the living archetypes and harmonics of light that weave together the threads of the fabric of life.

This union comes about through a process known to the Egyptians as Osirification. This process unites all parts of one's self into a living temple that could allow Source to be present within it. According to the Egyptian texts, we then have a complete body, where every internal organ and limb is in its perfected state. Such a being possesses their power; their heart-soul; their Ka, or double; and "their spirit which was the head of all the spirits."[1]

This uniting entails many changes in consciousness, for if we change one body of light, then all of them change, linking up like cogs in a machine to work in unison. This then was the purpose of the Nine: to create a unified body-mind and heart-soul based on an infinite framework of sacred geometry that connected the individual to the eternal and immortal bodies of light, creating a new type of human being.

## The Reawakening

The reawakening of this timeless Egyptian wisdom came about in the 1920s through the discovery of the boy king Tutankhamen's tomb. In his golden sarcophagus, he was surrounded by eight different concentric rings of artifacts, sacred objects, crystals, and funerary articles. These rings represented the Nine Eyes of Light and how we pass through

1. E. A. Wallis Budge, *Osiris and the Egyptian Resurrection* (Mineola, NY: Dover, 1973).

these layers in life and in death. These layers of feeling, form, shadow, sound, light, sacred geometry, perception, earth connection, power, love, and intuition create all the different aspects of our selves. In the massive public interest surrounding the mysterious boy king, last of the spiritual pharaohs, the art and science of this ancient wisdom reintroduced itself to the world.

As we head into a new era for humanity, this wisdom is being reintroduced through various teachings, piece by piece. This era we are living in now has been prophesized to be the revealing of all secret teachings that have been held back and kept in the hands of a few. The Egyptian sacred sciences are a big part of this revelation. All of these teachings are starting to come together now to reveal how to create a "new" type of human being—new to us, but known well to the Egyptians.

When the foundation of all these teachings are understood and harnessed, the interconnections allow us to understand and map the path to peace as the basis for an awakened civilization. Each of the light bodies connects and serves the others and can only truly be understood in this web of relationship. Without the knowledge and experiential awareness of all of them, the Egyptian Pathway is incomplete, like a puzzle with pieces scattered everywhere.

## Life Viewed through the Nine Eyes of Light: A Multidimensional Reality

The basis of the Egyptian worldview was the Nine lenses through which the Egyptian priesthood, nobility, spiritual masters, and pharaohs viewed and created reality. The Nine Eyes of Light are like nine unique lenses through which we can view life. It is like putting on a pair of glasses through which you can see life differently and create multidimensionally. In the following section, we will preview how each of the Nine gives you different perspectives on how to live, create, and shift your consciousness on guidelines used by one of the most advanced civilizations the earth has ever seen.

## Lens One: Khat/Aufu
### Your Physical Body and Its Connection to Light

If we see just through the first lens of Khat and Aufu, the body and flesh, we become identified only with the body and its needs. We think we are the body alone and follow what the body wants, which is simple, fixed, animalistic, and mechanical. We live purely in the three-dimensional world, influenced by the media, peers, fashion, and what others think of us. If we start to connect the body and flesh with the other bodies, our thoughts, words, and deeds turn to the connections between the body, the heart, and the earth and our relationship to it. We can either honor this relating, looking after the temple of the body and anchoring our connection to Mother Earth and her voice and wisdom, or we can abuse it, disregarding the ecology of the earth and our bodies.

As we step into the open, healed, and connected physical bodies of Khat and Aufu, we feel their transparency and ability to hold light. We absorb smells and feelings, feeling them with our body voice. This new openness and sensitivity allows it to be informed by the other bodies of light. Our blood, brain, and spine changes to allow in more light, and the many ascension symptoms we experience allow the body to change, sometimes gracefully and sometimes not.

## Lens Two: Ka
### Your Holographic Connection to Soul

Run on charisma, presence, personal power, intuition, and genetic resonance, Ka is our foundation for health and dynamic well-being, as well as being the first form of the soul that is most easily and readily available to us. The Ka body holds our vital connections to life, our family resonances and their gifts and lessons, and what we emanate, attract, and manifest to us. It is the first step into our multidimensional self and our energy field, or aura. As the holographic double of our physical body made of light, Ka connects us to the Gaian web of life and provides the interface to our Ba, or soul. Earth memories, past life memories, and deep healing lie in the Ka, for our task is to integrate the soul with the Ka so we can bring the soul into the etheric field of the Ka and then into our physical bodies.

As we use the awakened Ka, our power and ability to manifest rapidly increases. Everything comes to us. Our dynamic engagement with life in joy aligns with our ability to move, inspire, and transform others. We become connected to the web of life, and we create fluid, open, and clear relating with our families, friends, and lovers. There is no stickiness of attachment, needs, expectations, and projections, as we are self-contained, self-empowered, and connected to the earth and the stars.

## Lens Three: Shew
### Your Shadow as a Guardian to Source

The Shew, or shadow, explores and integrates our own subconscious as well as the collective unconscious. It is the reflection of the world you create. We see the deepest parts of ourselves and bring them back together again after being fragmented. To work with your shadow means connecting to the soul and the other bodies of light. Part of this is a mystical journey, part of it transpersonal, part very human. As we explore, embrace, and integrate the shadow as a valuable part of us, it opens up all our bodies to receive more light. We hold ourselves unconditionally and embrace ourselves as we are.

The essence of the shadow or Shew is accessed when we go on the deepest journeys into the emptiness of our bodies and cells to bring back the gold of awakening and physical transformation. We see the devil and god at the same time. Then our soul can be free.

## Lens Four: Ren
### The Science of Vibration and Sound

Ren activates when we see the languages and structures of creation through vibrational arts such as sacred geometry, light, sound, color, and shape. Looking at life through these languages means we look at how our thoughts manifest our reality. In Egypt, your soul name and the names of all things had a deeper significance, as each object was seen to have many layers of meaning to it—the physical form, the color form, the geometric form, and the emptiness of all forms. This multi-dimensional way of viewing every form allowed the Egyptians to create sacred architectures and multidimensional ways of using the powers of sound, vibration, and sacred geometry in order to enter the deepest states of consciousness and to utilize this in their technology.

As we start to surf Ren, we listen less to the words of others and more to the tone and pictures, and to the deeper meaning, that their words create. When we go deep into Ren, we experience samadhi, the highest form of meditative bliss.

## Lens Five: Ab
### The Human Heart Conscience, the Heart's Desires, and Heart Intelligence

The Ab, or human heart, allows us to accept and embrace all that we are, becoming an honorable human being with an open, pure, and cleansed heart. Ab is the seat of the still, small voice within; it is our conscience and our heart intelligence. As we come to think from the heart and feel with the mind, the domination of the mind and ego shifts and we become heart-centered. We feel others suffering, and do something about it from the place of sharing. Our moral values, the selfless and unconditionally giving aspects of our selves, arise from the human heart or Ab.

As we heal our mortal human heart, we give freely and generously with kindness and compassion. Our narcissism and possessiveness dissipate as we open the shutters of the heart to reveal the pain, loneliness, abandonment, and isolation there. We become heart-centered after healing the heart, so it becomes light as a feather and able to merge with the soul, Ba.

## Lens Six: Ba
### The Soul: Connector Between Individual and Universal Soul

Seeing through the soul, or Ba, we connect with, integrate, and embody our soul into our daily lives. We live and manifest our soul purpose, light and knowing with love. We feel the absolute purity of our soul, and learn how to integrate spirit and matter. Ba is the part of us that is free like a bird, soaring without restrictions, able to travel into many realms without being trapped by anything or anyone. It is inner freedom. It manifests uniquely for all of us, as it has no dogma or conditioning. As we fly with our soul Ba and the divine child, we play with our life and love more and more.

## Lens Seven: Sekhem
### Willpower, Bliss, and the Fuel for Love

Living through the life force, or Sekhem, we merge the power of life force with our soul to create transformation and open the gateway to Source. The power of kundalini merges with your personal power to create dynamic change, inspiration, and the ability to serve as a con-duit for life force to flow through you unimpeded to transform your-self and others. When Sekhem is unleashed, its fiery power dissolves all obstacles in its way, ruthlessly dissolving all attachments, needs, and obstacles to awakening.

As we start to use Sekhem more, we enter more bliss and love in a deep, almost drunken way. We use our willpower to accomplish things, to blast through any and all obstacles in our work or our own healing and growth. We use the power of fire to manifest, activate, and ignite.

## Lens Eight: Sahu
### The Immortal and Universal Body

Living in the immortal universal body of Sahu is to merge with the breath of Source, to become an embodied human being, with your feet grounded in the earth, heart open, and head clear and wide open to the stars. As we enter Sahu, our blood, bones, spines, DNA, brain chakras, and physical structures all change as we become more crys-talline. The body transfigures in order to contain the higher frequen-cies of light, and we actually become a different type of human being—genetically, structurally, and consciously different from most other humans.

Sahu is the transfigured Self. In Sahu, you connect and embody your own God form, your own Neter. Your own guide, or Higher Self, becomes embodied within you. It is no longer outside of you. One could say that the Higher Self descends and you become this. Sahu is the "last evidence of physical form, and the first evidence of eternity."[2] It is where the temporary human form merges with the infinite. In Sahu, our physical bodies become lighter than matter. We live on earth

---

2. Normandi Ellis, *Dreams of Isis* (Chicago: Quest, 1997).

but with a cosmic awareness. The extraordinary becomes normal as we become a holographic being.

## Lens Nine: Akhu
### The Shining One

Living in the ninth lens of Akhu or God Consciousness, we live as a conscious cocreator with God, yet if we spend too much time in this state we cannot function in the three-dimensional world. It is hard for the physical body to hold more than a drop of God in its fullness. This state is beyond words as it encompasses all life, and that which is beyond manifest creation. The full power of Source manifests in us through the union of all Nine, with Akhu directing and guiding all nine. In Akhu, we simply sit, and be . . . nowhere to go, nothing to do, no one to be, save a Shining One.

## The Holographic Nine Eyes of Light

The experience of the Nine is not linear: it is holographic, and we can move from one to the other without judgment or hierarchy. There are many ways to understand what a hologram is. The standard definition of a hologram is that it is a photographic picture composed of a great number of small parts, all of which contain the picture as a whole. When we break up the hologram into many pieces, we end up with many small but complete pictures of the whole. Poetically speaking, we can take the ocean as another example of a holographic reality: since the ocean is nothing but water, we can say that the whole ocean is contained in every drop of water found within it. Similarly, a ray of the sun contains the sun itself. A similar situation we find in a seed: the entire structure of the tree is contained in it, and all future generations of the tree are contained in a single seed.

An equally striking example of a holographic reality we find in ourselves: every cell of our body contains the complete information about the entire mind-body system. Each of the hundred billion cells that make up the body contains the complete version of the original DNA that was the source of the entire body! If we understand what the tiny lines on the palm of our hand have to say, we would understand our past, our present, and our future. If we really know what these tiny spots in the iris of our eyes have to say, we would know the whole condition of our mind, body, and soul. If we understand what the tiny sparks of light in the sky have to say, we would understand the past, present, and future of our lives and of creation as a whole. All light we see from these stars has already died in some reality.

Each level of creation is an expression of the whole of creation, interpreted through a different vibratory lens. All life forms, all human beings, all animals are a portal point into the total process: each being contains the whole. Here we see that the ancient dictum "As above, so below" is just one application of a more general holographic principle: "As it is anywhere, so it is everywhere." Only a 360-degree openness of awareness will sponsor the refined perception that is needed to see the tree in the seed, the future in the present, or the universe in a grain of sand.

As we integrate the holographic reality and union of the Nine, multitasking in multiple dimensions, not just in one, becomes commonplace. One looks after the children, does the cooking, pays the bills, and sees holograms at the same time. Time is seen as a form of energy, virtually unlimited. We grasp the essence of a subject, article, or book quickly and access instant knowing. We recognize other languages without having learned them by working with their energy fields. Symbols and art are used to access other dimensions to download knowledge and increase our feeling-intuitive capacities. What once took months to learn can now happen in days as we learn on multiple levels simultaneously. Our creativity increases exponentially in multiple fields as we tap into vast pools of wisdom lying latent within us that once were separate but are now united.

The Nine predate and gave birth to present-day subtle body categories, serving as a map of holistic or holographic communication. What is explored in this book is an easy-to-understand experiential knowledge of the original Nine lenses. Trying to box them into astral body, causal body, and so on can seem to be an appropriate and even wise move. However, even though they incorporate some aspects of these modern definitions, the Nine go well beyond contemporary descriptions of the subtle bodies.

The Nine are different language streams that coalesce to create a whole human being. To see through all Nine and integrate them is to experience life through Nine different viewpoints, attitudes, feelings, perceptions, and states of consciousness at different moments in order to reveal the whole you. Most people do not see through more than three or four of these lenses during one day; to see through all of them is to be a multidimensional being. The Nine are shining keys for us today to learn how Egypt managed to maintain a multidimensional civilization in remembrance and communication with all parts of itself, with all parts of its body.

This wisdom has become fragmented and misunderstood, despite the best efforts of modern scholars, Egyptologists, and spiritualists to piece it all together. The Egyptian light bodies are the culmination of love, power, and wisdom that can only be known by experiencing them and their shadows as well. Research, writings, and records give some clues and pointers, but it is only by going into the Egyptian arts and sciences of sacred geometry, breath, sound, light, meditation, and conscious use of sexual energy that one can understand what the Nine are and how they interconnect. One has to live them day-by-day, experiencing their unique voices, lessons, and nuances, and how they work in your life and relationships.

**Ancient rock carving of Anubis on the coast near Sydney, Australia. Elements of ancient Egyptian wisdom have been found preserved from the Americas to Australia, India, and Tibet. Egypt's global seafaring culture spread its wings far and wide indeed, and as you can see from this rock carving on the Australian coast, about two hours' drive north of Sydney, evidence of its influence is everywhere.** (Photo taken by Padma Aon in Central Coast, Australia)

In working with each of the Nine, we work on each part of ourselves. Having this map to guide us, we can journey and embody our highest potentials, as the ancient Egyptians did and many still do today. Some of the greatest beings on earth have used this wisdom in order to transform themselves, such as Thoth, Akhnaton, Magdalene, Isis, Pythagoras, Leonardo da Vinci, John the Beloved, Christ, and many others. So you are in good company.

Any potential for transformation occurs through awareness. When reading through each of the Nine, be honest, open, and aware. Which of the Nine do you still need to encounter, heal, and merge with fully? What resistance do you have to embodying each one? What do you need to let go of to do this? The awareness that all Nine exist within you, to be used at any time, means that you become a fully responsible cocreator with Source, on earth, here in your body, now. At their height, this is how the Egyptians lived, creating an awakened civilization from the basis of the Nine Eyes of Light. May it bless and illuminate you into creating a new and brighter future for us all.

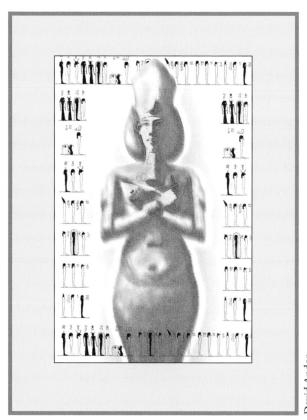

David Andor

# ~1

## THE PHYSICAL BODIES

### The Khat

The Khat is our physical form, the body that decays after death, the mortal, temporary part of us that was preserved in mummification by the ancient Egyptians. The forces of destruction are constantly working in the physical form of the Khat, as it slowly, gradually dies a little every day. Khat is an empty vessel waiting to be filled with the animating forces of the other bodies of light. At conception, it is the forming of the body; at death, it is the shell left twenty-one grams lighter by the departure of these bodies of light into formless realms.

*Khat* also means "form" or "appearance." It is the temple of the soul that the light bodies come to temporarily inhabit to learn their lessons, to complete their cycles of experience and incarnation. *Khat* is an ancient word also meaning "the fire altar"[1] within the sacred temple, the altar where offerings were made with chants, incense, and the offerings of one's physical self to something far greater than one's physical self. Khat is the place where change occurs for the temple of our spirit to land on earth.

The hieroglyph for Khat is the fish. The fish is the beginning of life in the womb. As we start life as a fetus in the womb, we resemble a fish

---

1. Normandi Ellis, *Dreams of Isis* (Chicago: Quest, 1997).

that then changes into many forms as it runs through the whole gamut of our DNA: snake, monkey, ape, elephant, and reptile, eventually becoming our human form. The fish is our first form as it first arises out of the primal swirling azoic soup of formless creation coming into form. In Egypt, the growing fetus in the womb created from the first spark of life and the lifeless corpse left after the light bodies have left the flesh, which is the leaving of this spark of life in physical death, were intimately connected.

The saying of Christ, "I am the beginning and the end," connects to this wisdom, for in the beginning of something also lies its end. In the beginning of life lies its potential end. In the beginning of a birth, be it of a project, career, or relationship, its end can also be seen, as both lie inherent within each other, and both are inextricably interconnected. From the moment of birth we also create death; from the moment of our birth, we are a death waiting to happen.[2] We do indeed die a little every day as the body decays gradually yet inexorably. Death and life are the twin forces propelling us into our human form of the Khat, for as sperm and egg merge, they die in order to create a new life. And we arise, born from the womb, through death creating life.

The Egyptians noted that as we journey through life and death in our physical bodies and our spiritual path, there are three different levels to the physical body functioning as it absorbs more light and transfigures itself into a vehicle of light. As it transfigures, it raises its vibration and ability to hold more light that comes through the interface of the Ka body, our holographic connector and the first form of the soul, which is closest to us. Each of these three stages is felt as a shift with distinct symptoms, many of which are known today as "ascension symptoms." We have much to learn from the ancient Egyptians'

---

2. Normandi Ellis, *Dreams of Isis* (Chicago: Quest, 1997).

knowledge of this as they too went through what many are going through today in their evolution, mapping out the three main stages of it.

The first stage is the Khat, or corpse, the body that is living and eating unconsciously. Khat has simple and fixed needs, has no self-consciousness, and is a machine, a system driven by mechanical functions, biological drives, sensations, and reactions. Khat is the light body of the Ka body slowed down in vibration so that its light becomes matter. Khat is actually a state of (un)consciousness, characterized by identification with the body's needs alone. In identification with the Khat, one sees themselves as "I am the body," divorced from the desires of the other bodies of light to infuse the physical body with their presence, which typically occurs through silence, nurturing quiet time, body-mind–spirit yogas, and meditation.

In a Khat-only reality, one's priority is to feed the body and emotions, with the shadow's need for distraction and hedonistic pleasure dominating one's life to ease the burdens of the mundane reality of work. Socializing and the fashionableness and ease of a place to eat, rather then the quality or light of food, are important. Looking outside for answers, attaching to the latest trends, finding heroes to emulate and adore are all part of this phase of consciousness. The herd mentality in choices of food, clothes, company, and ideas all keep one on the surface, rooted to the idea of body being the primary reality, with body consciousness and appearances dictating the way one moves in the world.

Connected to this is victim consciousness, allied with getting a fast fix to any problem, which arises from the need to escape the mundane nine-to-five worker-bee reality forced upon you by your not knowing what you are here for. Too many movies, too much TV, Internet, text messaging, and games are all designed to keep us distracted from the rich inner worlds we all possess and which are the greatest source of fulfillment. This phase of consciousness is literally the corpse: the light in Khat's eyes is minimal, and beings in this state can almost be seen as dead, as their life force is so slowed down.

## The Khat Scan: Scanning the Body for Healing

Unlike the CAT scan beloved of modern medicine, the Khat scan enables you to scan the physical body, organs, and spine for wounds, black spots, blemishes, and distortions that stop the life force from flowing through you at full strength. The Khat scan is a powerful healing meditation that is used to heal and dissolve blocks in the physical body by connecting to and using the energy of the subtle bodies to heal the physical. In this, you need no external technology—just your relaxed attention and focus.

Begin by lying down. Take a few deep breaths and center into your core, your *hara* or womb a few inches below your belly button. Relax and breathe. Feel the outline of your physical body, from the tips of your toes to the top of your head. Become aware of a gentle flow of energy caressing the outline of your physical form.

Now tune into your left palm chakra, and feel the sensation there. Feel the pulse, warmth, and energy flow. Now you are going to use this energy like an X-ray device in order to scan and see what is happening in your physical body, organs, and joints. You will be checking especially for wounds, black spots, blemishes, and any unusual distortions. Feel the energy like a laser that is clearing while it is scanning. From your left palm chakra, slowly bring this X-ray scanning energy up your arm, into your forearm, left elbow joint, upper arm, left shoulder joint, left collarbone, and down to end gracefully at the heart.

What do you notice?

Now tune into your right palm chakra, and feel the sensation there. Feel the pulse, warmth, and energy flow. Again, you are going to use this energy like an X-ray device in order to scan and see what is happening in your physical body, organs, and joints, checking especially for wounds, black spots, blemishes, and unusual distortions. Feel the energy like a laser that is clearing while it is scanning. From your right palm chakra, slowly bring this X-ray scanning energy up your right forearm, right elbow joint, upper arm, right shoulder joint, right collarbone, and down to end gracefully at the heart.

What do you notice?

Now tune into your right foot chakra, situated right in the middle of your foot. Feel the sensation, pulse, warmth, and energy flow. Again, you are going to use this energy as an X-ray scanning device to check for any blemishes. Feel the energy like a laser that is clearing while it is scanning. From your right foot chakra, slowly bring this X-ray scanning energy up through your ankle joint, knee joint, up the back of the thighs, to the hip joint, ending at the base of the spine. Relax and breathe into here for a moment.

What do you notice?

Now repeat for the left foot chakra.

Now tune into the alta major chakra, situated at the back of the head near where the spine and brain meet. The alta major is a major entry point and portal for Shakti, or life force, to flow. Feel the sensation, pulse, warmth, and energy flow here. Feel the energy like a laser that is clearing while it is scanning. From this chakra, slowly bring this X-ray scanning energy down through your spinal column, coming to rest briefly at the kidneys and adrenals, the base of the spine, the anus, the perineum, and coming to rest at your genitals.

What do you see and notice?

Now follow the inhalation of your breath up the front of your body into the third eye, between the eyebrows. Visualize this flow as a milky white color, and bring this flow to your throat, then down to your heart, riding the breath and the natural flow of energy. Do not push or force it, as all you are doing is tuning into what is already happening, not trying to make anything happen. Alternate this energy between the two breasts, feeling the flow like an infinity loop, between left breast and heart, and then right breast and heart.

From this infinity flow, slowly bring the X-ray energy down into your stomach, then lower into the pancreas, and then to the belly button. Here you see a wheel with four spokes emanating out from it. From the right-hand spoke, follow the energy into your liver. Feel the energy like a laser that is clearing the organ while it is scanning. What do you see? On the left-hand spoke, follow the energy into your spleen. What do you see? On the upper spoke, follow the energy into your heart. What do you see? On the bottom spoke, follow the energy down into your genitals. What do you see?

To end this Khat scan, follow the X-ray energy from this four-spoked wheel up to the heart and the throat, to end at the third eye. Feel the energy like a laser that is clearing while it is scanning. Breathe and relax into the third eye, integrating and absorbing what has happened in the last twenty to thirty minutes.

Ask yourself what you can do to heal the blemishes you have seen. You may also write down what you have seen so there is more clarity on what you need to do to heal and connect the physical to the other bodies of light.

*To accelerate your physical and psychic healing, the MAP, or Medical Assistance Program of the Spiritual Hierarchies, can greatly assist by helping to reconnect and heal the physical body to the other bodies of light if you ask them to do so. They can greatly accelerate any physical healing after you have done the Khat scan. This information is available online and in the book* MAP: The Cocreative White Brotherhood Medical Assistance Program.

# Aufu: The Fleshly Body

The second stage of the bodily transfiguration is the Aufu or Af, which means flesh, the organs, skin, blood, and bones that create the temporary vehicle for the soul to work in. Aufu is the fleshly covering of the physical body form. The hieroglyph for Aufu is three small bits of flesh. Many hieroglyphs use three to indicate many or multiple things. For example, the hieroglyph for gold is three grains or seeds.[3] In the case of Aufu, the three chunks of flesh represent the three different states of the physical body as it undergoes the process of transfiguration on the pathway to ascension, which to the Egyptians is the embodiment of the soul into the physical body.

The Egyptians viewed the body as a sacred tool and evidence of spiritual attainment. The lightness and clarity of the body's systems were a mark of spiritual growth, with the flesh being an indicator of how much light a person had brought into their physical body. The Egyptians did not denigrate or mutilate the body but rather worked with it so it could fulfill its purpose of transfiguration and light absorption. In this absorption, the body's task of transformation was seen as completed, with the full embodiment and grounding of the individual soul into full connection with the trinity matrix of Khat, Aufu, and Sahu, the universal body of light.

By itself, Aufu lacks consciousness, but it "transmits sensory images to the other bodies that act as food for the soul," as Normandi Ellis eloquently puts it. To feed Aufu properly is to eat foods that are life-nourishing and green, such as raw organic living foods and juices,[4] good water, exercise, and breath. In Aufu's case, we are what we eat. Aufu also adores nature, the greenness and abundance of life.

---

3. Normandi Ellis, *Dreams of Isis* (Chicago: Quest, 1997).
4. For a good book on this, read Mikio Sankey, *Support the Mountain* (Kapolei, HI: White Mountain Castle, 2008).

The connection of the Shew shadow to the Aufu can be seen in the dieting fads of today's world. Why can some people not lose weight no matter what diet they try? And why do they put the weight back on even when they do lose it? This is because the shadow wants nurturing and feeding: if the shadow is left untouched and unnurtured, then it will cause binge eating, wrecking any diets designed solely for the Aufu. If one deals with the shadow Shew first, and then goes on a diet, the repressed urges and desires of the Aufu-Shew connection will not rear up, and weight can be lost effectively. Perhaps this form of holistic nutrition that includes the shadow and the other bodies of light will become part of the new health paradigm.

Aufu is here to provide us with the pleasures of this world through the senses. If the body is not well maintained and looked after, our appreciation of this world will diminish, and we will be less able to appreciate the beauty in nature and ourselves. The more we look after Aufu and its close link to the shadow Shew, the more we can create graceful and light-filled bodies in harmony so that the flesh too can be enjoyed, just as the Egyptians did.

If Aufu is looked after, the heart is lighter and can make more peaceful, centered, and heart (Ab)-centered decisions. Aufu also affects the mind and emotions, as by having an open and nurtured Aufu we love ourselves more, which is when Aufu sends out signals of contentment and peace to the other bodies, weaving them together in biological harmony.

# The Seven Elements of the Body:
# Flesh and Light

*From self comes space, from space, air, from air, fire, from*
*fire, water, from water, earth. Out of the earth —plants,*
*from plants, substance, and from substance or anna comes*
*the embodied being.*

—Taittiriya Upanishad

The second stage of bodily transfiguration manifests as we delve deeper into the constituent parts of the physical body, which are the seven elements of the body and the thirteen joints of the body. In both the Indian and Egyptian cultures, many similar qualities and teachings[5] are shared. In yoga, astronomy, language, and spiritual teachings, both cultures resonated remarkably, prompting many to believe that both cultures originally shared the same religion in Atlantis. As the legends share, priests and priestesses fled from the sinking continent, taking their teachings to far-flung places such as Central America, India, Tibet, and Egypt, where much evidence still remains to this day of these teachings. What was originally one teaching then became many strands of one teaching, which are now being woven back together to provide a holistic understanding of consciousness and evolution.

In ayurveda, the five-thousand-year-old Indian science of health, well-being, and living wisely that has parallels to Egyptian health and medical knowledge, there are seven elements to the fleshly body. The first is *anna,* or the food we eat. The more we eat live organic foods and supplements that nourish and enhance the body-mind–spirit connection, the cleaner and more vital our whole system is. Drinking clean

---

5. To read an extensive commentary on these similarities, see Robert E. Cox, *Creating the Soul Body* (Rochester, VT: Inner Traditions, 2008).

water, preferably alkalized, helps the physical body to become neutral pH-wise, between acid and alkaline, allowing more light into our cells. The typical Western diet is acidic, which obstructs cell health.

Food is converted through chewing into *rasa,* a liquid form that nourishes all the tissues, organs, and systems of the physical body. What remains after this process is *rakta,* red blood cells that oxygenate the tissues and organs. The surplus of this is then transformed into muscle or *mamsa,* which protects the vital organs, maintains physical strength, and is responsible for the movement of the joints. Deep tissue massage, Rolfing, and other forms of yoga and exercise help maintain the spiritual connection and alignment of muscle to spirit and light.

Deep tissue massage on the thirteen joints of the body helps to open and release vast amounts of light and wellness deep into the cells of the body. This opening and release of the thirteen joints of the physical body allows it to align to the Ka body of light. These thirteen major joints or articulations in the body are: the ankles, knees, hips, wrists, elbows, shoulders, and the atlas bone in the neck.

These joints are reservoirs of energy that can be harnessed and utilized through spiritual practices found in tai chi, qigong, Egyptian yoga, and Tibetan energy practices. Our body's thirteen major joints or articulations connect our physical geometric structure to the geometric structures of the other bodies of light through movement and measure. In massaging and opening the thirteen joints, we release the crystalline deposits, stresses, and armoring around the joints, allowing more space into them. It is in this space that the light bodies can activate more into physical form, opening up spaces within the physical body to allow in more light.

Opening the thirteen articulations brings deep grounding, vitality, and empowerment to you. Each joint or articulation is aligned in pairs, so two ankles, two wrists, and so on are massaged and resonated over a two-hour period. Any conscious and talented deep-tissue bodyworker can work with this template.[6]

As the thirteen joints open and release to allow in more of the bodies of light, this released energy transforms into *meda,* or fat, which maintains the lubrication and smooth operation of the body system. This in turn transforms into lymph, which affects the blood and the body's immunity to disease. The lymphatic system is the body's sewage system, as it carries away the toxins, chemical and food additives, environmental pollution, and stress into the lymph nodes, which traps and neutralizes harmful substances if they are kept clear. As all seven elements of the body are interconnected, the clearing of the lymph nodes and channels also helps ease chronic muscle and joint pain and tension, as well as reducing the amount of fat on a person's body, leading to weight loss.

A fast way to clean and clear the lymphatic system is to have a few sessions on a lymph machine using the Electro-lymphatic Drainage Method, which uses sound frequency to open the lymph channels eight times faster than manual lymph drainage. In two sessions, you receive sixteen manual lymph drainage massages. As the lymph channels open, cleanse, and drain out, more joy, peace, clarity, and physical well-being result, especially if the lymph in the liver is cleared, in which case you will need a colonic afterward to clear the acid and bile found in the liver's lymph ducts. In addition, lymph-clearing activates and cleanses the blood cells, sending out seeker cells to destroy viruses and pathogens.

On a deeper level, lymph is a vital source of *prana* or chi used in advanced yogic meditations to deepen and maintain higher states of embodied consciousness within the body. The highest refinement of the lymph is into cerebrospinal fluid, the fluid responsible for bathing the brain and spinal cord in liquid.

---

6. For more, see Chapter 5 on the Ka.

Lymph then connects into *ashti,* or bone, for the skeletal frame. There are many ways to realign the deformities of the skeletal structure through atlas realignments, Network chiropractic, deeper forms of yoga, and depth bodywork. (See the "The Djed Pillar of the Spine" in Chapter 3 for more details.) Bone further refines into *majja,* or bone marrow, a source of prana and one of the focal points for advanced meditation, tai chi, and martial arts practices. Adept Yogis can tap into this energy at will, and once they have mastered it they can easily throw another person across the room using this focused force. This is because marrow maintains the motor and sensory impulses as well as the central nervous system of the body, which initiates, maintains, and adjusts our behavior on many levels. Infrared saunas actually heat the body from the inside out rather than the outside in, with the result being cleansing from the bone marrow itself, which then emanates outward into the other elements.

When the physical bodies transform to allow in more light, the bone marrow also produces different geometries in the blood cells, which transform into being octahedral in nature. The final refinement in our bodies of the foods and substances we ingest is through *sukra* or semen and ovum, the fluid force involved in generating new life. This fluid is highly prized, as once conserved and refined its vital force of light can lead to the connection of the earth element and the physical body to many of the other bodies of light. As it is refined and conserved, these fluids become hot to the touch, as they contain an enormous amount of energy to create with.

# Ascension Symptoms of the Second Stage

This state of consciousness is characterized in those who are moving beyond the appearance of the body and finding deeper meaning in foods to eat and activities that nourish body-mind and soul. Ecological concerns start to become important, and social meetings will include these issues. It is no longer taboo or laughable to discuss deeper things in life, and one will actively engage with these activities, deepening their inner space and becoming more aware of how the body and spirit operate. Good relationships become more important, and the need for this becomes a high priority as one starts to develop a deeper relationship with one's own self.

You operate from the heart and its knowing and begin to discover your soul purpose, starting to put it into action through your body's actions. Food and drink to nourish the body become more of a priority; eating out and socializing become less frequent as you look within and to nourishing company to feed you. Spiritual activity connected to the body becomes a routine and discipline as you actively feel the connection between body, mind, and spirit and discern what is right to put inside you and what harms you.

It is at this point that you will start to experience "ascension symptoms." As you take in more light, increasing your vibration and frequency, your physical body and emotions can experience illness because the body and the chakras are increasing their spin rate to assimilate this increased light. To release the debris and toxins that arise from this, the body will go through many stages and symptoms, which can be both confusing and worrying. These symptoms are a natural effect of the physical body and the Ka body (the first form of the soul closest to you) of light meeting and merging, which accelerates the process of you becoming a multidimensional being.

Some of these ascension symptoms can include:

- the need to sleep a lot and at strange times, and strange fatigue
- depression, anxiety, snappiness, panic
- a sudden loss of a job, relationship, and stability
- inability to do certain things that you used to do; inability to do anything at all
- loss of friends and relationships
- can no longer tolerate old patterns, people, or situations
- constantly changing direction and plans; extreme fluidity
- memory lapses and confusion regarding time and schedules; loss of identity, time, and space; becoming a "space cadet"
- sudden crying and being on an emotional roller coaster
- disturbing dreams
- weight loss or weight gain
- feeling out of body as your body identification shifts
- body tremors and shaking
- feeling like you are going insane for no reason at all; even suicidal feelings
- creating nightmare scenarios in order to move through deep issues
- shadow issues arising fast
- sensitivity to heat and cold, hot sweats, and cold shivers
- heartburn, digestive issues
- emotional overload, extreme mood swings for no reason
- extreme sensitivity to others, to sounds, to feelings, to environments
- headaches and blurry eyes, achy jaw, pains in the back of the neck
- revival of childhood ailments like emotional hurts and physical complaints
- old memories flashing back into your consciousness at strange times
- cold feet and hands, sudden temperature increases and decreases
- nervous breakdown
- aches and pains flashing through your body for no apparent reason

This can all be treated with meditation, rest, exercise, and healing treatments. Take time to nurture your body and spirit. Take sea-salt baths; make time for relaxation. Do nothing. Trust the process. Drink lots of water (with lemon juice if you are detoxing), eat healthy live foods and juices, and cut out alcohol, sugars, processed foods, and too many cooked foods.

Do cleanses like a liver cleanse, kidney cleanse, colon cleanse, and blood cleanse. See what vitamins and herbs you need to rebalance and reboot the body. Do some colonics. Move your body more. Breathe. Look into your shadow. Do not take artificial or prescription medication. Take liquid crystals to connect to the devic or nature worlds, which will help ground light into the body. Ask for assistance from the universe. Do not ignore repetitive symptoms; they often pinpoint an underlying blockage. As Aufu integrates more light into itself, it is important to honor the process and allow it to continue. You will know what to do, and if not, do nothing.

There comes a time in evolution when the physical body becomes the key to soul embodiment. Visiting a medical intuitive, or simply using your own intuition to discern the more advanced remedies and supplements you need, has never been easier, and with these advances we can evolve more quickly. Much of the ancient sacred traditions' ways of cleansing and accelerating the physical body's absorption of light is now being made much faster due to advances in technology and understanding.

Supplements such as monatomic or white powder gold (www.-zptech.net, www.ambayagold.com), trace minerals, cleanses (www.arise-andshine.com), and liquid crystals (www.theliquidcrystals.com) all help the body to transform and allow in more light. As we will see, however, this is all dependent on your shadow and the degree to which you have recognized, healed, and integrated it.

# The Third Stage: Earth Body, Human Body

The physical body is made physical by the earth and the earth element. The earth holds the key to the full embodiment of light in the physical in the third stage of embodiment. As the physical body coagulates all its cells, bones, muscles, tissues, and structures into form, it is earth that weaves it all together. We connect to this through the root, heart, and earth-star chakra.

The earth-star chakra is located just below the feet, as a golden star. When it is fully activated it connects to the core of the earth, and the spirit of the earth itself. As this occurs, it sends a web of light around the entire planet, creating your own link to the web of life and the matrix of Gaia, connecting your physical body through the heart to the earth.

As we deepen further in this realization, we come to feel that the earth is our whole physical body, not just our human form. We realize that the perfected human form is held in the blueprint of Gaia itself. In Egypt, the stone of turquoise was seen as the connector of humans to Gaia, the voice of the earth itself, and it was revered as the creator of the human body. By aligning to turquoise, we align to the creation of our physical form and the innate sacred geometries that our form possesses. These forces all meet in the human heart and are modulated by the soul-star and earth-star chakras. To actually speak to the spirit of the earth is to speak with the essence of your body, the body that is earth. This is an expansion of what we are used to, but nevertheless it is what we are and what humanity is remembering and becoming once again.

Earth is the final step in manifestation from the other elements; it is the element that is the ground of all the elements and the causal food for substance. Earth is the completion of all the other elements, holding the blueprint of all the other elements, the culmination of all their evolutionary efforts. Earth is our food, the supporter, nourisher, and caregiver of us all, the very cause for living beings, the ground, the foundation so that we may exist. Without earth, all the elements and the possibilities that they hold for creation would be circulating aimlessly without the possibility to create form, to manifest, to serve a purpose. Indeed, we come to earth from the formless in order to imprint ourselves onto the world.

> The element earth is the glorious end of one cycle where the absolute stands as the glorious beginning on the other side. The element of earth is glorious because it is only through earth that all things of the world are created.[7]

We connect the physical body to the earth element through the heart, the heart that is in tune with nature, our biology. The easiest place to access this energy is at sacred sites relatively untouched by people that lie in the heart of nature. The best place *now* to access these energies lies over the southern hemisphere, specifically over New Zealand,[8] where the ozone layer is thinnest, and where we are being bombarded by cosmic rays, light, and new information untouched by humankind's manipulations, electromagnetic and technospheric pollution, and energetic thought-forms and ideological constructs that have been built by a few well-meaning but ignorant men (without women) over the last few thousand years.

These incoming energies have not been felt on earth for many thousands of years, and there are many sites that hold this energy of pristine purity felt as a magnetic intensity in the heart. This can be

7. Shankaracharya Saraswati.
8. Also India, due to its unique gravity and morphic resonance of many thousands of enlightened beings present there over many thousands of years, and thousands still being there.

overwhelming, so pure and deeply resonant are the vibrations that connect the heart to the earth and to all people, felt in the whole body. The experience is felt in the heart as powerfully purifying, opening and releasing, opening our eyes to what lies beyond time, space, and the mind. We realize we love life.

Earth is the bearer of our foundation and the seed of all potential energy, the original wholeness from where life arises. Thus we have to keep our root chakra fed and nurtured through exercise, sexual healing work, an inner security and foundation, an abundant attitude, and intimate close relationships, the primary ones for the root or earth element being soul family, intimate ones, friends, and the earth itself.

In aligning to the earth's frequency and Khat, we experience and anchor a deep sense of humility. This humility gets infused into us at a bodily level; it is as if the heart and the body merge with the earth, where we come from, and where our bodies will crumble back into. Perhaps this is why many indigenous earth-centered peoples, like the Native Americans, are so humble and so earth-connected. They have realized the connection that their body is part of the earth, and align to that every day. This is a very particular frequency that every indigenous group recognizes: the earth heart. It is what they trust, and what is for them a universal language, as it comes from the earth, not the mind.

Think about the earth element and what it means to you. See where you are satisfied in your life, and where you feel you could have more, or less.

## The Technosphere

The Egyptians did not have to contend with one energy field that only we have today in the twenty-first-century world. This new electromagnetic field, which has only been in existence for five hundred years, is one that dominates all our lives, interfering with all the physical and

**The billions of communications happening worldwide every day.** (Courtesy Jim Channon)

psychic bodies we have, and that is now threatening to take over our planet: the technospheric matrix.

The globalization of information and communications technology, allied with the media, Internet, and 3G mobile phone networks, are cloaking our planet within a maze of electromagnetic noise, interference and pollution, wireless signals, microwaves, radio waves, cell phone signals and transmitters, among many others. Combined with the one hundred billion communications a day that occur as we talk, text, e-mail, radio, and surf the Web through landlines and satellite signals, the earth is becoming a ball of electromagnetic activity the likes and effects of which have never been experienced before.

The technosphere in the twenty-first century surrounds our terrestrial home of Gaia, the world of natural organic processes of the five elements in harmony called the biosphere. It is through our Ka bodies that we connect to the biosphere, but this connection has been diluted and in some people severed by the artificial sheath of the technosphere. In other words, the technosphere has literally created a new energy body around the earth, one that billions of people are connected to and influenced by. It interacts with the other energy bodies to create a new, purely artificial electrical wave fields around the human energy field and Gaia's energy field.

This artificial sheath weaving itself over the face of the organic, natural earth is a self-perpetuating mechanism. So indispensable has it become that now technological ease has become a part of our daily lives, while nature itself has become increasingly unnatural to us as we spend less and less time outdoors and more and more time with our computers, games, cell phones, and machinery.

The technosphere found its origins in the printing press, the industrial revolution, and the modernist movement, which was founded on a utopian desire to create a better world with technology the key to achieving social improvement and with the machine as a symbol of that aspiration.[9] Modernism fueled a fundamental disconnection from nature—from the organic order of things, from the cyclic process of nature and the feminine psyche, and from its laws, which create natural limits. By having natural limits, we can open to the unlimited.

By placing ourselves beyond and outside nature, by feeling we are superior and here to dominate and claim nature, to manipulate and control her constituent parts, imagining somehow that the whole will not suffer and can take care of itself whatever we do; we abstract life. The technospheric urbanized mentality is now almost completely out of tune with the key principles underpinning the health of organic life on earth.[10] Our children are growing up with little if any knowledge and experience of nature. Their experience is one of TVs, computers, cell phones, and video games seen from the inside of the house. They have already lost the connection they had since they were born, as it has been submerged under a cacophony of electrical and brain-wave interference.

_____

9. Exhibit on modernism, Victoria and Albert Museum, London, 2006.
10. Prince Charles.

Natural principles create harmony. Biology shows us that in all living things there is a natural and innate movement toward harmony. Organisms self-organize themselves into an order similar at every level of scale, from the molecules in your little finger to vast ecosystems like the equatorial rain forests. Life seeks and finds balance organically. This means there is coherence to the complexity of organic life on earth at every level of scale. All parts work together in a coherent way to produce a harmonic whole. And when it is in balance, when there is harmony, the organism is healthy. When this is not so, as in the case of the technosphere, the living organism suffers "dis-ease." It gets sick.

The rational, technologically driven, and secularist approach is completely opposite to the felt, intuitive sense of our interconnectedness with nature, which includes the realm beyond the merely material. In disconnecting ourselves from outward contact with nature, our inner nature also suffers. Our bodies become wired into the technosphere instead of what they are designed to be wired into: the biosphere, and the organic, more feminine web of life. The artificial web of life has taken its place for many, leading many to think that a new form of hybrid human—part human, part wired-in technobot—could arise. This could happen sooner than you think.

In cutting ourselves off from nature, we cut ourselves off from what we are, affecting our vitality, our health, our family connections, and our communication with other dimensions and realities. Losing connection to the environment and nature creates a big imbalance in the way we see the world. Humanity's natural tendency to consume leads to a deep dissatisfaction, as no thing can fill the hole that we try to fill, no matter how much we consume, no matter how much we try to fill the gap within us by getting things outside of us. Our tendency to consume is heightened by the worldview that we, as humans, are the center of the world, operating with an absolute right over nature.

This is far from the truth and natural order of things. In technospheric arrogance, we lose our humility and connection to the spirit or voice of the earth, instead imposing what we feel is right onto nature. Our mental ideas are not what nature wants and lives by. All the forms that Gaia wants to be built on her are already held in the Gaian mind, known as the "Dreaming of Gaia" in many traditions. This vision has been listened to and seen by many indigenous societies.

Listening to this voice, seeing what the Gaian mind has already placed into our landscapes, is accessed through the humble heart that listens and acts on Gaia's voice. Gaia in her wisdom was here long before us and will continue to be here long after us. To listen to her and see her forms in our landscapes is to defer to her. This does not mean we live in a technology-free age; it means that we work with nature and then use technology to help manifest the Dreaming of Gaia.

Many well-meaning people have conceived their idea of what Gaia needs. This is generally not what Gaia needs, which is why few new earth-based communities have really flourished and bloomed, as too many egoic agendas divorced from Gaia's voice abound in people's ideas of what they "think" is right for Gaia. Only Gaia knows what is right for her, and in following this voice we reach our own highest potentials and the embodiment of all the Eyes of Light.

## The Technosphere

*There is no great virtue in being well adjusted to a profoundly sick society.*

—Jiddu Krishamurti

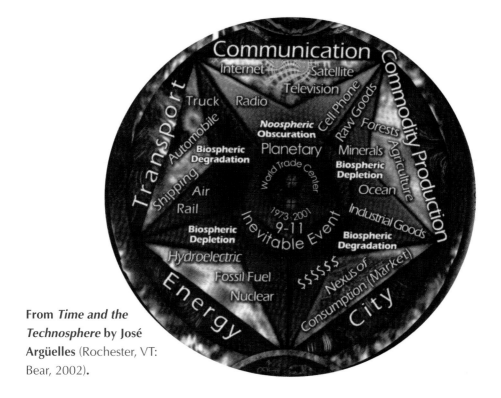

From *Time and the Technosphere* by José Argüelles (Rochester, VT: Bear, 2002).

The technosphere works in three main ways:

1. **Outer:** the outer skin of the technosphere is seen in the oil industry, commodities industry, the military industrial complex or "war machine," with the transport network being its veins and arteries. This kind of industrialization and globalization has led to the organization of cities and artificial environments for humans to cluster into, away from nature, and genetically modified foods that separate us from natural disease-free sources of energy.

   The drive for profit and the manipulation of money that is created from nothing that in turn leads to the issue of scarcity that drives prices up artificially is the motivating factor in the technosphere. Our current monetary system is an elaborate sham that depends on debt to govern its existence, binding many into a hidden form of slavery and control. Governments rise and fall by this manipulation of debt and control, and government links to the largest corporations mean they work hand in hand to maintain and control prices and the money supply. This control manifests in the political, social, economic, and environmental spheres. The creation of this worldwide economic empire is well documented in the *Zeitgeist* documentaries to chilling effect, as well as in the book *Confessions of an Economic Hit Man*.[11]

2. **Translator:** the translator of the technosphere is the corporate- and government-controlled media. Media of all kinds, from the Web, news channels, TV, the media from Hollywood, the papers you read, the text messages on your phone, are all examples of this form of communication.

3. **Inner:** the inner equivalent in our brains is uncontrolled electrical signals known as the monkey mind or mental chatter, seemingly random streams of thoughts in the mind that dominate many people's waking existence. This "babble" of thoughts and reminders from every direction dominates this mind. The nearest outward equivalent is gossip, talking too much, and distracting oneself from any form of silence or aloneness. Interestingly enough, it has been scientifically documented that spending forty-eight hours in nature clears the mind, allowing deeper brain wave states to arise and stillness of mind to be experienced, even without any structured meditation activity.

As we enter the twenty-first century, humans have created an expression to collectively bring awareness of the power of perception into focus. This is the media simulacrum, where media in all its forms has

---

11. John Perkins, *Confessions of an Economic Hit Man* (San Francisco: Berrett-Koehler, 2005).

become the tangible, immediate expression of mass consciousness thought. Television, the Internet, film, music, books, magazines and newspapers, radio, and billboards all compose a living simulacrum, a mental interface that large numbers of the global population are daily engaged in. It shapes, infiltrates, and dictates the thoughts and expression of a populace, infusing and reflecting our dreams, a mirror that reflects back the entity of the mass consciousness.

Where is the line that divides? Do we create it, or does it create us? What feeds this media mirror? On one level it is the sophisticated use of archetypal symbol, the knowing strike of image, soundtrack, and sound bite by those who seek to meld the media to their personal or collective advantage, feeding on the energy and electricity of human emotions and the drive of acquisition, status, power, money, fear, and desire. The advertising industry in particular specializes in the distillation of image and sound as "trigger points" that will get results—that is, get you to believe in and buy their product. Individuals who have mastered the media embody archetypal symbolism in order to transmit to millions. For example, through the decades pop stars like Madonna feed on and reflect the changing faces of the mass consciousness feminine, expertly manipulating images, sounds, and neural linguistic cues.

This is because only 7 percent of what we say is understood through words. Thirty-eight percent is through voice modulation, and 55 percent through body language. On the phone, 23 percent is understood through words, and the rest through voice modulation or feeling. So if we want to understand another's full range of communication, we have to feel with both these qualities.

Today, however, "the mind is working at such a pace because of modern lifestyles that face-to-face communication is found to be slow and wanting."[12] With SMS texting, phones ringing, the short attention span

---

12. Priya Devaraj, *Times of India,* March 2005.

influenced by watching TV and playing computer games, cursory e-mails pumping out information, our communication seems to be evolving, but the actual depth of communication is decreasing. Not much of what is being said is actually being heard. There is precious room left for deeper interaction due to this decrease in sensitivity, with the art of listening to feeling and tone sacrificed to the rapidity of information transmission. We are becoming information rather than the feeling, the higher experience that created the information in the beginning. In losing touch with the source, the cause, we are becoming the effect.

The technosphere works by keeping the mind fixed into the banal, the mundane, the details and minutiae of life, the problems and issues of living in the third dimension that then dominate other dimensions of experience and can then exclude other ways of being. The technosphere is the external manifestation of the monkey mind, an endless stream of thoughts and anxieties, lists of things to do and how to behave properly that keeps babbling in the background of your head space. The physical body fuel for this are unhealthy, processed, acid-forming chemically and genetically modified foods that when combined with pharmaceutical drugs keep the physical body in a kind of stasis mode, unable to communicate or feel all parts of itself and the voice of the body's wisdom.

Another part of the fuel for the technospheric matrix mind is the sexual impulse looking outside of itself for a sense of gratification and fulfillment in another, fueled by personal needs and inner holes and wounds that are then easily manipulated by the media and the advertising machine. This can then push one into desiring more money even when you have enough, amplifying the desire for possessions and status symbols. Technology helps to share this message, all filtered through the ancient laws of how an empire rules and controls the mass mind: through food and entertainment, which in ancient Rome was bread and the circus, and now is credit and the TV. Again, economic reality is manipulated by leaked news reports and media manipulations that create the rise and fall of the economic empires of false credit creation.

All of this excludes any form of inner journeying, any form of meditation, any form of questioning that looks outside the box, any form of inquiry that questions the status quo. Any kind of looking within oneself for answers, rest, or nurturance becomes externalized, for in the technosphere nurturance comes from the outside in the form of a pill, food, TV, drugs, alcohol, or sex. This is the state of the collective consciousness.

# Babble: The Inner Technospheric Mind
## A Typical Technosphere-only Day

In the technospheric vibration, humans tend to look but do not see. One can get so focused on the banal, the mundane, the everyday, that one can forget about everything else. Most importantly, one can tend to focus only on one's own self, desires, hopes, needs, and expectations, for the technosphere is not a selfless way of being unless it is connected

**From a Morgan Stanley Bank circular sent to its customers in 2007.**

to the other bodies. In the technosphere *only,* one can get trapped in a bubble of self-reflection, of selfish action, of survival. Here you can see and hear only what you want to see, what conforms with your own views of life.

A typical technosphere-only day would start with a man reading the newspaper while eating a genetically modified breakfast. As he travels to work listening to the news and playing with his PDA, answering e-mails and phone calls, a stream of same-sounding electronic pop music drones on his radio, and work problems and irritants cloud his thoughts. As he sits down in his office, watching the Dow Jones index flash past him in a blur of numbers and code, he starts to pursue the contract he has been working on that will cut a thousand jobs in order to automate his boss's factory. He sighs and signs the deal. Swimming in a sea of words makes his eyes tired and his mind dull.

He yawns and rubs his eyes as his boss comes in. "Yes, sir, of course, sir, how may I help you?" At lunchtime, he walks along with thousands of others through the concrete streets eating a tasteless sandwich made with special genetically modified tomatoes. Coming back home in the smog of traffic he scratches his chest and coughs, wondering why he has been wheezing recently. "I must go to the doctor—the air here is terrible." Of course he never will, for time is money in the technosphere from nine to five.

As he settles to watch the news on TV for the fifth time that day he feels the glow and hum of the TV lulling him, numbing his brain. A friend calls and says, "Let's go for a drink and watch the football game." Several drinks later, the day is forgotten. Time to start again.

The simplest way to avoid being caught in the technosphere is to connect into nature and listen to the still, small voice within, set against the background of incessant mental chatter. Going beyond the mental chatter of thought requires a bridge of vibration, a gateway across the waking and dream states. In Hebrew tradition all the sounds that a person hears during his life continue to vibrate within his consciousness following the death of the body,[13] like clanging coins or rattling seeds in a gourd. The nature of this "static" or mental chatter can be compared to the inner disturbances experienced by someone trying to meditate on a crowded street. In order to rid the soul of this debris, it is shaken in the *kaf ha kela,* the catapult. Hebrew sages say that "two angels stand at each end of the world and toss the soul from one to the other," with these two opposing forces trying to rid the soul of its accumulated psychic dust by putting it through a kind of cosmic centrifuge until only pure consciousness remains.

Were this treatment not administered to the soul, it is believed it would be unable to silence all the sense images, noises, and mental chatter that are carried with it from this world and mode of communication into the next, and the soul would then have to wander in the world of Tohu (confusion and emptiness) forever.

## The Technosphere: Its Present and Its Future?

Cold technology and the spread of its support systems are moving so fast because of our ransacking of nature. In Native American teachings, this ransacking is directly equated to the cutting down of trees. As the trees are cut, they go from the vertical to the horizontal plane, creating a different energy in the biosphere. As the trees hit the earth and bounce, as nature is cut and sold to support our ever-increasing military, industrial, global transportation and communication networks, it creates a frenetic energy, a more active culture, a culture more in need of externalizing, producing, and using more technology. This occurs because the balance is no longer there between nature and people.

---

13. Zalman M. Schachter.

The introduction of 3G high-data Internet, video, and computer phones and their large-capacity transmitting and receiving towers is one of the main instruments for the creation of a wired-in world. The volume of extra signals being transmitted is akin to a twenty-lane high-way of radio signals and waves passing through the center of every major city in the world every day, bombarding everyone all the time with microwaves, other radio waves, TV signals, wireless Internet con-nections, and so on. These invisible highways of electromagnetic pol-lution are literally changing our thought processes, gradually yet inevitably, as we biologically adapt, as mammals do, to working and incorporating them as part of our daily lives, habits, and routines.

This ascension of technology is becoming the answer to all our prob-lems and even the answer to death itself in the form of cryogenic freez-ing, organ transplants, immortality elixirs, and new experiments to transfer consciousness into computer hard drives. When everything of value is found outside our selves, and when technology holds the answers to our evolution, allied with the speed and spread of artificial intelligence, there is only one chilling but logical conclusion: the body itself will become part of this cyber-artificial construct and electronic web, as seen in the film *The Matrix*.

In humanity's wish to create new forms of life that combine both, the microchip—the building block of the technosphere—is the key to this merging. The microchip has the distinction of "being the first prod-uct mentioned in the Bible"[14] (Revelation 13:17), where it is stated that "no man will be able to trade without the mark of the beast in his hand." The first major step toward this was through José Delgado's experi-ments in the 1960s where a bull was implanted with a microchip trans-mitter and stopped dead in its charge. This experiment and its present day expression is the culmination of all technospheric evolution, the

14. Jake Horsley, *Matrix Warrior* (New York: St. Martin's Griffin, 2003).

culmination of all human technological development that first started with the use of rational communication.

This culmination of technology becoming part of the human form is now happening, bolstered by the U.S. government through the Food and Drug Administration's approval of microchip insertion into the human arm. As Reuters reported on October 14, 2004,

> A computer chip that is implanted under the skin won U.S. approval for use in helping doctors quickly access a patient's medical history. The VeriChip, sold by Applied Digital Solutions Inc., is placed in the upper arm in a painless procedure that takes minutes. About the size of a grain of rice, the chip contains a patient's identification number that corresponds to health information in a computer database. A handheld scanner can retrieve the patient's number from the chip, which emits radio waves when activated.

Proponents hope doctors will use the technology to find vital information about someone who is unconscious or having trouble communicating in an emergency situation. The FDA's approval of the VeriChip for medical records paves the way for alternative uses described by the manufacturer's CEO as "authentication for electronic commerce" via identification. This means anything like phones, credit cards, and being tracked by Global Positioning System (GPS) technology, which is now so sophisticated that it can easily differentiate between locations as close as your kitchen and your bedroom so that you can be tracked all day and all night.

According to the company,

> VeriChip is a device that can be used in a variety of security, financial, emergency identification, and other applications. Once inserted just under the skin, the VeriChip is inconspicuous to the naked eye. A small amount of radio frequency energy passes from the scanner

energizing the dormant VeriChip, which then emits a radio frequency signal transmitting the verification number.[15]

This twenty-first-century technology was originally developed for the pet and cattle industries to keep count of animals. In 2005, Wal-Mart tested a similar technology in Texas called Electronic Product Code (EPC). According to Katharine Albrecht, a leading campaigner against the use of such Big Brother technology, "In the post 9/11 world, we are racing down the path to total surveillance. The only thing missing to clinch the deal has been the technology. This may fill the gap."

The first wide-scale test of the chips and how they can be used to track humans and all their information was already successfully carried out in Iceland from 2001 to 2003, when a thousand Icelanders were successfully monitored by GPS over a yearlong period after having chips inserted into their arms.[16] In alliance with the media and the other aspects of the Matrix, this chip technology could easily be in place within three years worldwide.

The technosphere has a definite purpose: to serve as a catalyst, a point of tension. In any state of heightened tension or friction there is a greater possibility of transformation as well as a new creation as we are accessing deep emotions and energy in this stretching. We have to stretch and challenge ourselves in order to really grow, to reach our full potential. The ways that this stretching, or additional tension, is occurring is obvious on a planetary scale: ecological crises, wars, terrorism, mass extinction of species, loss of nature, pollution, mass media controls over public thought and opinion, and personal upheavals and transformations. All of this is designed to wake us up to what is happening so we can do something about it in our own way.

---

15. VeriChip press release.
16. *Sunday London Times,* 2001.

The technosphere is a chrysalis constructed by our own thoughts, fears, desires, and subconscious, preparing us for the next phase of evolution—the next wave. Its dissolution can happen once we have learned and mastered the lessons from it, which is when it will have served its purpose. The Matrix is the training ground, which Jesus himself exhorted us to "not get lost in, for it is only a way station, the in-between stage to heaven and the higher worlds." In essence, we are now rapidly externalizing and manifesting the collective thoughts and subconscious of humanity through thousands of years, through these memes and technologies, in order to experience something new.

## The Technosphere Is Watching

In today's world, with the proliferation of digital cameras, music recording devices, home film studios, YouTube, Facebook, the Internet, CCTV, and reality TV programs, we are constantly watching ourselves all the time, constantly recording everything that we as humans are saying, doing, and thinking, all over the world. From the events of 9/11 to the activities of indigenous people in Papua New Guinea, from how Joe Average lives his life in New York to how a group of strangers behaves when thrust together to live side by side in a Big Brother situation, we have a unique window into the world where we can now see much of what is occurring on earth all the time.

In this 24-7 culture, the human mass consciousness is constantly on display, witnessing and observing itself through a lens—a lens of consciousness. Today we can see who we are and witness our actions on an unprecedented scale. In effect, we are witnessing our own subconscious expressed in the external world for us to see and potentially learn from. Now we can see who we are, and maybe who we might wish to be, with all parts of the mass psyche on display.

This information circuit or information loop is accelerating, revealing and bombarding more and more information to all of us about ourselves. We are witnessing the darkest sides of our subconscious becoming fully revealed to ourselves through the media. It has been speculated that this information loop of the information age, where we are exposed to an almost endless supply of data, is accelerating exponentially. From the time of Christ, circa 1 AD, to the nineteenth century, information flow doubled with the invention of the printing press; from the nineteenth century to the twentieth it doubled again. From 1900 to 1940 the information flow doubled again, and yet again between 1940 and 1970, and again by 1985, until 2009, where information flow is doubling every five months. By 2012 this information loop will become virtually infinite, predicted to double every second, faster that any human can possibly assimilate, process, or understand.

The logical conclusion to this information age is that humanity will then literally become information, starting a new cycle of history where humans no longer exist as individuals but rather as nodes and carriers of information, hooked into the giant circuit board or net of knowledge known as the universal web. This can be the artificial Web or the organic web of life. Very few people will be able to do either, unless they are working holographically using the Nine Eyes of Light.

What can we do with all this data? There must come a point when something breaks—when we stop hoarding and collecting data, when we cease to have new experiences from the data we are collecting and maybe start to use it all in a new way. The only logical conclusion is that we will stop collecting and start transmitting data.[17] Just before this point is reached, it will seem as if our reality has just become a repetition of old experiences, old patterns, and old information, recycling old data and

---

17. This acceleration process is dependent on the four modes of gathering and storing information and communication through the technology of the human form.

perspectives over and over again until there is no more novelty or learning in it. As this occurs, as it is starting to now, humanity will realize that there are other ways of communicating and experiencing, such as the Nine Eyes, and will access them in order to evolve and expand further.

This can occur through humanity's witnessing of itself. The Witness, unchanging and still, watches everything that happens without reaction, without going toward it or running away from the thought, information, or emotion.

> True awareness is a state of pure witnessing without the least attempt to do anything about the event witnessed. Your thoughts and feelings, words and actions may also be a part of the event—but you understand precisely what is going on because it does not affect you. Once you are in the Witness you find that you love what you see, whatever may be its nature. This choiceless love is the touchstone of awareness.[18]

In the Witness, we are spirit having a human experience, for the creation of the mind itself starts through observing. As the wisest of Indian sages, Patañjali, describes, "Patterns of consciousness are always known by pure awareness, their ultimate unchanging witness. Consciousness is seen not by its own light, but by awareness." Consciousness cannot see itself any more than a TV picture can watch itself, even though it is capable of displaying a vast number of different channels and programs, each offering a realistic view of life.

When humanity en masse develops this ability, which sages of all traditions have taught and developed for thousands of years, "once consciousness calms down to the point of becoming still and transparent," we can sense our own presence for the first time—self-awareness. "As mind

---

18. Sri Nisargadatta Maharaj.

is now colored by witness awareness it can represent itself back to itself—for the world is the ground for both experience and liberation." [19]

This meltdown of self-awareness, when humanity fully witnesses itself in its totality, is the meltdown of the information age. We will soon reach this saturation point with this form of information and will need other ways of communicating. As this gets exhausted and taken to its ultimate degree, we will start to access universal mind as the information age feeds back on itself by fully observing, seeing, and witnessing itself. Indeed, we have created the technosphere in order for us to see ourselves fully, to witness all our thoughts, deeds, and actions. As we exhaust the limited possibilities of the technosphere, we will find new forms of communion and transmission in the Nine Bodies, where communication is more fluid, holographic, and experiential. This is part of the legacy that the ancient Egyptians wish to pass on to us now.

---

19. Maharishi Sadashiva Ishaya, *Enlightenment!* (Waynesville, NC: Ishaya Foundation, 1995).

Anaiya Aon Prakasha

David Andor

# ~2

## REN: NAME AND FORM—
## SOUND, VIBRATION, AND
## CREATION

*In the beginning was the Word, and the Word was with
God, and the Word was God.*

— John 1:1

As the creation myths of many cultures share, when God created form, he named or sounded each form in order to bring it into existence. As Adam saw the world around him, he named each object to bring it into manifestation. As Brahma looked into the void, he named each potential that he saw and brought that object into existence. Without naming, things do not exist, or rather things remain unknowable, mysterious, beyond understanding or form.

Name creates form. The moment we name something, be it a person, attitude, object, or way of being, we give it a form. Giving something a name gives it a form, which defines and labels it to give it meaning. Name creates form. Naming things creates thoughts. Thoughts arise from language, the basis for communication and relationship. Thought creates a certain reality, a consensual reality that we can agree exists as we all give it the same name and meaning. How could we ask another person to pass the apple without all of us knowing it was called an apple and all agreeing that it was an apple? This is why the ancient Hawaiians, on seeing the great sailing ships of Captain Cook on the horizon, could not comprehend what they were seeing; to their perception these ships did not exist.

Thoughts are names, and names create and define objects through their vibration. Thoughts are objects, known as thought-forms. Without names, there are no thoughts, no objects, no language, and no way of communicating. Without names, our reality and everything we do everyday would literally cease to exist in this dimension as we know it. Without names, all objects dissolve into a mass of vibrating formless energy.

As soon as you name something, you bring forth to you *all* the associations you have created in your entire life about that object. It is all there in that moment, the whole field of energy connected to the meanings you have given to that object. The only way to truly and purely experience that object is to see it in innocence, without name.

We first experience Ren through our own name and its resonance to us. Our name defines our relationship to the world. Our name connects us with our ancestry, with the resonance of people long dead and still to be born. Name links us all. Name creates identity and form. When we name something we bring it into being. Conversely, when something is unnamed it is unknowable, a mystery. This is why the secret name of Ra and the unnamable name of YHWH contain the greatest power, only known to a few, who can then wield the power of God to create or destroy.

Ren is your true spiritual name, the name that you resonate to most: the name of your soul. This name leads you forward into becoming your true being. It is a reminder of your essence when you forget it. It is the sound of your soul, our God-given name that creates resonance each time it is said and that holds great power once you learn what it is and how to use it. Mantras connected to your real name hold great power for you, and remembering your original name brings forth your soul purpose, grounding you into manifesting your heart's desires.

Teachers throughout time have given their students names. Yet today it is more important for you to remember your own name through prayer and meditation. However, when you are in a sacred site or temple, in a ceremony, your original name can arise more quickly as your soul opens up and delves deep into its essential sound vibration that unites it with all creation. When you sing spontaneously in abandon, in connection with the currents of creation, when you let go of yourself, then this sound, your soul song, can arise. The purest sound you can make is this song of your soul, connecting your heart, or Ab, to your Ka, or power.

As thoughts become forms so can you unite the Ab, the heart, with the willpower of life force, Sekhem, to create reality from the heart. This power, known to the Egyptians, came from the understanding that all thoughts are names and sound vibrations, and these names, meanings, and sounds create our manifested reality. From these sounds all names and thoughts are created and destroyed. This understanding also highlights the ways in which we as humans, through the technosphere, are creating, manipulating, and veiling deeper realities through the indiscriminate use of sound, name, and meaning.

## Finding Your Ren: Making the Mantra for Your Name

To find your own Ren name, simply sit down and clear your mind for a moment. Take a few deep breaths and clear your mind. Now read, and sound, these nine vowel sounds out loud. Which ones most resonate with you?

## Nine Vowels

ah

a

e

i

oh

uu

ai

au

am

Place the vowels into an order that feels right for you. Do you feel like adding any consonants between the spaces? Play with this for a while.

Now sound these vowels and consonants in different pitches, up and down the scale. Have fun with the sounds in different pitches, lengths, durations, and even timings. Some sounds can be shorter or longer, faster or slower; even different accents can be fun. Deep bass sounds and high-pitched sounds can also resonate. What sound goes with what pitch? What pitch feels best overall to you? This pitch is your keynote, where your resonant frequency lies, the frequency you are most comfortable with and able to create the most from.

To know the true names of a person, entity, or god/Neter was to have its power, and to have power over it, for the name, or Ren, contains its owner's complete identity and essence. For this reason, each Neter has secret names that embody their power. The commonly known Neteru names are titles more than actual names. For example, Hwt-Hrw translates as "House of Horus," Nebet Het translates as "Lady of the House," Ast or Isis means "throne," and so on.

This is why sacred languages have seven layers of meaning: each layer reveals deeper and more profound energies that transport your consciousness into the essence of a thing, person, or object. Each of these layers gives you clues into the nature of the power being referenced. The secret name, or Ren, embodies the spiritual essence of the individual at its seventh and final layer, only accessible by the immersion of your consciousness into samadhic or superconscious states, or by permission of the Neter itself. It is a being's Ren or name that contains its uniqueness and distinction, setting it apart from others while providing the means to express itself in the world as an entity unto itself.

Ren is the power and science of name, mantra, and sound. As in many sacred traditions, when one calls the name of a particular being, Neter, god, or goddess, that being is compelled to come to you. In evocation through a mantra to deities, the name holds their power, and by evoking and opening to them through your open vehicle, you can commune with them. By calling to these beings in the right way, with the soul, Ba, and your power, Ka, united, they will come and present themselves to you tangibly. They may even ask you what you want and how they can assist. I have found that with the right intention and correct feeling and pronunciation of their names, they come and are glad to be present.

Another example of the power of Ren is to use the name of a deity or master to reveal and dispel veils. For example, if you enter meditation and encounter a figure you cannot see, or it is cloaked, you can call on the master or god you feels most connected to in order to reveal the true intentions of that figure. For example, "In the name of Christ Yeshua, I command you to reveal your true form and name now." When you do this with your power three times, the being is compelled to reveal itself; it is a universal law.

Name is power. Calling and using the name is part of the science of mantra and sacred sound: the deeper part is to focus the mind and enter one pointed consciousness or samadhi, to go beyond any and all gods and enter the Source from where all names arise and dissolve. Ren is the pathway to this.

## Sound and Consciousness

In Egypt the Great Pyramid was constructed as a vibratory chamber to harness Ren energy, whereas in Europe, great cathedrals and stone circles were constructed to amplify the sound vibrations of group ceremonies in order to tune into this primordial matrix. In Ren, sound vibration conveys the idea of an object. Every thought, idea, feeling, and vibration originates in sound. The moment we feel, an unheard sound forms. The moment an idea appears in one's mind, a sound occurs.

Delving deeper into how sound works, we have to look at the brain and how it translates vibration and sound. If the brain is an intermediary in the way a TV set is an intermediary that turns waves into sound and images understandable to us, then the brain acts as a translator for different wavelengths of vibration and different wavelengths of consciousness, each of which produces different images, sounds, feelings, and thoughts.

It is in the four different wavelengths of Ren and sound that we access the sparks of intuition, flashes of insight and deep wisdom that provide the major changes in our lives. It is no accident that the greatest discoveries in science have been made at these moments, including the discovery of the benzene molecule by Kekulé, who fell asleep and saw its ring structure; the sudden breakthrough on the nature of gravity by an apple hitting Newton's head; Archimedes cry of *eureka* on discovering the principle of buoyancy while bathing in a tub; and Poincaré's mathematical problem-solving, not to mention the many musicians, artists, and inventors like da Vinci among many others.

These breakthroughs happen when the rational mind switches off, allowing the other wavelengths of vibration to become known and work through the scientist, artist, philosopher, or musician, allowing the new revelation to occur. Science has recently shown that these breakthroughs or radical insights happen when the right hemisphere of the prefrontal cortex (the brain's conductor) is triggered, resulting in gamma bursts of brain activity.

These breakthroughs throughout history in human consciousness and endeavor are also mirrored by another breakthrough in the human life journey: the phenomenon of near-death experiences. Research into near-death experiences (NDEs) shows that when a patient's consciousness transitions from the physical body, many report vivid imagery, light, and feelings of love and comfort. Most pertinently, patients report traveling down a tunnel from this world to enter another world where the laws that govern communication are vastly different, outside the normal causalities of time and space. When we are about to die, our life flashes before us in this series of images; a whole life of love, loss, fear, pleasure, and pain is told in a heartbeat, in one moment of self-reflection.

This act of reflection occurs when we step across the boundary of our own mind's perception, entering the unknown, the near-death experience. In this moment of self-reflection we enter multiple layers of the Ren and communication. When we access these different modes of Ren, the world and our relationship to it seems different; our connection to all we perceive is vivid and undeniable. What the Egyptian tradition shares is that what we cannot see "out there" in the universe is what we cannot see "in here" in our consciousness. Ninety-five percent of our selves is unknown, but it has been explored before in human history and by many people today. This mysterious 95 percent is found in our own consciousness when we enter the four modes of Ren, which arise from us developing our perceptual and multidimensional abilities.

This untapped potential can be tapped by accessing the brain's ability to function as a holographic data storage and retrieval system, a "hard drive" that employs different light angles to read information or "software." *Holographic* here implies an unlimited ability to access infinite amounts of information from multiple dimensions simultaneously. The simplest way to understand this is through light.

Laser beams, concentrated beams of light, occur in a variety of colors, much as your thoughts and emotions do. A fascinating characteristic of holograms is that different images can co-occur within the same space if they are placed there by different laser colors. You see the red image when you shine the red laser through it, a different yellow image with the yellow beam, and so on. If you do not shine the right color, you will not see the image with its information. It will remain hidden until the right frequency is shone upon it.

One frequency can reveal information on your relationships and feelings; another frequency can reveal subconscious memories and patterns; in another lies your hidden wisdom, insights, genius abilities, or intuitions; in yet another frequency you find your ability to access multiple dimensions, and so on, ad infinitum. There is no limit to the number of layers or frequencies we can access. In each light of perception, each color or searchlight of consciousness, another facet or layer of information is "seen." The structure of the brain, like many sacred texts such as the Egyptian *Book of the Dead,* the Indian Vedas ("sacred knowledge"), or the Hebrew kabbalah, have many enfolded and hidden layers, like the many skins of an onion, each being "lit up" and understood through a resonant mode of vibration or a different state of Ren.

What we are understanding now is that the brain is a holographic biocomputer that operates through electromagnetic frequencies and fields of possibility and potential. Each electromagnetic field interfaces with a specific dimension through geometric matrices that access different ways of seeing, perceiving, and interacting with life. This science of the expansion of perception is what it means to become multidimensional and to communicate holographically. This communion and communication happens through the four stages of Ren, the four stages of sound.

# The Four Stages of Sound

All Creation is sound. Sound creates consciousness. Words of power, or mantras, generate energy. This energy can be used to go quickly and deeply into focused states of consciousness that lead into all the light bodies. The initiation into the mantra or words of power is crucial, as without this you will not be able to go through all four stages of sound into the soul, Ba, and the power of life force, or Sekhem.

Using mantra is the fastest way to focus and concentrate the whole body and mind on one idea or strand of vibration. As everything in creation is sound, if we focus totally on one aspect of sound, or one aspect of God, be it Isis or Osiris, Shiva or Shakti, we can access that energy and immerse our whole self into it. We can become it.

The first stage of Ren or sound vibration is the written and spoken word. This is when you repeat the mantra out loud. This form of sound is seen in newspapers, media, the Internet, the news on TV, the way you speak to one another politely, the way you speak to strangers. It is also the babble of uncontrolled thoughts in your mind, the monkey mind of thoughts and things to do or be that are externalized in our lives through the babble of TV and the chatter of radio; it is the background noise of our brains.

The manipulation of this form of language manifests through the terminology of law, impersonal bureaucratic speech, and political doublespeak. Simply switch on the TV and you will see this language unfolding. However, words can also be used to express truth in its highest form through self-expression, as a conduit for truth, compassion, and the highest ideals of life. Sound here is a double-edged sword, showing that this mode of communication can be limited, or liberated, by the consciousness that we bring to it. It can be a tool for manipulation or liberation.

The second stage of Ren is the picture that the sound creates, or the internal mental repetition of the mantra. You take the mantra inside your mind, repeating it, allowing it to become more subtle and penetrate deeper into your consciousness. Traditionally we have accessed this state of sound through creating pictures in the mind through sacred sound and through mystical poetry, sacred geometry, and art; that done by Monet, J. M. Turner, and Bridget Riley illustrate this.

This second mode of Ren is the translator, the bridge between the 5 percent of the brain we normally use and the 95 percent we still have not tapped into in the wider spectra of consciousness. In this dreamlike, fluid, constantly shifting medium, we are in flow, in "the zone," never staying stuck or inert. Water, sound, and darkness are the mediums that our ancestors used in order to enter this expanded reality, and the ways we express this mode are through metaphor, art, paradox and poetry, music, dreams, and sacred languages.

In the twenty-first century it is through immersive multimedia entertainment. Generally, when we access the second mode of Ren, we enter joy, our consciousness expands and appreciates life more, and we feel a pulse of perfect rhythm or synchronicity that is always present in each one of us, occurring when we are stripped of the boundaries of thought, the monkey-babble mind or technosphere, and judgment.

The third stage of Ren is when the mantra begins to dissolve from internal repetition. It starts to fade away, and light starts to overtake the sound, until there is only a hum within you. At this stage the mantra may also start to repeat itself without you doing anything. This is when we enter deep meditation, where the mind stops and all sound as you know it dissolves into currents of light vibration that slow the brain-wave patterns into stillness. This third mode of Ren is where the mystical experiences and knowledge that are the basis of all sacred traditions is accessed through a process of divine revelation or "universal download."

It is in this mode of Ren or sound communication that the writing of the Egyptian *Book of Coming Forth by Day* or the *Book of the Dead,* the Vedas, the Koran, parts of the Judeo-Christian Bible, and many Buddhist sutras and *termas* were transcribed. In ancient Greece this state was known as *hesychia,* or the silent transmission in which messages from the gods were revealed to selected humans, known as heroes. This knowledge has always been available and was universally applicable throughout history in our acceptance and immersion in these higher modes. This "true sight" of knowing has no boundaries of space, time, or perception. This mode of communication-communion is where word and object are identical, where the division between subject and object, you and me, does not exist. There is only the light of consciousness, moving at a very high frequency.

The fourth stage of Ren and sound is when mantra and mind dissolve completely. The breath stops, one-pointed focus of mind dissolves into no mind, and the Sekhem or life force unites into Akhu, or God/bliss. You enter silence of body, mind, and soul, and the idea of separation also dissolves. You dissolve. This is the point, and aim, of all mantras: to use sound to enter silence and total bliss; to use sound to dissolve the mind, merging Osiris and Isis, Shiva and Shakti, into one. To know you are God.

This fourth mode of Ren is an infinite consciousness that contains in seed form all the other modes of sound vibration before they become manifested. It is a spherical state of being where you can access everything in creation at any moment through your own transparency, fluidity, and openness. In this field, people are indivisible from their environment, and affect the environment as the environment affects them. This field encodes all information, providing instantaneous communication to everything everywhere through quantum resonance—the resonance found in all living things.

Everything is interconnected. It is from this field that the three other spheres of communication are generated in order to express the inexpressible. Wave fluctuations of what quantum physics calls this "zero-point field" drive the motion of subatomic particles, which in turn drive all the particles of the universe to generate the Universal Field in a self-generating feedback loop across the cosmos. This field is "a self-generating, grand ground state of the universe"[1] that is continually renewed through the movements of life. No energy is ever lost; it just takes on a new expression through Ren.

Through Ren we enter Sahu and Akhu, the immortal and infinite bodies, in a state of indescribable bliss, which is the name, or Ren, of God. This journey is one we can all take with this guidance and with a guide. On the journey into death and through its many portals, only by sounding certain names can we travel through the veils that lead us to eternal life and the end of reincarnation. In Tibet this was known as the layers of the bardo, and in Egypt the levels of the Duat. These veils are guardians created by sound: wrathful, fearsome, and protective, yet blissful and light when we have conquered our fears and are joyfully vigilant to the voice of the ego.

## A Sound Practice of Ren

Stop everything for a moment. Take a few deep breaths.

Now sound out the mantra *au or hu* aloud, at full volume, twelve times, at your keynote, the pitch and frequency you find most comfortable.

Now whisper it twelve times.

Now take this current of energy you have created and repeat the mantra twelve times in your mind silently.

Now let go of the sound, and relax into the current of energy created by the sound. Relax and let go of the repetition of words, letters, and language. Focus solely on the current of energy weaving its way through your brain and consciousness. Follow it loosely, and relax into its pathway. What happens?

---

1. Hal Puthoff.

# The Architecture of Ren

Sound and form are portals to enter innocence. Enlightened architects have utilized the science of Ren—of sound, form, and harmonic proportions—to create physical spaces where we can enter the luminous worlds that Ren cloaks and reveals. In many Indian temples, intricate carvings in marble capture the moment when matter starts to vibrate, the moment when we experience movement in that which appears solid. In temples such as these, such as the exquisite Jain temples in Mount Abu, India, and Harlesden, London, the experience of the temple is one of constant movement and vibration, where every object is dancing. In many traditional Christian cathedrals, when the sounds of the choirs reverberate, your eyes become entrained by the patterned light of stained glass windows. These combinations of color and shape vibrate in resonance with the sound, creating oscillating afterimages and expansions of consciousness.

The most powerful sacred buildings and architectures have been constructed with the knowledge of the Ren, which involves sacred geometry, harmonic acoustics, and the four stages of sound vibration. A sacred building is a harmonic structure built to journey through the four stages of the Ren. One of the most powerful examples of these four encoded into a building is in Chartres Cathedral in France, a temple to the Mother and Isis.

Chartres has a powerful design, as its specific purpose is to bridge a perceived gap between the finite and infinite. In essence, it is created to resonate the true harmonic ratios and proportions of the human body. As one walks into the cathedral space, one activates and aligns to inherent geometries of vibrations and shapes of sound that resonate and inform our consciousness. These shapes of consciousness are mathematically encoded into the sacred space.

Entering Chartres is like walking into another world, vibrant in a silence that contains many possibilities. Orbs of light hang suspended in darkness; pristine geometries cloaked in symbol ripple in blood-red and blue waves throughout the mindscape. Throughout the day the light constantly changes in intensity and color. Certain windows within Chartres are coded to catch the attention only at certain times of the day, conceptually reflecting and reminding me of the Indian *raga* musical scale, whereby particular sets of notes and modes are played at specific times such as morning, early afternoon, twilight, midnight, and so on. So, each window, like music, is played differently by the light at different times of the day, immersing the interior in a different atmosphere. This provides us with a new facet, a new chord, and a new face every hour, every day of the year, with light, shade, and color subtly combined or dramatically contrasted.[2]

Chartres Cathedral is built to reflect and explore this dance of light and shadow. In the view of the alchemists, matter was mind, and it was the immaterial that was real, with the shadow or echo of matter being unreal.[3] As the creator of Chartres, Abbot Suger said "the loveliness of the many colored gems calls me away from external cares.... I see myself dwelling in some strange region of the Universe which neither exists entirely on Earth, nor entirely in the purity of heaven."

When we see, hear, and reflect on the beauty of material objects, we can then take them within the mind and become able to "see" through them and perceive their counterparts in the invisible world. In this transformation, we are transported to an intermediate place where our consciousness is neither completely material nor completely spiritual, but both at the same time. The "dull mind rises to truth through

---

2. These effects are deliberately designed to open the heart by direct opposites, similar to the point in a movie where a hero is killed tragically and unfairly with strains of soaring angelic music playing behind.
3. Plato.

that which is material and, seeing this light, is resurrected from its former submersion."[4] Here we can travel from the seen to the unseen worlds through the many layers of Ren, using the visible as a gateway to the invisible. In this journey we are transformed.

The science of Ren in Chartres uses a simple vocabulary of squares, diamonds, triangles, and circles (the shapes of the Ka body) to create simple progressions made in color generating movement, light, and space. One moment there will be nothing to look at, and the next second the canvas of your perception seems to undulate and morph. Energy releases from the forms via the relationships between them.

When we see this point when color, light, and form momentarily precede mental interpretation, we fully experience their purity, immediacy, and freshness beyond their three-dimensional appearance. We see them as energy itself. Here, the perception of color is entirely relative and unstable—each one influences the other in a mesh and web of interconnectivity. The eye becomes seduced, transported into a deep relaxation that readily receives a diffusion of colors. Color links the inner and outer worlds.

To increase this bridging effect requires the curve, or toroidal spiral form. When colors are twisted along the rise and fall of an enfolding curve, their juxtapositions change continually in innumerable sequences that create different sensations. From these clusters, which flow into each other, arises meaning. The curve of the torus creates a more pliable structure, evoking rather than describing, bringing to mind the rhythms of nature rather than describing them literally. As the eye flows along the curve, it loses its linear thread as shapes fuse, dissolving like a mirage into a shimmering chromatic field.

At this hinting of what lies behind the surface of the senses, behind the first layers of Ren, lies the quantum state, or fluid mind. In investi-

---

4. Abbot Suger.

gating the energy or visual potential of such shapes and colors, one can journey into what lies behind the appearance, which is why the cathedral builders built this space.

Ren is an important aspect of the light bodies, and it dominated much of Egyptian thought, writing, architecture, and ways of perceiving and interacting with the many worlds around them. All the worlds and dimensions can be placed into a space far smaller than the point of a pin, and they are far vaster then you could ever measure. The ways to interact with these many dimensions is through applying the science of Ren, the science of name, sound, and form.

## Meeting the Ren

RD states that as he went deeper into the Ren journey,

> It was a returning to the source of all things. Following the mantra deeper within, I forgot it and was taken into the hall of records and shown cases of information on *everything,* all moving in geometric patterns. Behind the moving patterns were subtler and subtler forms of sound and light. Eventually all sense of time ended and there was only light. . . . I felt this as the level of God and all-knowing wisdom. I also became aware that I needed a physical partner to ground this energy of samadhi into the earth.

As CO shares, "Working with the Ren and the mantra took me through the veils into emptiness, stillness, a place of no breath, no movement in the physical, and yet fluid breath and movement in the void." MT shares that it is a place where the Master Yogananda resides and met her, whereas EP simply dissolved into white light and passed out. SMC shares, "I have always loved and responded strongly to sound. Feeling the words reverberate throughout me is wonderful. Today was the first time I went behind the words to feel and experience *being* with the mantra. My body felt such peace and openness. I could have sat in this state all day."

For a complete understanding of the vast nature and meaning of the Ren, see the forthcoming book *Holographic Communication* by Padma Aon Prakasha.

# The True Nature of Sound

## By John Reid

Spiritual traditions from many cultures speak of sound as being responsible for the creation of life. The words of Saint John's Gospel are a good example: "In the beginning was the Word, and the Word was with God, and the Word was God."[5]

Around 4.5 billion years ago, sounds louder than we can imagine were at work shaping the earth. Immense sound "storms" reverberated within the earth's molten iron core and mantle, pushing up the early landmasses, creating mountains and valleys. Then, around 3 billion years ago, following the formation of the oceans, the first primitive life forms are believed to have evolved in the watery depths.

The structuring and organizing force that triggered life has eluded theorists, and many competing theories abound. Many scientists have come to believe that the fierce lightning storms that tore open the early atmosphere were the magic ingredients that literally "sparked life." If there comes a time when this theory is proven to be correct, it would fail to explain how the helical nature of DNA evolved, *or* how the building blocks of life were assembled. What force was at work to cause the building blocks of life to coalesce and begin to create form from the formless? We believe, just as the ancient seers do, that the creative force was the most obvious and potent of all: sound.

---

5. John 1:1.

It is generally believed that life began in the harsh environment around hydrothermal vents. These ocean-floor vents were where water came in contact with the heat of molten rock. The hydrothermal vents spewed mineral-rich gases from earth's core into the water. The gases came in contact with hot lava, causing bubbles to form that ranged in size from melons to microbes. It is the microscopic bubbles that most concern us.

The elements that poured out of the vents found themselves in highly turbulent water and in an ocean of rich bubbling sounds. It is important to know that although sound is invisible, it actually carries structure, both in air and in water. The watery membrane surfaces of the microscopic bubbles were the perfect places for sound structures to imprint. The patterns of energy on the surfaces of these tiny bubbles were created by areas of stillness, called nodes, and high-intensity sound, called antinodes.

Naturally, the elements found a safe haven in the nodal areas of the bubbles. In other words, life formed in the stillness, on the surface of microscopic bubbles. The patterns of stillness were regular, such as a dodecahedron. Adjacent to these still areas were areas of dynamic vibration, which we could think of as the dynamic creative force or the Shakti aspect of God. If this model is correct, then it may be the reason that many people meditate in stillness to reach God within: some subconscious part of the brain may remember the time when life formed in the stillness of those ancient seas. Sound and stillness, of course, still reside within all of us.

When we study the geometry of sounds, we see that they include many of the mathematical constants of the cosmos, including phi, the "golden mean." This ratio is approximately 1 to 1.618, and it is found in all living things. Sound geometry is based on definite angles that form on a membrane that is "imprinted" with the sound vibrations, thus allowing us to observe them. It is interesting to note that recent research is suggesting that the earliest life forms may have been viruses, life forms that are often highly angular in their outer shells. Cells, according to this theory, evolved much later. The angular aspects of the earliest primitive life forms and organisms are strong evidence that sound was involved in the shaping process.

The reason that all living things have the phi ratio imbedded in them may be because phi is imbedded within a pure sine tone. Pure sounds are devoid of harmonics and do not feature the rich complexity of a musical sound. An example of a fairly pure high-pitched sound is an organ pipe, which causes air to spin into a vortex. Such pure sounds contain the phi ratio, and they create sonic scaffolding that, we believe, organizes, structures, and triggers life.

But how could a pure tone originate in the oceans of earth? Wave action creates sound known as "white noise," all frequencies of sound jumbled together. As those sounds impinge on the watery depths, they are filtered naturally by the water. The deeper the sound travels from the surface, the purer it becomes until, at great depth, it is a very pure low-pitched tone, resembling that of a church organ. It was these sounds, we believe, that were the driving force of creation. They formed "sonic scaffolding" on all micromembranes they interfaced with.

Viktor Schauberger, the brilliant Austrian scientist, may have been the first to study microvortexes in water. Interestingly, microvortexes carry the same basic structure as DNA. More recently, scientists in Hong Kong have demonstrated that microvortexes can be created in the laboratory and are used to manipulate single DNA molecules. In other words, the bore of the microvortex approaches that of the DNA double helix. It seems like divine irony that the very mechanism that may have created DNA is now being employed to manipulate it.

Perhaps the first strands of DNA were created in the microvortex environments of primordial hydrothermal vents. Should microvortexes be discovered within microscopic bubbles, we have a model that begins to resemble living cells: a membrane (the surface of the bubble) with strands of DNA within. If sound was indeed the trigger for life, it follows that sound can heal life. The sound of ocean waves is certainly calming, but the sounds embedded within them may be healing at a level we can currently only guess at.

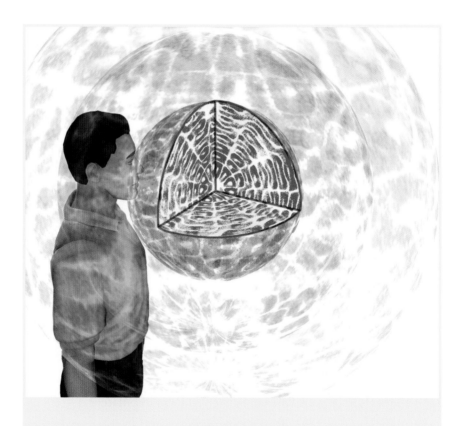

**How sound is created through the voice.**
(Courtesy John Reid)

# Portals to Innocence

*Anyone who will not receive the kingdom of God like a little child will never enter it.*

—Luke 18:17

Imagine, there is no such thing as language. Imagine, there are no words to describe your thoughts. Imagine . . . you are totally innocent.

Now look at an object right in front of you. Just gaze at it, without any labeling of what it is, what you have thought it to be, or even what it could be. Look at it like you have never seen it before, like there are no words to describe it, like it is completely new. Gaze at it like it is the very first time you have ever seen it.

Stay like this for a few minutes. What happens?

When we take away the Ren label from our perception, whole new levels open up quickly. As one begins to realize and dissolve the layers of name and meanings that create the forms and perceptions of your world, the value that you have given to them also starts to fade and dissolve.

Everything, and every event that occurs, is neutral. What you observe around you and within you is neutral until you make a decision as to what it will mean for you. You give the event a value, usually good or bad, helpful or not helpful. To stand back and see this mental process, of naming and defining what values and associations you give to that object or person, allows you to let go of what you think, allowing you to be truly present to the object or person.

The idea of "you" is removed from your ideas, attachments, and judgments about what reality is, which colors the surface of your perceptions. Without attaching any meaning, any value, toward these thoughts or objects, your mind becomes a blank canvas, an empty page.

You can experience this. Try this practice with a friend you feel open with. Sit quietly, center yourself, and follow your breath. Open your eyes, the windows to the soul, and truly gaze at your friend, eye to eye: you will see, as you do every day, that they have a form, a body. Keep gazing and you will see them blurring, becoming indistinct, a mass of colors, shapes, and vibrating patterns. As you keep gazing and concentrating, you will eventually come to see that he or she is a blank canvas, an empty space, not even "existing" as you would perceive "'existing." They disappear completely into emptiness.

Witnessing this, what is already and always here, allows you the direct perception of reality behind matter, behind appearance. When you experience this, and literally see another person or object dissolve right in front of you, how real can this body-mind, this reality, be?

Anaiya Aon Prakasha

# ~3

# SHEW: THE SHADOW

The greatest light casts the greatest shadow. Integrating this within you leads to your greatest empowerment. The Egyptians understood that the Shew or shadow is your ally, and in many cases your adversarial ally, teaching you through adversity your own lessons, judgments, and misperceptions. As everyone's shadow is unique, the general rules and principles found within these pages are here for you to inquire into, master, and guide your own shadow into integration, healing, embrace, and harmony in alliance with the other bodies.

The shadow is what we make it. The Egyptians saw it as having a two-fold aspect: one is what it is in its essence, and one is what we project onto it, what we project it to be. It is this projection and self-creation, generated by our individual personalities and the collective human personality, that covers the essential nature of the shadow. This essential nature is not self-created, whereas the layers and coverings we dump onto the shadow are entirely our own self-creation. This dichotomy reveals the inner battle that we all feel at different times in our lives—the inner fight between human and divine. Nobody is perfect, we all have our foibles and our lessons to learn, and this is what provides our own unique bridge into the immortal.

The Shew shadow works in the personal and collective unconscious, manifesting in our lives and relationships to show us what we have left out, what we have not embraced, what needs our attention, what we have cut off from, and what we have ignored, rejected, and buried under the carpet. (Perhaps this is where the word *shoo* arises from—to push away that which we do not like or want to see.) Sometimes we may feel we have done these actions, and sometimes we may feel they have been done to us. This is an essential aspect of the self-created shadow: the victim that cannot own the great responsibility that you are creating everything in your life, whether you are conscious of it or not.

Shadow wants to work with us, to be included. Once it is harnessed, included, and listened to, it has a voice that actually guards, protects, and aligns the soul to Source, to Akhu, as it lets us know when something is in integrity or not. This voice is often played out in our intimate relationships as our shadow projects itself onto others so it can be seen. It wants to be seen no matter what, however it plays out.

Shadow brings forth your dualities, helping you to balance them in your life. Being aware that there is duality present in the moment can lead to a choice to dissolve that duality through a remembrance and expression of unity, be it in your own meditation, through correcting your thinking, by witnessing, or by communicating honestly and self-responsibly if it is in the context of relationship. Duality is an artful reminder of how we can be more whole and more conscious, for when we are reminded of duality in our own actions and behavior we can be reminded of our own innate nature of unity. Duality becomes our greatest ally, our greatest friend, in serving to show us the moments when we are not aligned to love, and in this sense duality becomes the ultimate tool for remembering who we are.

Duality and the shadow, Shew, can be amorphous and illusory, painting pictures of many realities that it senses and draws from. It draws and acts on all the feelings, thoughts, and emotions from your entire personal experience held in the Ka body (your energy double) and the collective experiences of humanity. In order to reveal the true essence of the Shew, at some stage you have to feel and experience the collective unconscious and transmute its feelings through compassion: the function of the soul, Ba. This then aligns with the Hu, or immortal bodies, to fully integrate the shadow.

In order to work with the shadow effectively, the Ka body of light (your auric charisma, light, and presence) has to be subdued so the shadow can be brought out without being rationalized or spiritualized in any way. This is a temptation, as the light and power of the Ka can blind us to our shadow, because the human tendency is to identify most with their light and power, not paying attention to the shadow that lurks in the background. This ignoring of the shadow occurs because the light of the Ka is seductive and easier to identify with than the suffering of the shadow, which we naturally do not wish to delve into but which we are inexorably meant to face at some point.

The brightest light blinds us. To allow yourself to delve into the shadow, stripped of the power and light of the Ka, and fully experience and meet it, is the beginning of the integration of the shadow into all your other bodies. This takes humility, honesty, and vulnerability, which then paradoxically makes you more complete, stronger, and softer.

The amount of shadow we integrate brings us closer to the Hu, or immortal bodies. The more you integrate the shadow the closer you get to Source. The more we investigate and face it, the more it integrates, feeling safe to be accepted and dialogued with. As this process deepens, we become more vulnerable, open, and human, as our divine aspects meet and merge with our human side.

The amount of shadow we integrate can be measured as a percentage and is a marker of your balanced and holistic evolution. To have a large percentage of shadow or a large percentage of light, power, or knowledge leads to an unbalanced state of being, showing you that you have been missing a vital piece on your path. This is quite common, as not many people really wish to actively explore the shadow, partly out of fear for what they may find and partly because integrating the shadow leads to integrating soul consciousness into the body. This is a scary thing, as you now have nowhere left to hide: no rationalizations, words, belief systems, or spiritual philosophy can mask the shadow, which is clearly there for those who wish to see it.

To deal with the shadow takes humility, vulnerability, and the ability to drop out of your power and light source, the more "spiritual" parts of you, to enter those parts of you that are not illuminated. As we integrate our shadows below 15 percent, that is, we have integrated and dissolved 85 percent of the shadow, we start to work actively with the collective shadow and begin to make a difference on a global scale. As we go below 3 percent we start to make a conscious impact on the galactic level, and once we go below 1 percent the shadow can enter into communion with its source and maker: Akhu. At this point, you integrate the shadow into the spine. This allows a deeper transformation or Osirification of the body to occur through the Djed Pillar of the spine. In this process, the light quotient and colors within the spine change from white into golden-green light as the spine transforms into its awakened and original template.

Shadow is a gateway to Source, a gateway to Hu, and there are different stages along the way to integrate and incorporate this. The original Egyptian understanding of the Shew, or shadow, as a blank featureless figure standing at the tomb of the deceased looking out into the sun of Ra has been misunderstood and mistranslated, because this experience has been lost from the minds of modern humans. Instead, modern people have focused on the emotional and mental aspects, with more awareness starting to arise in this century about the effects that the shadow has on the physical body and on the transpersonal level.

However, even this knowledge is only a part of the whole picture, as the shadow itself extends into cosmological, mystical, and spiritual realms that were mapped out in the Duat of the Egyptians and the bardo realms of the Buddhists.

# The Ghost

One of the first aspects of the shadow is its ghostlike appearance. This aspect of Shew is an earthbound entity closely attached to the physical body, which manifests after death as a ghostlike residue of the former self. This ghostly residue is formed from the individual's attachment to the earthly realm and the inability to let go of earthly attachments such as family ties, romantic relations, unfinished karmic business that has a strong emotional charge to it, or a strong quality of desire that cords one into those people or ideas.

Another reason why the shadows of the dead get stuck in earth's fields is that as people physically die, they are scared of going to hell or of being judged by God, thanks to the religions of this world. This fear of judgment is the core pillar of the shadow: how we judge ourselves. As the light bodies of Ka and the soul Ba begin the journey after death, this fear prevents them from continuing beyond the earth's fields. They can then get stuck in the earth sphere as earthbound spirits, or ghosts, particularly if their death was sudden or violent.

For most people, it takes about three days to realize they are dead. That is why people have to go through ceremonies and rituals as pre-scribed in both the Egyptian *Book of the Dead* and the *Tibetan Book of the Dead* to help them realize they are dead, to prepare them for their journey in the Ba and Ka to (maybe) return to Source. Once these souls move away from the earth sphere, the remaining family members and loved ones can actually feel the release and liberation; they feel a lightness.

In Egypt, priests and priestesses used to specialize in these moving-on rituals for souls who were stuck in the earth's fields. It was seen as a matter of spiritual hygiene to keep the earth plane uncluttered by these spirits, as well as a matter of compassion and importance for the Ba souls of the deceased to find their way through the Duat or underworld. This is another reason for the importance of the *Book of the Dead,* for the more cluttered the earth's fields are by people's shadows roaming around disconnected and ghostlike, the more toxic earth's environment becomes, as psychic clutter clogs up the energy meridians of the environment, the earth, and the community. Similar to the human body, when meridians are blocked we feel unwell, sluggish, angry, or fatigued, so it is the same with the earth's meridians and the larger effects it has on all of us, which is why the Egyptians paid so much attention to it, so that their communities could remain clear and connected.

This clearing work is still undertaken by a few, who perform it after major disasters like the tsunamis or earthquakes that have rocked our planet recently. However, this is literally just a drop in the bucket compared to what really needs to be done. Perhaps as our cultures learn and remember more, this practice can be done more regularly to benefit all our communities, and clear the cluttered shadow-fields of our planet.

To counteract this cluttering, we can manage our earthly obligations, relationships, and duties without getting stuck or tied down. In grounding and connecting to earth, we open to a bigger love on behalf of the planet and humanity in a real and tangible way, regaining our soul foundation and power. Opening the foot chakras, visiting sacred sites, walking barefoot, and breathing in nature accelerate this connecting process.

## The Golden Shadow

Working with the Shew on all its levels of connection is a living mystical journey. The lessons of tension, conflict, and suffering can and do change into a more graceful way of learning once Shew is integrated with the soul Ba. This means that Shew becomes an internalized process, guided and informed by light and the evolutionary impulse of your soul. To do this, the shadow has to differentiate itself from the other bodies while at the same time integrating itself with them.

This does not mean that there will never be any more conflict in your life. It just means that the signs are there before full-blown conflict happens, allowing you, through skillful means, to work with opposing forces and bring them into a unity. This integration requires simultaneous awareness of the bodies and the voices and intelligences that belong to each body. The shadow's voice can be strident and loud or quiet and subdued as it resides deep in the places you do not wish to go.

Shadow will let you know when you are not being true to your heart's desire and soul purpose, as it too wants to experience this. Once aligned and connected to the other bodies, they all work as one, focused and wanting the same things. They communicate in their own unique ways that we have to become attuned to, so we can hear their voices and act accordingly in their dimensions, with their rules and behaviors.

Shew is often easily contacted through sex and drugs as instant tools to access its reality. It is pleasure-seeking, always open to sensations and ways of self-indulgence. Its will is feeble, and it is suggestible and ill-disciplined. When it is in this state, it can easily be worked with or manipulated, both by you and by others. If one is marooned in the shadow, one is gullible and easily led. However, once it is aligned and put into its proper place and integrated, it is a tool to create from and with.

In this aspect, the shadow is a master artist and can create as many worlds as it is able to imagine and can then experience that world. Multiple different parallel realities lie before it, and it paints each one convincingly, as its natural function is to create. However, the shadow paints and creates its realities from a sense of self-imposed limitation rather than from the limitless expansion and possibilities of the soul Ba. One can see these limitations in modern-day mass culture, art, and literature, which are essentially forms of catharsis and expression of the shadow divorced from the other bodies.

Shadow creates its own realities, creating future pathways based on its present condition. It creates its own myths, its own legend, its own story that it clings to. All other realities pursue and follow this course until one meets the shadow, embraces its central or pillar myth, witnesses how it plays out in your life, and integrates it. This central myth of the shadow is the pattern that recurs again and again in our lives until we heal it.

This is our crucifixion, what we carry with us until we heal, conquer, and integrate the shadow with our other bodies, looking after it but not banishing it. As Yeshua said, "Get thee behind me Satan."[1] He did not banish the shadow; he allowed it to guard his back, to protect him and keep him in alignment with all the other bodies. If we banish the shadow, we strengthen its myth, burying it deeper and making it more inaccessible in our own subconscious.

It is interesting to note that Christ started his ministry in earnest *after* meeting his shadow, and the shadow of the world in the form of Satan, while he fasted and meditated for forty days in the desert. Meeting these forms of the shadow and integrating them while conquering the aspects of his lower self enabled and empowered him to then start teaching and putting his own unique soul purpose into full action—a lesson for us all. For Christ, this manifested in the revealing of the Ten Beatitudes, a mystical teaching that carves a pathway through the collective consciousness to lead one into Christ Consciousness. (It is also interesting to note that his predecessor Osiris became awakened by conquering and literally "sitting" on the inert form of his shadow self, Set. Set then became his seat and throne.)

It is important to remember that the Shew only has a limited set of possibilities when one is living within it. It cannot expand beyond this set of possibilities, as this is all it can see. All future realities have to conform to this pattern, and nothing else can be seen. The shadow does not wish to listen to or hear anything outside its parameters and will

---

1. Matthew 16:23.

ignore what other possibilities are presented to it. Instead of opening, it will contract further into its myths and beliefs, strengthening its belief systems at all costs. It is irrational until it is exposed by embrace and cognition; it only lets go when it is assured that it will survive and be included with all the other bodies.

When it feels this, it relaxes and lets go, allowing itself to integrate with the other bodies, allowing the light in the darkness to shine. In this lack of opposition, it comes into harmony, and its myth and legend can be dissolved. As this occurs, one comes to understand that the shadow exists to inform us of our evolutionary lessons and why we have incarnated. It holds gold within its recesses as it allows us to be both human and divine. It is the bridging point into spiritual maturity and human responsibility.

It connects both and makes sure we do not leave out either one, as we cannot sustain living in the higher bodies until we are integrating the shadow, and we cannot include all the other bodies without the shadow modulating and communicating all its rich mines of wisdom to all parts of Self.

Shew is the communicator and interface between conscious and unconscious. It is the voice that warns us when we are becoming too complacent, and it is the voice that guards us when shadow becomes too rampant. It is the meaning applied when we no longer seek outside ourselves for anything. It holds the wealth and power of darkness within it and reveals its treasures to those with dedication, compassion, wit, and wisdom. It loves conflict as a means to self-discovery, yet it runs away from those who try to run away from it. In this mutual escaping, both the human and divine sides of self lose.

Parts of the Shew world are the shadows cast by higher realities. This is why they also have so much allure: there is good in evil, and evil in good. This is how harmony and balance work together. The shadows of higher realities that lie unexpressed attract us to it, to see what

**Angel and demon of the shadow.** (Amaya Du Bois)

it is, to somehow access it. And this accessing requires we communicate with all the parts of the shadow to access the gold of the shadow.

## Shadow, Power, and Soul

Having too strong a Ka body, your double, veils the shadow underneath the light of the Ka. The brilliance of the Ka power and light can blind us, acting as a blanket through which we cannot see the shadow underneath. When Ka is allowed to be present but not dominating, the weaker-willed shadow can come into the foreground to be seen, met, embraced, and understood. This is a delicate balance.

The shadow needs to develop its own will and constructive voice and learn how to use its mental powers. When its will and creativity are strong enough, its relationship with the Ka can deepen. As this dialogue between the bodies grows closer, the shadow can let you know what it needs, and then proceed to do it, letting you know what is occurring for it. You can then act on integrating it into your other bodies once you know its voice and promptings, without being a victim of it or being overtaken by its needs and desires. You become a master of its desires, not mastered by its desires.

As this deepens, the shadow gets to know itself and its world. Shadow is an explorer. It tests, experiences, and indulges in all sorts of behaviors until it has had enough. This can take a long time, as the shadow's world is vast and there is much to be learned within it and many experiences to be had in many different situations. It builds up its strength throughout these extreme or polar experiences, eventually managing to see itself, to fully recognize itself and become self-conscious of its workings. This happens when the other bodies of the Ba soul and Sahu, your universal body, are brought into operation with it, as the full seeing of one's shadow can be a devastating experience that cannot be endured unless Ba and Sahu are present.

Ba and Sahu guide the shadow. If they did not, it would avoid self-reflection, as shadow is essentially self-indulgent and too lazy to go beyond its world, with its many pleasures, extremes, and distractions. This also means it avoids the dangers of looking too closely at itself, which can lead to great fear and wild swinging dualities that are almost schizophrenic in nature. Eventually, as you connect the Shew to the Sahu, you will confront what previously could have led to thoughts of suicide, panic, and madness.

Shew is content to be on the surface and the center of its world. Shew itself has no real self-awareness. It becomes aware through accessing information for the requirements of the soul, Ba, and universal body, Sahu, to incarnate and be known to you. It becomes self-conscious through these lenses and can then act as a unified part of you as a conscious person. To work with it in balance and to sustain any integration with the light bodies, Ba has to maintain the shadow's drive and interest by giving it some form of pleasure so that the pleasures outweigh the negative experiences. Conscious lovemaking is a direct way of doing this.

In these interactions, shadow Shew deepens its relationship with the Ka, making Ka more adaptable, fluidly intelligent, and creative. It learns to bring about healing and other positive changes in both Ka and the physical body of the Khat. The unconscious influences the conscious mind and creates your reality until you make it conscious. Once you tap into the vast power of the unconscious, you become empowered and able to manifest your heart's desires with this power and awareness. As this occurs, you can change the health of the body.

When the shadow becomes self-aware and able to establish its relationships to the other bodies in acceptance and mutual equality, without judgment, then these powers can manifest to be wisely used in the moment. However, shadow will project its inequality, an inequality generated by you in the seeing of it as somehow inferior to the other bodies. It is up to you to remedy that by including the shadow, for fundamentally, Shew works by seeing itself as less than, which we then identify with, creating various forms of ego control.

## The Power of Aloneness

The power of aloneness is something we all have to integrate in order to achieve our deepest heart's desires. Being alone means you can center fully in your core Self and discover what brings you the deepest joy according to your own knowing and integrity. Aloneness helps you to fully understand yourself and what works for you. It helps you to work out and explore your shadow, to get to know its voice intimately within you.

Too much of life is spent outside without quiet time alone to nourish and reflect the soul and shadow. It is in this time that we truly get to know our shadow through the lens of the Ba soul. In alone time, you come to recognize the shadow's workings, needs, and longings as well as how to connect it to the other bodies. You come to feel what is missing and give that to yourself. You come to truly love yourself and the shadow, which is the guardian of love. It is wise never to work solely with the shadow isolated by itself, by you being immersed in it to the exclusion of the other light bodies, as this can lead to isolation, despair, sadness, grief, and chaos.

Shew is the denial of truth that we suffer from most. Where do you feel love missing so much that it hurts, or that you project this lack outward? It may not be easy to face the truth of your shadow.

Truth is something you get to embody and know alone. As the Sufis say, "The Flight of the unknown is the journey of alone, to be with the Alone (All-one)." When we sit with the pain of the shadow in the heart, the shields and armoring around it can gently open so we no longer feel the pang of loneliness but surrender to love's softness, which is breaking the heart constantly yet gently.

Judgment is the yardstick of the shadow. How much do you judge yourself, others, and life? If you are living in a state of nonjudgment, you are living unconditional love. Maybe this is what it is to be a human being.

Shadow shows us where we do not love, highlighting a part of us that is isolated, cold, forlorn, fragmented, and separate: a part of us that we have not embraced about ourselves, what we judge. When we love and accept ourselves as we are, when shadow is acknowledged, cognized, and allowed to be, harmony and the integration of God consciousness occurs . . . eventually.

If you treat Shew with friendliness, respect, and an open giving heart (Ab), it will work with you. You have to tend, nurture, and bring the shadow into maturity through loving acceptance, like a flower you tend to and watch bloom, or like a child and its mother. You have to give it attention so it can grow up. As long as you judge it, you can never meet it or see it. You can only meet the "devil" by not judging it, and at some point we all have to meet our own "devil" in order to become all of who we are.

In fully embracing Shew you go beyond sense or gross experience, which can lead to a form of madness as seen by the rational mind, for madness is simply an "absence of sense." Everything dissolves in embracing pain fully, and peace is the reward for living the truth of this moment. However, the obstacle to this is that we constantly avoid the void within ourselves that we have to journey through to reach this peace. We fill up the empty spaces in our lives with activity, distractions, socializing, and anything outside of ourselves to stop us realizing the truth of our shadow and our heart. So much of our existence is an escape from ourselves, whether it be in fantasy projections or in ideas of our own specialness, goodness, or rightness.

If something is *behind* us, such as fear, it does not help until you make it conscious. The work is to bring the shadow forward and face it. When you look at it in the face, you embrace the pain and embrace the truth. As you come to know your innermost workings, you can then receive your heart's desires and come into congruence with all parts of Self. This is evidential: when you get it, you know you have succeeded in your shadow quest.

Aloneness makes you stronger and more whole. It focuses your light within and helps you to relate to others from your own center, your own truth, and your own rules and integrity. As there is no one else to project onto, you feel your suffering and become accountable to your own soul and shadow. They then become your markers for progress and growth.

Being alone tunes you into the soul's desires as in solitude you get to know yourself the best and can give yourself the best, what you deserve. When you set your boundaries with power, as taught by the shadow, you create more space for your individuality to blossom and for self-love to actualize. In loving yourself you give to yourself what you most need. This will then reflect in the outer world.

When one is cut off from friends, family, loved ones; when one is placed in an unfamiliar environment far away from what one knows; when one has no means of getting anywhere to escape; when one is truly in the unknown, this is when one can discover the merging of the Shew with the other light bodies. Rich inner worlds lie within, waiting to be explored, and it is only in certain opportunities given to us that we can benefit from this most greatly. Staying in this space, even while surrounded by others, is what makes us whole and able to relate to others as a whole. If we rely on others to make us who we are, to enable us to express who we are, then we will always live in reflection and in need of others.

Christ spent forty days and nights doing this: meeting his shadow, being alone, strengthening and fortifying himself without distraction, without others to make him feel comfortable, without a set of circumstances and known environments that could bring his personality into play, into a comfort zone. We are addicted to comfort, so we will do anything to avoid discomfort. Every living being has to go through the pain of their limitation in order to evolve to a higher level of consciousness.

When we stop thinking from our everyday mind, we get a glimpse of reality. Our shadow asks us to go into the most uncomfortable places and stay there. Sometimes in order to do this we have to leave our present day webs of relationship that we have woven in order to find a new web of life, a new web of relationship acting from a new set of rules that arise from the solid bedrock and foundation of having found out more about your shadow and who you are. This then allows you to contribute, express, and create your reality from your own authentic expression of Self. The trick after this, then, is to stay with this knowing in the midst of other people, your culture, society, and its norms and pressures.

## Protector and Separator

The shadow as protector is found alone. In chasing our shadow we get more confused; in sitting with it, facing it, despite the pain, it integrates. As VS recounts, " I remember reading a story about a man who had lost his shadow; he could not find it anywhere. He even got the police to help him search for it. Even though it represented his deepest fears and darkest desires, he felt incomplete without it. He needed it to feel whole again: to feel human once more." One can also observe this in the way in which cats and other animals actually chase their own shadows. They never catch it but have a great time trying, until they flop down exhausted. In sitting with the shadow alone, facing it, bringing it forward, and creating a friendship, it can integrate.

The shadow keeps you on the straight and narrow; it keeps you on your path. It teaches you how to keep boundaries and differentiate between the different bodies so that they are all in right proportion, right relationship, and harmony. Shew acts as our protector, ensuring that others' shadows do not encroach onto us. As Jesus said, "Get thee behind me Satan,"[2] to the shadow. He did not abandon or dissolve it. He used it to "get his back," to protect him and his light. Shew is what makes us whole when combined with the other light bodies.

Shadow rears up in feelings of irritation and fear that can guide us (when we are conscious of this voice) into a state of balance when we are out of balance. For example, perhaps we are descending too far into the body and shadow, or perhaps we are ascending too high into the soul Ba, leaving the body or shadow behind, neglecting them. Shew helps to keep the balance, and balance leads to wholeness.

Shew helps to preserve our individuality from melding into others, which primarily manifests with family, children, or community concerns that can dissolve our sense of individuality into the greater whole. While this is a beneficial thing, many times we can lose ourselves in service to others, forgetting to nurture ourselves. One can become too busy and lose one's center. The shadow comes in to remind us, to keep the balance of our individuality, as this body too needs to be taken care of.

Shadow is the middle ground between all the light bodies, the balance between coherency, order, and harmony and chaos, death, and the temporary worlds. It is the gatekeeper to embodiment. The more we delve into the shadow, the more a treasure trove of wisdom, power,

---

2. Matthew 16:23.

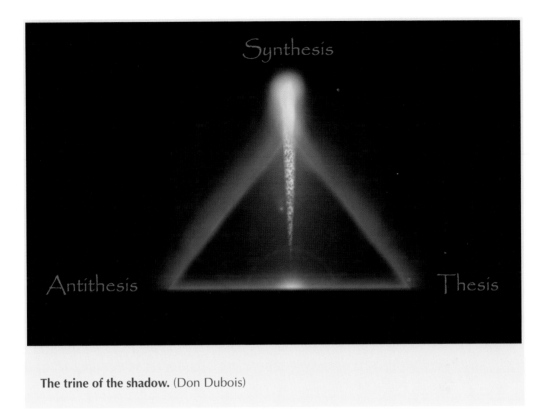

**The trine of the shadow.** (Don Dubois)

and self-love is found. From self-love, unconditional love can arise, again when it is held in balance.

Shadow teaches us the power of limitation in order for the unlimited Self to manifest. It limits certain actions in order for itself to be known, felt, and worked with, ensuring that you learn how to differentiate between each body so that each one can be whole and therefore connect effectively. One has to separate in order to unite, and in the alchemy of the Nine Bodies, one has to separate the shadow so it can be seen and worked with in its world. In its world, one discovers what drives it, for this world is run through your subconscious processes.

In separating and contemplating the different bodies, and then synthesizing and consolidating them, we create a pyramid: thesis +

antithesis = synthesis. Mutually opposing forces unite precisely because they have been separated, and they can come back together again because they are known and brought into conscious differentiation. As Jung says, "This task entails the most painstaking self-examination and self-education. The process of psychological differentiation is no light work; it needs the tenacity and patience of the alchemist who must purify the body from all superfluities in the fiercest heat of the furnace."[3]

The separating of personal from transpersonal is necessary because the physical body is a dwelling place of the shadow. Shadow is the key to embodiment. As this occurs, one cycle of ascension completes up to and above the crown, connecting the Ba to the earth-star chakra below the feet. As we embody more of these light bodies, the shadow becomes a gateway and key for us to see and discern the most appropriate action to take. It keeps you aligned, protects you from yourself, and serves to reweave you into all the light bodies, integrating with all other parts of ourselves so we can be divinely human or humanly divine. To leave it out is to lose a vital part of ourselves.

## Remedies for Reconciling the Shadow and the Physical Body

Every body casts a shadow. It contains, and is a reflection of, the body-mind. Form is defined by shadow. Once your physical body dies, you can return to be seen in your Ka, soul Ba, or shadow body, all of which retain vestiges of the human personality, or you can return to be seen through the Sahu immortal body, as a blazing perfected light form. Perhaps the most well-known example of this is Christ, who resurrected after the Crucifixion in his Sahu body.

---

3. C. G. Jung, *Psychology of the Transference* (Princeton, NJ: Princeton University Press, 1969), 132.

The shadow teaches what can make you whole by sharing how to spiritualize that which is material and unconscious. To do this, Shew acts as the function that seeks out the negative or dense in life by judging. Judgment is the yardstick of the shadow, as it is how it operates. When this function is balanced, it allows us to grow and develop by learning through discernment and duality. When it goes in excess, it becomes a way of seeing life, of contracting into fear, and of placing too much pressure on ourselves to grow.

This can happen because one is not connected to the higher lightbodies and stays stuck in a shadow loop. This loop feeds itself, recycling the same pattern until one relaxes into the higher light bodies, which modulates the shadow as a useful form of evolution. Duality becomes an ally and a friend, once aligned in its proper perspective, for you to see where you need to grow.

To let the shadow run your life is to lose connection. Seeing too much of the polarities in life, either too positive or too negative, keeps you stuck. To be aware of it, work with it, and allow the soul Ba to guide it, gently but firmly, allows the integration. The body is a tool to see this. For example, when the body is in pain or parts of it are stagnant or blocked, Shew is manifesting itself as mental or emotional residue to be seen, experienced, and learned from. The shadow will let you know if it is being ignored by influencing the body, letting you know through pain, disease, or discomfort what the unconscious is trying to make you conscious of and bring your attention to.

Shew lurks in the deep recesses of the body. Color illuminates its feelings, allowing us to work with its structures, easing them into fluidity rather than rigidity. Color allows the black-and-white shadow to be seen and its nuances explored and highlighted, brought into the visible from the unseen world lurking within. By recognizing the shadow, especially its central myth and pillar, it can be taught to work with the body and Ka. Perhaps one of the greatest roles it can play in this respect is not to introduce conflict and chaos into the conscious mind, and to stop negative effects occurring in the physical body.

This is a challenge, as the voice of duality and the greatest human fear is held in the physical body. Throughout the ages the body has been called the devil, the Antichrist, and the greatest obstacle to spiritual growth. From Christian flagellation to Buddhist denouncement, anti-body practices designed to repress, subdue, and take one away from the shadow have dominated many cultures. The greatest duality is held here because the greatest prize is also held here, in the body.

The physical body is the last step to full spiritual embodiment. This can only be realized when the shadow is connected consciously to the five "lower" bodies. Once illumined and consciously worked with in alliance with the body, Shew becomes a light in the darkness, a tool for bringing light into matter and recognizing this presence and voice held deep within the frequency of matter. God is everywhere, even in the darkest frequencies. Recognizing the frequency of matter itself is a big step to this . . . noticing the frequency of the body. This then allows consciousness held in the soul Ba and immortal bodies of the Hu to work with and absorb the shadow Shew.

Shadow is key to matter. It holds the key to open the recesses of matter and to accelerate and raise the frequency of the body. It holds the door to sexual realization and connection, and it guards the way to allowing the full release of ascending currents of kundalini and descending currents of light. Sexual realization occurs when we allow the shadow to be guided by the Sahu and Ba, which in turn aligns to the other light bodies. This form of sexual realization arises when we are aware of our shadow myth and are working with it consciously to express it from the body, giving it form and color so it can be seen and live out of the shadow that has been imposed on it. As this happens, the shadow too can play, which is what it wants to do.

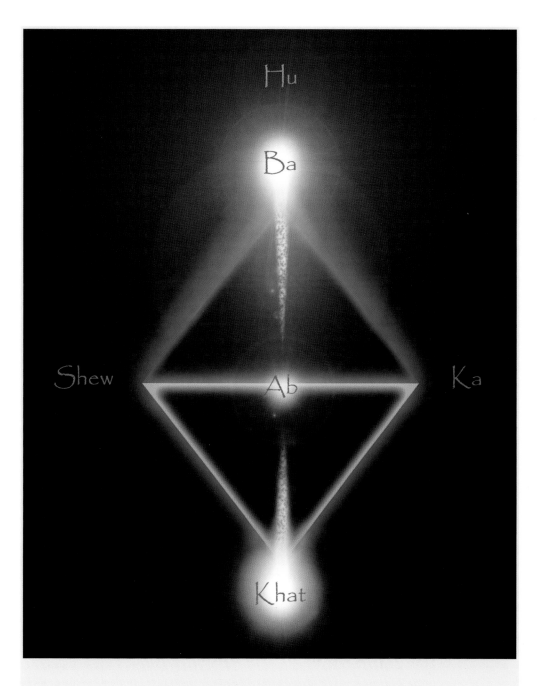

**The five bodies connecting.** (Don Dubois)

Shadow connects deeply with the physical body and can positively or negatively affect it. Appeals to the shadow can be made to alter the physical body once you are in close dialogue with it. However, both the Ka and the shadow can mistreat the physical, as if it was unworthy of being loved. Breaking through the idea that the body is all there is while simultaneously honoring the body as the temple by which all other bodies can manifest is a blessing, for even to have a body to use is to be able to grow. In looking after this temple for the soul, we include and appreciate it for the service it is providing as a holy vessel and sacred temple, that while useless until animated, provides the vessel for all forces of animation, light, and creativity to perform. Thus, in looking after it, treating it well, giving it the right foods, exercise, and connection to its larger body of Gaia, which is our true physical body, it can be happy and included among all the light bodies.

To break out of the paradigm where the shadow determines one's awareness is another major breakthrough. In dealing with the increased physical changes that occur from this, the very structures of our brain, DNA, blood, and spine also change to provide an expanded structural framework in order to integrate the changes happening in our emotions and our consciousness. With these physical changes we need assistance to facilitate and integrate these shifts. Green and raw live foods, massage, juices, and exercise all help in this shift. However, the deep structural shifts in our skeletal structure and the Ka body of light need more work on cellular and atomic levels. The Egyptian culture knew this and invented some powerful techniques to open the body up to receive more light; these techniques have now resurfaced in a modern context.

## The Djed Pillar of the Spine

Set is the shadow of Osiris. Osiris is the resurrected and glorious light form of the shadow that is integrated into matter to reveal the full embodiment of your Ba soul and universal Hu bodies of light. Both Osiris and Set are opposite and necessary twins. Set is matter, the spine that holds the shadow in place, whereas Osiris is the Djed Pillar of the spine, the Tree of Life of the spinal column that is a clear, open conduit between the heavens and the earth.

The importance of the spine, and its polarity between Set in the shadow state and Osiris in its fully conscious Djed or Tet state, was well known in ancient Egypt. Initiates used the pathway of the spine, the Tree of Life, in order to bring their life force and kundalini into the brain unimpeded. However, this Tree of Life in most humans is the damaged and stressed nervous system, holding onto defensive postures, emotionally hard-wired into limiting patterns that are stuck in the shadow and the unhealthy, untuned, and unresponsive body.

In your nervous system are stored your deepest stresses and tensions that prevent the soul Ba from fully flying free. The most primal fight-or-flight and defense responses as well as deep fears and traumas all get stored in the spine. Perhaps most importantly, our karmic issues from previous and present lifetimes get lodged into the central channel of the spine, to then play out in our lives.

Many ways of dealing directly with the causal issues of karma, stress, and suffering that lie in the spinal column were developed in Egypt, with some of the most powerful being initiations directed into the back of the brain and the spine using the ankh as a conductor for superconscious energies, and lovemaking techniques that allowed the potent energy of orgasm and love to rise up the spine into the brain. In order for this to happen most effectively, initiates would first have to clear their spines. Various healing modalities today directly address this causal form of what can be called karma, which helps unbind the shadow from being lodged in the spine and nervous system.

These modalities include:

- karmic knots healings

- atlas realignments
- central channel breathing
- advanced craniosacral work
- Network chiropractic adjustments

Clearing the central nervous system, the Tree of Life, of its stresses, strains, and its karmas can be vastly accelerated through these modalities. In Egypt, this Tree of Life was seen to ground one into the earth. When you are sufficiently grounded, the more rooted you are, the more you can fly. Your roots lie in the pillar of the spine, the spinal base, and nervous system, and its holographic counterpart, the Ka. As these merge, you rapidly integrate the shadow and are able to "soar" at will into higher dimensions, different states of consciousness, and expanded wisdom, peace, stability, and presence, as well as a new lightness of body and mind.

## Karmic Knots

Karmic knots are the seed causes of many karmic issues. They are held in a thin white line of light in the middle of your spine, and they can be seen, felt, and intuited as black seeds or knots that obstruct the flow of this white light in the spine.[4] These karmic knots are the causal reasons we reincarnate from lifetime to lifetime, as they carry the seed of lessons we still have to learn, actions we have performed, and consequences we have reaped from our actions. Emanating out from each karmic knot held in the spine are weblike patterns that fan out into the physical, emotional and mental realms as well as the Nine Bodies. Each karmic knot is a "seed" from which the "tree" of karma arises.

---

4. While most of them are situated in the spine, others are situated in the brain or held in the different light bodies.

Most spiritual work on the path is based on cutting, embracing, and healing, one by one, the branches of this tree until we reach the seed.

It is at this point that the energy from a karmic knots transmission can help push you to dissolve the final residue of specific karmic issues. This liberated energy, once released, can provide further "fuel" to help you to resolve your other karmic issues. Karmic knots transmissions can help you to complete certain issues when you have learned enough and are open to complete the issue to allow you to move on.[5] Karmic knots transmissions are powerful transmissions of light that dissolve up to three karmic knots in one hour. If you consider that most people on a dedicated spiritual path can have between five and twelve knots that they are working on, this can be quite a shift in one's path. If this work is combined with the other healing modalities that deal directly with the spine, acceleration becomes quantum.

Many people have been receiving these karmic knots transmissions, and their various effects depend on what karmas you have learned enough from and are ready to release. For example, a common experience of first receiving this transmission is feeling "a tangible infilling of light and loving energy flowing in through my crown and into my heart center," says CR As each knot unravels, different issues arise to be cleared, and resolution can be brought to karmic issues that you may have been working on for many years. "At a point, I began a journey through my most primary relationships (parents, siblings, children) as though I was attending a gathering or parade ... to clear up the karmic entanglements of the past. The feeling was of love, acceptance, and freedom to move on."

Similarly, MT shares that as the energy descended into her, she felt "in a wave of movement, a snakelike form move up my spine, undulating

---

5. Having an unbalanced male- or female-only approach will not complete all karmas. In addition, some karmas can only be lived into and cannot be dissolved solely through energy work.

up and down from the base to the top. I became aware of specific points that were blocked. They manifested as intense points of sharp pain. The areas were: the small of my back area, a middle point opposite my heart on my spine, and the large bone at the top of my spine."

As GH noticed,

I was pretty unconscious until midnight, then I woke up completely wide awake and energized. The only thing I remember is at one point waking up, finding the density of my body too heavy to even lift a finger, then sinking back down into the ground once more in a deep void. The next day I gently awoke with the awareness of witnessing myself in my heart. All day there was a heightened sense of vibrations all around, as my day seemingly spun in slow motion— calm, peaceful, almost surreal. I find myself supercharged upon my return, living in my heart, creating with love and presence, walking in my truth.

Many people also report physical sensations. As PJ shares,

I was sitting in a space of deep, deep meditation in some unknown spaces, and at the same time very present here and now in my physical body. I remember I got really burning hot at a certain time. I remember visualizing clearly a tube of light connecting the center of Mother Earth to the cosmos through my spine, and I was surprised and really amazed how this tube was so fluid, full of a light, crystalline free-moving energy. I was feeling so good during this transmission that it was hard to come back, feeling light and peaceful. It was so clean inside.

These kinds of sweats or chills are quite common, as the body-mind releases pent-up stress and tension on a deep level, purifying itself of the karmic knot obstacle. This can also be the first time that many people experience a unified energy directly in their central nervous system.

The movements of energy into the knots can be very apparent for some and gentler for others. Again, this is a unique and individual thing. As KD states,

> Amazingly powerful stuff there. I felt as if I was in between states of consciousness—not quite here but not quite there either. I definitely became "aware" of several particular parts in my body . . . I then felt my body erupt along my hara line, like an explosion into a billion magical little fragments. I could see/feel lights and sparks shooting out from me in an explosion of life force as my fragments were realigning themselves within me.

When the karmic knots unfold gently, it can be felt like "a soft breath of air coming from the sacred crown to my sacred womb, awakening it . . . and a radiant heat took place" (EL). One can also experience "wavelike movement around the crown with my whole body enveloped in a warm cocoon sensation . . . very peaceful and comforting" (NP). Similarly, one can also experience "a wave of very warm energy going through the lower part of my body, down and out of my feet. Then the same happened in the top part of my body out of my crown chakra. After an hour, the overall feeling was a deep sense of peace and harmony" (AH).

Parental, family, and ancestral issues seem to be a big theme in the dissolution of karmic knots. Many times, the clearing of karmic knots can start the day before, the day during, or the week after the actual transmission. MW shares that the dissolution of his karmic knot happened in the five days during and after the transmission, allowing him to truly love and appreciate his partner. Similarly, BG shares,

> In recent weeks I've come to see my excessively invasive and controlling mother, who I learned not to *ever* say no to or have any kind of boundaries with in order to survive as a child. When the transmission

began I felt a cool energy come in down my spine, but it seemed to get "stuck" in the area of T1–T2.... I sensed it was attempting to untangle a knot there.... It made it's way through until it came to another knotted location further down my spine. I felt self-pity and victimized, which came with tears ... and then rage at my mother. I kept seeing an *enormous* knot at that protruding bone there. At one point I saw my mother's face; she'd come to apologize.... She really did love me.

The week after this healing, the rest of the karmic knot with her mother healed. Similarly, as VR shares,

The previous karmic knots transmission had to do with my last life partner. We separated ten years ago, and for many years I was not able to let go of him. He was still in my heart, and there was no space for a new man. Immediately after this transmission I noticed that something had shifted. I felt so liberated, as if I had finally "divorced" from him. During the transmission I could feel a big knot dissolving in my neck/throat chakra. I felt nauseous, extremely tired, and I had a slight headache. Right after the healing I noticed that something had happened in my heart chakra and solar plexus as well. I now know I will have the courage to open my heart and reunite with my family and talk to them again.

Releases of the knot can be dramatic or subtle. Some people, such as JM, experienced

pain with three balls of light making their way up my spine to my throat, where I gasped for breath, inhaled, and released ... then a deep, sharp pain from the middle of my back and into the front of my chest at the top of my diaphragm and below my heart ... a huge gasp for air, a shudder, a convulsing, exhale, and release from the back to the front and out....

As AA experienced, "everything seemed to happen very quickly. I felt a dynamic thrust of energy toward the base of my spine and literally saw two huge knots, like thick ropes, break open and release."

The potency and visceral nature of these experiences occur because the body begins to vibrate at the frequency of the unified consciousness that is being poured directly into the spine and its karmic gateways. Many people can pass out because they have never experienced a unified consciousness directly in their central nervous systems before. To experience this directly is a big opening to the central nervous system that goes well beyond the time of the actual dissolution of the knot itself, for once the spine feels this, a pattern begins to be remembered—a pattern of unity.

Some people have deeply mystical experiences replete with masters, archangels, and aspects of their higher selves with lights, colors, and multidimensional travel all being quite common. Ancient memories from past lives can also manifest, as more Sekhem and life force flows throughout all parts of you. Each transmission is unique.[6] It does not matter what country, race, or religion you are from to receive this. We all have the same spine, and almost everyone has karma. The results are the same for whatever country and religion you are from, and these healings have been done on people of at least fifteen different nationalities with similar effect.

These transmissions are available on www.christblueprint.com.

## Network Chiropractic

Network chiropractic spinal adjustments are a direct way to release energetic blockages to induce healing of emotional, physical, mental, and

---

6. I trust that by sharing these many and varied experiences from the thousands of karmic knot healings I have facilitated that you can sense what it is like and the acceleration it provides.

spiritual issues at their source. The adjustments are done with minimal physical touch and are integrated through the breath and spine gently realigning back to their original posture. By directly working on open gateways in the spinal column, the spine releases areas of tension, and depending on how deeply one goes, these releases can also connect into the light bodies.

According to the Network chiropractic Web site,

> Gentle precise touch to the spine cues the brain to create new wellness promoting strategies. Two unique healing waves develop with this work. They are associated with spontaneous release of spinal and life tensions, and the use of existing tension as fuel for spinal reorganization and enhanced wellness. Greater self-awareness and conscious awakening of the relationships between the body, mind, emotion, and expression of the human spirit are realized through this popular healing work.

Techniques like this were practiced in Egypt in alignment with the atlas technique (see below) to dissolve key stresses in the brain and spine, creating more space in the spine and revealing more connection between body, brain, shadow, and soul. Actually receiving a Network adjustment feels very gentle, yet very lightening of your load. You can feel a new rhythm enter your spine and permeate throughout your body, which allows a deep sense of relaxation within the core of the body to occur. This then allows more peace and stability to arise so that previous issues can be dealt with from a calm, centered, and clear state of balance.

For more information, see www.associationfornetworkcare.com.

## The Atlas

The atlas is the connection between the spinal cord and the brain, lying at the first vertebra at the top of the spine. If the whole spinal cord were to be taken out of the body, its interface into the brain would be the atlas, the interface between the body and brain. In Greek mythology Atlas is a Titan and demigod condemned to forever carry the world on his shoulders as a punishment from Zeus for daring to challenge him. His back and neck are crushed by the weight as he stoops over, crushed by his duty and heavy burden. *Atlas* means "he who suffers," "the bearer," or "endurer."

Ninety-nine percent of us are born with an atlas defect, which means that the atlas is incorrectly positioned. Instead of the atlas bone being straight to allow the spine and brain to meet properly, it is at an angle, which prevents the full and correct flow of energy through the spine. This skeletal atlas defect then keeps us trapped in the stress patterns of the body-mind that prevent more energy from traveling down from the atlas and its associated chakra, the alta major, to the rest of our central nervous system and body-mind.

Atlas alignment was discovered in 1993 by disabled Swiss doctor R.-C. Schümperli. In his research, he found that in several advanced ancient cultures, particularly in the Mayan and Egyptian cultures, manual repositioning techniques of the atlas were practiced. He further discovered that the atlas is dislocated within almost all humans from birth, which can entail a chain reaction of symptomatic complaints such as back problems, migraines, psychological complaints, and complaints of the neck, spinal column, knee, and hip joints.

This dislocation has a direct effect on the psyche and organs, creating pressure, contraction, and disruption of the brain and muscles. This disconnection disturbs all internal body and nervous system communication, resulting in the spine being unable to send out its signals at optimum value to any part of the body-mind. Ultimately, this stops you from embodying the descent of light down the spine and the ascending current of kundalini energy up the spine.

Our bodies compensate and adjust to the incorrect position of the atlas from birth, creating a "false body" attitude. This incorrect positioning causes a disturbance of the sensitive, static equilibrium of the spinal column. By correction of the dislocated atlas, this long-disturbed internal communication can perfectly function in the nerve channels on all levels. As the Atlas is fixed to the suspension of the spinal column, the body's own healing forces are self-activated, resulting in decreasing stress responses and increased centering.

This makes the body-mind freer, lighter, more fluid, and connected. The heart feels freer to open, more breath and space are available, posture improves, you feels taller, and the organs and skeleton realign, dissolving old tension patterns. More energy becomes available to all parts of you because the central nervous system is now able to transmit and receive energy more efficiently throughout the whole body-mind-soul. As this occurs, growth accelerates as the missing screw in the brain-body connection is realigned.

The atlas is the physical opening to the alta major chakra, referred to as the Mouth of the Goddess in the Asian tantric traditions. Located at the back of the head at the base of the skull, it is the chakra where Shakti ignites and travels down the spine, sending waves of vibration throughout your brain, neck, and body like a tuning rod. It is the major chakra where the higher aspects of your body of light activate and enter into your physical body.

In Egypt, initiations were given to people through the alta major. If you see ancient paintings from Egypt, the high priest is standing behind the initiate aiming a copper rod at their alta major, transmitting sound and what is known as the "negative green" spiritual carrier wave of pure consciousness into them, turning their whole body-mind into a tuning rod. In these initiations the Alta Major was aligned and therefore could conduct vibration easily throughout the whole nervous system and brain in ascending and descending currents of light and kundalini. Indeed, the alta major was seen as a galactic doorway to these higher forces, a portal to concentrated high-frequency beams of light that unite our alta majors and pineal as one.

The atlas and alta major chakras were seen as evolutionary doorways to allow in these frequencies and to actually allow the expansion of the neurological centers. The depictions of the large-headed and highly evolved Egyptian race, also mirrored in some modern-day Tibetan lamas, were predicated on these centers being open to allow in higher frequencies of light. These higher frequencies emanating from the Galactic Center are returning to earth once more, as seen in the Mayan prophecies and in new healing modalities like Reconnective Healing and Ilhanoor, all of which tap into super light waves, as physicist Paul Violette describes.

These super light waves account for the recent increases in solar flare activity and the changing of magnetic grid lines on the earth. Gregg Braden points out that these super light waves can actually change DNA structures because of the increased resonance in the amino acid complexes in our physical bodies, which higher frequencies of light activate. All of this is helped by the atlas being realigned so the alta major can open to receive these incoming light sources comfortably. Without the atlas being realigned, this process can be uncomfortable and less effective as the increased frequency has nowhere to conduct safely through into our bodies.

Both of these areas at the back of the brain are connected to the subconscious and the feminine lunar entrance or "back door" to the third eye pineal. When they are consciously connected into, these chakras accelerate the embodiment and enlightenment process. When the alta major is aligned, both physically and energetically, your physical body and light bodies also connect on a deeper level, accelerating the awakening, ignition, or "descent" of your light bodies into the physical.

Embodying light into matter is part of our evolutionary imperative as a species, and it is precisely why the separation of body and spirit has occurred in the major religions of the earth, for within this union lies our ultimate freedom and creation of a new type of human being. This union is feminine-centered as it is a natural part of the feminine consciousness to work with both matter and light as opposed to the more transcendent and detached masculine consciousness.

For more information see www.atlasprofilax.ch and www.atlasevolution.com.

## Central Channel Breathing

The flow of the soul's energies occurs through the spine, and where body, mind, and soul all connect is through the perineum and the central channel of the spine. The perineum is a soft opening between the anus and the genitals that is the entryway and exit point for your spinal energies. It is the site of many blood vessels and nerve endings, and it is sensitive.

The perineum is part of the root chakra that generates and grounds all of the energy into the physical body. It stands in the middle of our personal, sexual desires, holding them in balance, flow, and harmony with the top of the spine: the impersonal crown chakra and third eye, centers of light and intuition. The perineum holds these polarities together and unites them through the spinal flow. It enables us to experience, live, and realize that sexual energy and light energy mix and merge within us to create one flow of living light.

The perineum grounds the spine through the central channel of the pranic tube, the tube that runs through our spines from the top of the neck down into the earth and then into the center of the earth. Like the spinal base, it provides a platform, a solid foundation for energy to ascend and descend up and down the spine. The central channel or pranic tube ensures your spine is kept connected to everything. When it is open, energy runs smoothly. When closed, energy becomes lopsided. It anchors the middle way between male and female energies in the spine, providing the basis for unity and neutrality, where male and female dissolve into simply being energy without polarity.

The perineum anchors the body-mind by grounding us into our human bodies with love. It holds us in place to allow the human and divine parts of Self to flow together as one. It is through the perineum and central channel breathing that many healers help to heal others, allowing their bodies to become conduits.

## The Practice

This is a simple but powerful breathing practice designed to open the central channel of the nervous system, where many stresses, tensions, and karmic positions are held. It also accelerates your mastery of the breath and the conscious control of the body-mind reactions and responses—the seat of the ego. It serves to take you deeper into stillness, the witness consciousness, and the more refined qualities of the soul light found in the center of the spinal column. It helps to open the third-eye chakra and is also used in tantric lovemaking to channel energy up the spine into the heart and brain.

Sit up comfortably, spine straight.

Focus your index and middle fingers into a pointing position, and point them at your root chakra perineum.

Focus on the thin white line of light that runs through the center of the spine.

Purse your lips like you were going to blow out a candle.

In this position, inhale light up the front of the body and spine for seven seconds, using your fingers to direct the energy of breath and light up the spine.

At the count of seven, cross your eyes gently and raise them to the third eye.

Hold your breath for seven seconds at the third eye.

Exhale down the spine for seven seconds, using the fingers to guide the energy.

Repeat the whole process 12 times.
How do you feel afterward?

## The Djed Pillar of the Spine: Gold and Green

When the spinal column becomes clear of its karmic knots and stresses, it becomes a "column of gold swimming in a sea of green." This is one of the stages in the Egyptian *Book of the Dead,* or the *Book of Coming Forth by the Light of Day,* where the soul's journey through death is mapped. These stages can also be seen as stages of transformation, of the embodiment of light into form, or enlightenment.

This transformation, when the spine becomes a "column of gold, eternal and in harmony,"[7] is when all your chakras fully align to the spine and all its energies flow and circulate in balance throughout your whole system. It is at this point that your physical body allies with your consciousness to become anchored and situated in the "for-giving," that is living without being enslaved to need, desire, and attachment, which is your natural way of being. You no longer live to get from others but to give. You have mastered all need, desire, and attachment and are refined enough to discern the subtlest threads of these energies within you.

---

7. Normandi Ellis, *Awakening Osiris: The Egyptian Book of the Dead* (Boston: Phanes, 1988).

This presence includes the sexual energy, refined, sublimated, and harnessed within it. As the sexual energy is the deepest source of need, desire, and attachment, this is a vital step. It does not mean that you will not feel desire: it means that it no longer controls you and drives you, and you are fully conscious of it. As you become fully conscious of it, you can use it to its highest potential, which is combined with love and wisdom and the vigilance needed to sustain this.

Making love in this state means that you unite all your chakras along the golden column of the spine, merging sexual energy with light through giving, consciously harnessing the force of desire. This necessarily means that all the holes of need and getting from others, the holes of the shadow that you used to fill your own holes within, are seen and healed. This allows the true potential of sacred or holy desire to manifest within you, as loving giving and sensual bliss merge your Ba and Sahu: your "Higher Self."

This transformation and "Osirification" of the physical body as it embodies light is the purpose of Egyptian tantra. Once all knots and stresses are gone, then one can really work with full embodiment. As long as knots and stresses are there and the atlas is misaligned, then one is limited in how much light one can bring into the body.

As the white light within the central column of the spine transforms[8] into a golden stream of liquid light, clarity, immovable centeredness, and strength, it becomes supported by a sea of green, a sea of aliveness. This green sea is then surrounded by a thin film of white on its edges. The metal and crystal associated with this are gold and green tourmaline, both of which can be used directly with the central nervous system to clear, align, and open up its channels directly.

---

8. In addition to these modalities, the Egyptian sciences of biogeometry and liquid crystals were also used in the clearing and regeneration of the spine. For more information, see www .biogeometry.com and www.theliquidcrystals.com.

## Higher Harmonics of Gold

These colors were seen as primary in Egypt for many reasons. Not only are they the frequencies, waveforms, and colors of the transfigured spine and Osiris, they were buried with nobility to assist them in their afterlife journey in the form of green tourmaline, and a version of gold that had been treated and refined to become a higher harmonic of gold.

The Egyptian science of biogeometry shows us how shapes, colors, symbols, and geometries moving in harmony together create sacred temple spaces and architectures, with this science also being used to heal any dysfunctions within humans as well. The basis of this technology lies in the three primary colors of the resonant waveforms that create harmony and higher frequencies, with these biogeometrical shapes having three primary vibrational color qualities: (1) negative green, (2) a higher harmonic of ultraviolet, and (3) a higher harmonic of gold. These three frequencies are the common energetic colors found in sacred art, sacred architecture, and sacred power spots on the earth, as found by Dr. Ibrahim Karim.

The higher harmonic of gold clears and strengthens the nervous system, strengthens the immune systems, and is beneficial to the space it is in. Higher harmonics of gold are also present in the relics of saints, in holy places, and in sacred sites and structures. It can be found in spiritually aware people and in some forms of music. The higher harmonic of gold is in resonance with physical gold and is depicted by the halos around the heads of saints. It enhances wisdom and prosperity.

You need to use gold and its higher harmonics when you are in negativity, tension, stress, disease, and toxicity. In using gold, your inner beauty and highest potential can reveal, clearing negativity and providing stabilization at a holistic level. Gold regenerates and stabilizes you, smoothing out the distortions so you become Self-contained. Gold also opens the crown and third eye chakras, and is a master healing stone anchoring purification on all levels. Physically it boosts the endocrine system and helps with spinal alignment and neurological problems.

## Monatomic Gold

Classical science teaches us that the three phases of matter are gases, liquids, and solids. Recently, humanity has become aware of plasmas, condensates, and liquid crystals. Another "new" yet ancient discovery is another phase of matter called "monatomic." These are also known as Ormus and m-state elements, and many civilizations across the world and throughout history have used monatomic elements in many forms for natural healing and awakening.

Monatomic elements work on creating superhealth within you, which begins at the level of your cells. Not only do your cells communicate via chemicals and electricity in your nervous system but also through the exchange of photons or light particles through the biophotonic network, known in Egypt as the Ka body of light. Light is innately intelligent and carries higher quantities of "purer" information as well as being superconductive. The more of it you can bring into your system, the more you can transform your body at the cellular level, from your organs, muscles, and tissues to your brain and nervous system.

Monatomic elements are superconductive, and when they are ingested into our bodies they change our cellular structure into a superconductive matrix because they are the cause of energy at the cellular level. This means that the cells become superconductors for an increased flow of photons that increase your electrical and electromagnetic field. "Put another way, you could say that monatomics transform the body's 'wiring' from being simple copper cable to being wired with fiber-optics, where the same 'width' of wiring is able to carry a thousand times as much 'process' information."[9] This then allows all the bodies of light to flow in harmony with the physical body, accelerating the alchemical and transformative process of embodying soul presence or Ba.

The energy produced by monatomic gold flows through the body with little resistance. They are extreme concentrations of superfood that release a flow of light to heal body-mind and soul by creating a trinity of balance. David Hudson says that these powders behave as superconductors at room temperature, and tend to "ride" on the magnetic field of the earth.[10] As the Ka is attuned to the magnetic fields of the earth through its geometric structures, which are also part of the biophotonic network, monatomic elements can be said to enhance the connectivity of the Ka, the closest form of the light body to physical awareness, to the physical body or Khat.

According to Hudson, monatomic elements connect with nonphysical realities, or the bodies of light, through the zero-point field or the void, which holds endless potential for new and unlimited energy. The basic idea of alchemy is that you cannot create something out of nothing. Instead, one transmutes consciousness into whatever it is that you wish to create. If you wish to transmute something that already has a solid form, for example your body-mind and soul, then that object has to undergo a process of disintegration and transformation to move toward the zero point. From the zero point it can begin moving toward materializing its new, transformed being.

The "nearer" one is to the zero point, the higher the vibration. So, in order to prepare your physical body to receive all the other bodies of light, you must raise the frequency, clarity, and spaciousness of your

---

9. www.zptech.net.

10. Under some circumstances, monatomic elements weigh less than zero. That is, a container full of monatomic matter could be observed to weigh less than the empty container. See www.zptech.net.

physical body, bringing the physical closer to the vibrational levels of the more formless bodies of light.

## Negative Green

Negative green is a spiritually intelligent carrier wave that creates resonance with many other dimensions through the bodies of light. It is an integral and important part of spiritual energy fields and increases with the spiritual evolution of the person. (It is the resonance with gray, between white and black.) It is at the core of the energy centers in the body and power spots in nature, with structures such as pyramids and domes producing this vibration along their central axis.

It is connected to green tourmaline, which acts on the nervous system to solidly anchor high levels of consciousness into the mind, anchoring powerful healing abilities and self-awareness. It raises our ability to carry light and is a highway for light to conduct into the spine and nervous system. Along this journey, it can heal the energy bodies and open the heart to infuse peace and patience. One needs more negative green and green tourmaline if you find it hard to bring higher consciousness into thought or if you are emotionally closed and lack peace, compassion, and patience.

Together, the harmonics of -green and +gold create not only sanctified inner space within you but also outer space in the architectures and temples that the Egyptians lived and worked in. To have both integrated is to be living in harmony with all your bodies of light, which is how the Egyptians designed their civilization, their architecture, and their spiritual work. The best technologies are already working within us. As we evolve so too our bodies reflect this change. Our cell geometries change, our spine changes, our brains change, even our sexual organs become different as they become clear, light, and free. This was all known and mapped by the ancient Egyptians, and now that knowledge is being revealed again so we may embody our highest potentials, individually and as a collective.

## Shadow Myths

Myths are temporary stories that lead us into the infinite. In this they have their use as tales and lessons to be learned on the initiatory journey, as gateways into a deeper reality and understanding. In these accelerated times, once these myths are known they can be experienced and learned from relatively quickly, coupled with your own willingness and commitment.

Our shadow has its own unique myth or legend that sustains it, that keeps it alive. All living beings want to survive, to keep existing: this is part of life's basic programming, which we eventually come to terms with as we face and overcome the fear of death, which leads to true fearlessness. For each person, their shadow myth may be different. Each one of your myths is unique for each body of light. You may have already conquered some of your myths, and you may still need to become fully aware of some of them and choose a new course of action to heal and integrate that myth forever.

Embodying all Nine Bodies is not done in isolation or seclusion. In today's climate and evolution in human potential, and in the forms of enlightenment itself, one has to unite and work with all nine in the world, in the community, and in relationship as well as alone. While there are periods of seclusion, these periods are to stabilize certain aspects of the bodies of light. It is hard to merge and unite all nine without following both of these paths, as this is the divine plan for this age: for humanity to demonstrate its love with each other, not just for a God outside but with a God in each other. This, then, is the meaning of the Sanskrit *namastute:* the God in me recognizes the God in you.

## The Myths

At a certain point, the ruling principle of our shadow life must be encountered and dissolved in order for a new center to emerge. In its world, the shadow creates and lives out a myth, a legend, a recurring theme that keeps repeating in your life. The world of the shadow can be complex, but once its central myth is understood, the shadow can unravel in all its nuances. Its myth is one of the central meanings of your life, a key pillar, and it is revealed when you are ready to deal with it. The circumstances for this myth can arise during your childhood and become reinforced throughout its repetition in your life, primarily in what brings you the most passion. In this passion lies intertwined the shadow myth in the attempt to find this soul passion and the heart's desire to manifest it.

The myth will continue until you come to terms with it, and it is important to understand that you are the creator of this myth. For example, one myth may be judgment. One can continually create the myth of judgment by judging others and being judged, sometimes fairly, sometimes not. This judgment leads to isolation from a part of self that one cuts off from, manifesting in close relationships where one would also cut off emotionally or spiritually. In seeing this clearly, it can be healed and repaired through humility, forgiveness, and communication.

It is our task to discover this myth, heal it, and love it in whichever way is appropriate. This does not negate the shadow or destroy it. Rather, the central pillar of the shadow that has been kept intact for aeons can now be replaced so the shadow body can align to the other eight bodies. The myth can only change when there is recognition and conscious awareness of the soul Ba. It is through the soul that the myth can be dissolved and rewritten, for Ba and its higher self of the Hu are the master programmers for all the other bodies.

Before this is done, the shadow rules you. After this, the soul works with the shadow in right harmony and proportion. The roles get reversed: whereas before shadow ruled soul, now soul rules shadow— the right balance with no negation, rather integration; everything in its right place working together like a well-oiled machine running in divine will.

You heal and integrate the shadow's central myth when you are relaxed with where you are, allowing all to be and sufficiently connected to the soul. This can be a painful thing to experience and accept and to sit in. You have to face not only your deepest fear and pain but sit in it while it is being reenacted within and around you. This can also take on the form where other people play out your greatest fear and shadow myth for you.

Other examples of shadow myths can be abandonment and rejection, feeling unworthy, and so on. These are all painful experiences, without a doubt, and they are healed by venturing deeply into them. (This can be done in ritual but will happen spontaneously on your path when you are ready for it.) It is one thing to be aware of your myth; it is quite another to venture into it, connected to your soul Ba, and dissolve it by being centered and inclusive of the shadow through loving peace: the power of love. When there is no reaction left, the myth is gone. There is no need to rush or think about it. It will happen when it is ready to happen, organically and spontaneously, when your awareness differentiates between the physical body, the conscious mind, and the unconscious shadow.

The myth lived by the shadow in its world influences both the physical body and the Ka. You can understand your own myth by looking at the recurring patterns of your life, the recurring stagnant and painful parts of your body. What keeps happening to you that demands love where there is no love? Where does this manifest in your body?

## The Myths in the Bodies

There is no shadow in Sahu or Akhu, the immortal and universal bodies of light, which means there are seven gateways that the shadow holds into your full embodiment. These get subtler and subtler as you evolve and integrate the aspect of the shadow that is preventing you from *fully* embodying. We each have our own myth in all of the bodies. Only you know what it is, and this can be accessed through an honest appraisal of your life experiences through the lenses of the seven bodies.

For example, a common myth in the world regarding the shadow held in the physical body is what we look like, and many people's obsession with this results in cosmetic surgery, vaginal surgery, dieting, worry over the body, and so on. Whether your body looks fat, skinny, or misshapen are all the domain of the Khat, and behind this is the shadow's urges and need to consume that will sabotage any diet. On a deeper level this manifests in whether you are connected to your bodies and the earth, to the voice of the body and the voice of the earth, and whether you love and accept yourself just as you are. If you are in your body, you can feel it and hear its wisdom and what it needs. If you are disconnected from the body, it falls ill to let you know to pay more attention to it and its needs, which are connected to your shadow.

In the Ren body of name and form, people name themselves and their children after heroic, divine, or mythical figures, hoping to imbue some of that legend or magic onto them and their child. This resonance can either stimulate or burden a person. Many people change their names as they grow and evolve to more accurately reflect their vibration, the meaning this has to them, and where they are on their journey. The myth of a name does have power, as people call your name every day. If your name resonates to a collective myth or story, you have to ask yourself: do you want to be associated with that myth forever?

In the Ab or the human heart, seat of the heart's conscience and wisdom, you have to find the balance between love, power, and wisdom in your human experience. This is a delicate balance that can lead us into harmony with both earthly forces and celestial forces, for all the chakras balance in the heart. You can either become too earthly and ignore the higher aspirations of the heart, or you can become too spiritual and love and serve all without tending to your own heart and those close to you.

In the Ka you find personal power, vitality, charisma, and the ability to influence others, as well as a connection into expanded and luminous realities. The myths here can be over reliance on power, as Ka gets fed by the attention and adulation of others, or in the case of the negative Ka it gets fed by the judgments of others. One common myth between Sekhem and Ka is the feeling of invincibility and power beyond the cares and concerns of others, divorced from the heart and soul, Ab and Ba.

The central myth of the shadow is judgment and separation.

In the soul Ba, shadow manifests as living without compromise to the soul, which can cut off the need for self-love and self-nurturance and lead to a loss of grounding and the human touch.

In the life force of Sekhem, you discover and use power and what it is. Your ideas of power come to be examined here: what does power mean to you? Do you feel you have enough of it? What does it look like to you to be fully empowered? What are you scared of to step into this power? Have you ever felt universal power? What did it feel like? Was it true power?

It takes personal power to fuel unconditional love; power is the engine, and love is the substance of all of it. Humanity's ideas of power have been distorted since ancient times and are starting to come back into a true context for its use. Women in particular are discovering this feminine power and are learning not to compete with masculine power.

If you are a woman, how have you learned to compete with men for power, and how are you now stepping into and using the feminine power and center instead?

## Meeting Your Shew Firsthand

In meeting your own shadow Shew directly, you begin to see the parts of yourself you have been holding back, repressing, or hiding out of fear. Its power, your power, brings up fear at first, but as you learn to tap into and become allies with the shadow, this fear becomes transmuted as you work with the deepest archetypal subconscious power that you hold.

However, shadow, when initially contacted, can swing in wild polarities and dualities. If it is not embraced, any realization can be swiftly forgotten as it rears its head once again, demanding to be seen and met with compassion. It wants to be worked with consciously, not just left festering in the corner. If one approaches the shadow too directly, without openness, humility, and self-responsibility, it will flare up and defend its position. It will vociferously defend and attack its rights and will project all that it is onto its supposed attacker.

Each person's experience of the Shew is different as we are all unique souls. However, certain similarities do present themselves in everyone's shadow, as they are all linked to the collective shadow of humanity. Within each experience are also the keys to working with the shadow, for the shadow will show you where it comes from and, with some inquiry, how to work with it.

The shadow is androgynous[11] and can shift between male and female forms depending on what part of you that you have left out. It will show you what you have not even dared to think, see, or feel, and it is

---

11. Interestingly, frogs can change sex at will and are androgynous.

wise to have this initial meeting in a safe and guided environment, as it can be shocking to who and what you think you are. Seeing it is believing it.

The shadow Shew is an experience that you live every day as the subconscious guides the world for those who have not made it conscious. Making it conscious means that you live it, experiencing its depths and extremes in your life, learning to befriend it as an ally and protector, understanding its purpose and honoring it by listening and checking in with it every day, and giving it pleasure in an integrated way. Expressing it through art, music, lovemaking, and shadow theater are a few of the more direct ways to tune into it, and once integrated it becomes your protector and gateway to full embodiment.

As MT shares,

Meeting my shadow was a powerful and empowering experience. The Shew was androgynous, and while I could see features that resembled me, the form was translucent. Inside the Shew was filled with this gray, charcoal color of billowy smoke that swirled around inside the body. The lower part of the Shew's body had red, orange, and yellow coursing and flashing like a lightning storm. The eyes were void, like the dark cosmos.

At first the Shew was standing over me, staring at me. I felt that it was quite angry and did not trust me. I asked the Shew if it would please sit with me. I apologized for ignoring it and said that I wanted to listen and understand. When the Shew sat across from me its eyes changed to a fiery white. Shew wanted to be acknowledged. It wanted to move and create from the place of the feminine divine with great power and certitude. As I sat with the Shew it's fierceness lessened, and I began to feel the softness of its power. At that point, its eyes changed to a beautiful red ruby gem color, and it smiled.

As SMC shares,

When you asked us to embrace our Shew, I felt raw unbridled power enter my body and fill me with an incredible, uncontainable fire. I have never felt that amount of desire and passion, so palpable, in my body before. This fire was not just about sexual energy, although I did feel that very strongly. It was so fierce in me that I think the words that came out were "Come here! I own you," and I even felt the feline growl in my throat as I voiced the words. Wow! I realized that for a long time I have shied away from claiming the power of the truth of who I am. I have always known this in my heart, but never have I felt the intense fire, the raw power, in my physical body.

CO shares the repression of her Shew:

My Shew appeared as a cloaked and hooded figure. I could not see the form until I commanded that he/she unveil itself. As it pulled back its hood and dropped the entire cloak, I was taken aback by what appeared before me. My shadow appeared as an androgynous figure with an eyeball hanging from its socket, sporadic tufts of hair left on the skull, burned flesh, stab wounds, joints out of sockets, and other assorted wounds.

I asked what its pillar, its core emotion, was. It showed me abandonment. I felt the pain, the self-abandonment and rejection of power as well as passion. I felt my cloaked and hooded self. I felt my Shew's desire to be loved, embraced, enfolded in harmony and forgiveness into my Khat, my Ab. In meditation with this, two very powerful cellular memories of "overmothering" and abandoning self in the distraction of serving others arose. The awareness of these memories seemed to bring forth a clarity, a release of something forgotten. Yet I failed to honor the call to allow quiet time to embrace more fully these powerful cellular memories. My shadow then arose in frustration with my ignorance and played itself out with others around me. The lesson is to allow the time to fully integrate and embrace what is unveiled within one's shadow.

RD recounts,

The shadow came to me from behind. I was taken to an Egyptian temple in a torchlight ceremony. A man emerged from the shadows cast by the torchlight. He came to me as a shape-shifter with red glowing eyes, asking for forgiveness. Forgiveness meant releasing the shadow from its obligations to do "dirty work" on my behalf without conscious awareness. Its role as a protector had been ignored. The shadow then transformed into a beautiful sensuous woman and came physically very close, within sharing breath. She desired true intimacy and had the desire to have her needs heard, which had been ignored or turned away from as too physical, animal-like, or dark and sexual in nature—deeper earthly needs as opposed to high spiritual goals and states.

She made it clear there would be no route to enlightenment without first meeting the darker side of life and embracing it. She asked to be in daily communion and that her role as protector and confidant would be assured. The shadow has needs...and it is important to listen to and honor those needs from that place, or it becomes distorted into irritation and unconscious anger. The shadow projects its own needs onto the world and everybody else when it is not fulfilled.

You have to take time to assimilate and understand the first conscious meeting with Shew, so rich is it in its archetypal associations and connections with the deep subconscious power that has been hidden within you. Shew will give you what you need to see and know rather than what you want. It will show you the parts of yourself you need to work with in order to become whole and truly empowered. As AW shares,

My shadow appeared in the distance and glided toward me like one magnet being drawn irresistibly to another. Various aspects of its body manifested one after another. Its skin seemed to be made of an icy, crystalline material, glasslike, transparent. As the emotionless figure, part angel, part devil, part human, part beast, stared down at me with its large white eyes spiraling with light, a wave coursed throughout my body like an electric shock or the aftermath of an orgasm. My shadow, devoid of human passion or emotion, was terrifyingly beautiful to behold and powerful beyond reason. One of its legs, that of a goat, reminded me of the ancient god Pan, complete with a cloven hoof.

My shadow stretched its feathered wings as mother's breasts emerged from its chest, became engorged, and then violently spewed out star milk. A gigantic, fountaining male erection, half the length of its body, simultaneously expanded skyward. At its base, in place of testicles, a yoni, glowing with light, opened wide, and the crown of a child's head appeared from the birth canal. A geometric star appeared in my shadow's hand. The other hand held a chalice aloft, overflowing with blood as if offering a toast. At that moment I felt tears streaming down my cheeks, yet no emotion seemed to have caused them.

On one level, I understand that my emotionless shadow has functioned as a protective shield for me for many years, allowing me to realize my dreams and succeed in many interesting endeavors without the risk of emotions deterring me from my goals. My central myth, which has been one of abandonment, is becoming one of transformation. From meeting with my shadow, I understand that in order to survive and succeed on this journey, my heart must grow much larger in compassion. More passion! More tears! More love!

# The Collective Shadow

The shadow is a collective construct shared by all humanity. The collective shadow is created by all the thoughts, fears, beliefs, and projections of humans for hundreds of thousands of years that have coagulated and coalesced into archetypal patterns and constructs. These living thought-forms carry all the emotional charge and fury, pain and fear, fight or flight of humans.

See if you can name a few more of these right now.

These thought-forms create a literal blanket over the collective of humanity, informing, feeding on, and being fed by billions of people. To be fed by the shadow is to be fed by a mother that we know very well, very intimately, and that we are reluctant to let go of. It is almost like an umbilical cord that connects us to the collective shadow, and because it is all that we have known, to go beyond it, or to integrate it fully, can be scary. It is the total unknown to go beyond this mother of the shadow that nurtures our fears, our holes, and our justifications for not being loving to ourselves and consequently to others. To leave this mother behind takes time, discipline, refinement, and discernment.

Love has no attachment in its purity. The love you may think you have for others in your life, and for the shadow, is oftentimes conditional and attached. This is a humbling knowing to face once you are radically honest about your holes and needs, and it is a necessary step to take before you can detach from the hooks and snares of the collective shadow. The first step in this process is to dialogue and strike up a friendship with your own personal shadow. Get to know it, what it wants, what it needs, and what it feeds on within you, or what it asks you to do.

How do you feed your shadow?
How does it feed you?
Which chakra does it live in most for you?

The next step is to begin the divorcing process, that is, to disengage from the collective hooks that we plug into that prevent us from full and conscious integration of the shadow. To become conscious of the shadow is half the process, and becoming aware of exactly how it manifests in your life is a key. Contemplate this for a moment.

The collective shadow influences your daily life. It is like the whole of humanity has a blank, featureless face looking out to the rising sun from an earthly cave of its own making, waiting to leave the cave, the den, and its mother. To leave this mother of the shadow, this hiding masquerading as nurturing, is to reclaim your power and integrate the shadow so it is not left out, rather included, embraced, and brought into the heart of Ma'at: harmony, order, and alignment.

This harmony and alignment works on many scales: on a collective scale it is found with the moon. The moon influences the collective and personal shadow, bringing both emotional chaos and lucid clarity. By losing our connection to the thirteen moon cycles and natural time, which leads us into the infinite timing cycles of the Galactic Center, we have also lost conscious connection with the shadow, distorting it into a twisted, unbalanced reflection.

In ancient Egypt this was not the case, as they recognized that the power of the subconscious is immense, and by consciously tapping into and programming it like a computer, a lot of power can be released and harnessed in your life that was previously being wasted or squandered. The shadow was seen as an ally to be worked with, included, and gently led, like one would do with a child, as it left the mother of the subconscious and returned to its source in the earth and the sun to then function as a connector, gateway, and reflector of the sun to the Galactic Center.

All human beings live, to greater or lesser degrees, in the shadow Shew. In Egypt and later in Palestine the constructs of this collective shadow were known and mapped out by sages and shamans so they could carve a pathway through the collective shadow mind. The shadow guards our higher light bodies for very good reasons. It is not just a transpersonal or Jungian phenomenon (it goes into many dimensions), and to approach it just through these means is to leave part of the shadow untended to and still veiled.

To integrate the many layers of the shadow is a mystical journey that requires awareness and work with the Ba and Sahu. Once combined with the transpersonal work and awareness of the shadow, the shadow realizes its integration. In addition, just as there are spiritual hierarchies of light, known as Ascended Masters, so there are dark brotherhoods of shadow that are the parallel of the Ascended Masters. These practitioners of power, control, and greed also have a structure to their organization, just as the Ascended Masters do. Some of these levels are listed below for you to become aware of and disconnect from.

## 1. The Personal Hole

The shadow first manifests in you through the personal subconscious, which then feeds into the collective shadow, finding parallels, hooks, and comfort zones to hook into. Most of us have deep-seated wounds in our consciousness that create lifelong patterns, habits, addictions, and behavioral tendencies that cover a black hole in your body-mind, veiling a need in you. We can cover these holes in our subconscious, which leak energy, by denials, justifications, excuses, and hiding the cause of the issue under the carpet. These veil the core seed of the wound and can often keep us bound in these cycles for lifetimes.

These deep-seated wounds are often hidden and masked, even when much spiritual work and inquiry has been applied, and prevent us from fully accessing the body of light. When these holes are cleared and sealed, a sense of empowerment, more energy, and a feeling of being whole can arise. The feeling of there being something missing, or a sense of something lacking or being deficient, can also disappear.

Exorcism is rapid soul healing and clearing from these thought-forms of fear, loss, and holes within you that you seek to fill through external sources. What has been hindering you that still persists? What seems unhealable within you? What situations arise that do not go away and keep repeating? What thought-forms still hold you in their grip?

Yeshua, Moses, and John the Baptist, all of whom were trained in Egypt, were masters of exorcism as soul healing, demonstrating the importance of removing the veils to pure consciousness. In essence, awakening is simply letting go of all the veils that stand between you and presence. Exorcism rapidly clears intractable blocks and obstacles that no other form of growth, healing, inquiry, or personal transformation can achieve. An exorcism is the removal of specific entities or thought-forms that feed off your wounds, needs, desires, attachments, and fears. An exorcism can completely clear an issue or reveal a deep wound that will then need additional inquiry to reveal its subconscious grip on you.

Entities feed on your wounds, holes, and needs, veiling them, making it harder to heal. Each need and wound you have creates a hole within you through which other life forms can come to feed. These holes, once cleared and sealed, and once the entity is removed, will dissolve the issue, or clarity will arise to exactly what it is. Sometimes you may know what the issue is but be unable to move through it no matter what you do. This also is where exorcism comes in: to remove the block and dissolve the veil of illusion that has been hardened over time.

## 2. The Genetic Unconscious of Your Ancestry Stored in DNA

Ancestral distortions, attachments, patterns, belief systems, thought-forms, and manipulations are all passed down through your bloodline.

This can manifest as deep unconscious sufferings, conflicts, unhealthy resonances with family members, and negative thought-forms and lifestyle choices. Feeling that you are a victim to your DNA often manifests through the claims, "That's just the way I am," or "My mother is exactly the same." These thought-forms keep you bound to the matrix of the family consciousness and the genetic unconscious of your ancestry. DNA tampering, distortion, and draining of energy can also be present from outside sources.[12]

## 3. The Seven Rulers or Planetary Ego Supports

For thousands of years the human consciousness has had seven main supports for its ego structure, which over time have become living, breathing thought-forms or sentient beings. These have become planetary-level entities that create, manipulate, and feed on these archetypal forms within the human matrix. These seven living sentient beings of lust, fear, greed, envy, sloth, ignorance, and pride feed on the life force from people to keep these thought-forms alive and to keep people imprisoned within the planetary light body and incapable of expanding outward into their other light bodies.

For millions of years humanity has lived within these seven primal supports of the ego mind, and year by year these seven grow in size and power as more and more people feed and are fed by these living thought-forms in a vicious cycle of parasitic interdependent relationship. For example, after 9/11 the rise in fear expanded the ruler of fear tremendously, resulting in the United States living at the frequency of fear. All seven rulers are based on false body-mind identification, which,

---

12. Various forms of healing can deal with this; for more detailed information see Padma Aon Prakasha, *The Power of Shakti* (Rochester, VT: Inner Traditions, 2009).

if not rooted out from the depths of the psyche and ego, results in us being unconsciously controlled and manipulated by forces buried deep within the collective human mind-set.

## 4. Reptilian, Solar, and Galactic Entities

The primordial ancestry of the human brain is part reptilian. It is a part of us. However, there are unbalanced humans who rely on this part of the brain, cutting off from the energies of love and compassion in the other parts of the brain, instead relying on power and sharp intelligence to drive them. This ultimately results in a cold, heartless, profit- and greed-driven society intent on survival at all costs.

These unbalanced reptilian beings, as mentioned in many best-selling books by David Icke, among others, have been here on earth for millions of years and are said to control a large part of the world's economic and social systems. They also plug into and harness the energy of the emotions of human beings, using this energy to feed themselves in many and varied ways, primarily through generating and then harnessing the powerful negative energy of fear. To disconnect from this influence with understanding and ruthless compassion is to free yourself of their Matrix, a matrix designed to ensnare and trap you into systems of financial manipulation and control, media influence, fear tactics, and heartlessness.

On the solar and galactic planes there are many civilizations, deities, and rulers in various planets and constellations who can prevent you from entering the fullness of the Ba and the Sahu, or universal light body. These false deities, or "celestial demons" as they are known in the East, can give you a false sense of power that imprisons you by telling you that the temporary and phenomenal experiences they offer you are genuine experiences of sovereign freedom and selfless power. If you have not had the experience of solar mastery or freedom, then you can fall prey to these false lures and subtle temptations. These can be removed through awareness and light healing.

## 5. Archons or Ancient Earth Rulers

Archons are demonic rulers and are mentioned extensively in the Gnostic Gospels. They have been behind the scenes for millions of years, manipulating and orchestrating the movements, fears, and emotions of the collective consciousness in order to feed themselves and keep separation in place. Archons are ancient, powerful demons that live at a high frequency of power between the seventh and ninth dimensions, inaccessible to most people who are not fully conscious of the galactic body of light. Several Gnostic Gospels, and much of John the Baptist's and Christ's work, focused on dissolving many of these demons' hold on the earth and its people. However, many are still left.

Archons are attached to almost every human's body of light, preventing the crown channel from being fully open. They form a thick, black oily blanket 1,300–23,000 feet above your physical body in your light body, preventing light, love, and full empowerment from reaching your body-mind consciousness. When an Archon is removed, major changes can happen in many areas of your life, particularly a loss of fear.

Archons are also attached to all twelve planetary fields, several star constellations, inhabit many countries, and can be several miles across in size. They are drawn to zones of terror or war to feed off the energy flows there, with some of the biggest Archon numbers on earth being in Auschwitz, Iraq, Sudan, and Israel. Conversely they are also drawn to areas of great light to create conflict there, such as Kashmir and Palestine.

All of these shadow constructs can be dissolved through light transmission; see www.christblueprint.com for details.

# The Mystical Shadow: Hell Realms

As one travels deeper into the shadow, one comes across the hell realms, dimensions resonating at frequencies of discord, chaos, and suffering. Known and mapped by the Egyptians and the Tibetans in their *Book of the Dead,* these realms are very real within the collective shadow. To clear and learn the lessons held within these realms, and release the aspects of you that are stuck there, requires skilled guidance and awareness of your shadow and your other bodies. This is a mystical journey that involves you traveling consciously into these realms to see and experience this part of self. Those among you who are inclined to bodhisattva work can also help release trapped souls from here or dissolve certain thought-forms.

This is not a question of a belief: just as there are heavenly worlds, so are there demonic ones. Just as there are spiritual hierarchies, so are there demonic hierarchies; just as there are Ascended Masters, so are there demonic masters who live on shadow. As above, so below. As Thoth says in the *Emerald Tablet,* "A Masters Work is Three-fold: The dissolution of evil, the promoting of the good, the spreading of wisdom."

Each hierarchy has its purpose, and if we are to integrate the shadow, this is a journey one has to take, because it is only by going to the depths of suffering that one is able to generate enough compassion for self and others. Feeling the greatest suffering breeds the deepest compassion and wisdom.

There are two types of demonic thought-form: ones created by humans over time that become living thought-forms that feed on and are fueled by human ignorance, fear, greed, lust, sloth, envy, pride, and hate; and the second type, associated with the formation of the universe and earth, and the beings that were created by this explosion of light and the antimatter or darkness that was simultaneously created. These spirits are ancient, powerful, and talked about in the *Book of the*

*Dead* in Egypt and Tibet, serving to create various veils and gateways through the collective consciousness.

The hell realms have been ventured into voluntarily by many beings throughout history, various bodhisattvas, Buddhas, Christs, and other evolved beings who understood that to ground and sustain their awakening, they had to integrate the shadow. Now it is your turn, as now it is easier than at any other time in history to work with these worlds, as quite literally many of these hell realms exist on the earth plane. They have manifested from the unseen into the seen world so that those who can "see" can work with them to free themselves. Today, this is manifesting in your daily life and relatings in many ways. Others less fortunate are now swamped in these worlds and frequencies, unable to see any way out and not even knowing that they are in it.

This is a choice time to work with these worlds of shadow. Never has it been easier to see, and never has it been easier to navigate through with skillful guidance, courage, and fearlessness. As CO put it,

> I asked to be taken into the deepest hell realms to meet, recognize, and discern my shadow piece that is there; to use whatever tools necessary, dissolving or cutting with the cord of ruthless compassion, embracing with heart and integrating with mind, so that I may be in the knowing of the nature of shadow with a clear mind without need, desire, and attachment.
>
> As my shadow reached out to take my hand and escort me deep into the bowels of the earth and thus deep into the bowels of my own being . . . I saw many dark aspects and experiences in the descent, all within my being and simultaneously within the earth's being. Whenever my mind would begin its distractions, I would command my full presence and ask to be taken deeper. We descended to a realm that I have only imagined in brief moments. This time I stepped into it fully.

She showed me the aspect of my Self that was powerful beyond anything I could have imagined within the darkness of sexual abuse, manipulation, lust, anger, rage, and many other aspects that I have veiled. Even in first seeing my shadow, I only saw one side of it, the wounded, pained, and abandoned side. I did not allow myself to see the full presence of my shadow. . . . I see now that I cannot step into my true Self until I have fully embraced all that which is in me. The Two Truths.

## The Culmination: The Antichrist

Imagine this: all the aspects of the shadow embodied into one living thought-form, the polar opposite of Christ Consciousness. This is the Antichrist, an energy field that surrounds the earth and is anchored by various beings (mentioned in the Gnostic Gospels as being Archons and Aeons). These are the rulers of the collective consciousness of humanity, the manipulators behind the scenes of our unconscious, that which we cannot see or do not wish to see.

Until we are resonating at love and joy, we are still feeding this shadow and have a negligible effect on the collective consciousness. As soon as we rebirth and step into joy, we can change the collective, balancing thousands of people by our mere presence alone.

From an evolutionary perspective, the Antichrist has to fully embody on earth before Christ Consciousness can fully reappear. The darkness is necessary in order for the light to appear. Circumstances have to get so critical as to reach a climax point in order for a more enlightened civilization to sprout, phoenixlike, from the ashes of the old. Therefore the Antichrist has a definite purpose: to serve as a catalyst, a point of tension. In any state of heightened tension or friction (at a certain wave band of consciousness) there is far more possibility of transformation, as well as a new creation, as you are accessing deep emotions and energy in this stretching. We have to stretch and challenge ourselves in order to really grow, to reach our full potential.

The ways that this stretching, or additional tension, is occurring is obvious on a planetary scale: ecological crises, wars, terrorism, mass extinction of species, loss of nature, pollution, mass media controls over public thought and opinion, and personal upheavals and transformations. All are designed to wake us up to what is happening and do something about it in our own way.

The Matrix created by the Antichrist is a chrysalis constructed by our own thoughts, fears, desires, and subconscious in order to prepare us for our next phase of evolution: the next wave. It has been created to provide the tension, the friction, the push and pull of duality to propel us into unity consciousness. Its dissolution can only happen once we have learned and mastered the lessons from it, which is when it will have served its purpose. This is when humanity as a collective issues the cry that "enough is enough." In essence, we are now rapidly externalizing and manifesting the collective thoughts and subconscious of humanity over thousands of years in order to experience something new.

In order to fully embody all Nine Bodies of Light, one has to meet and embrace the Antichrist and know it in its fullness. Both Buddha and Christ Yeshua did this, and we all have to do it in our own way at some point in the unfolding of our soul journey. This can take many forms, but rest assured it will be both a personal and universal unfolding felt on all levels of your soul. In your own unfolding, you have to embrace the darkness of creation, the antilife force that is also Christ. It is all God. In this, we embrace and surrender to the All, extending love to those who are extending the cry for help and healing.

Antichrist is antilife, love, and flow, the rigidity of matter without the conscious awareness of light, the opposite to being in the present organic ever-unfolding moment. It is that which we have created over millennia that has said no to love, no to life, no to embrace, and no to surrender, the fear that was birthed from the first thought and feeling of separation. It is the ancient mind of man built on fear. It is the forgetting of the truth of who we are, the demon that Shiva dances on, the demon of ignorance and forgetfulness. This demon is seen as epileptic, spastic, and prone to fits of rage and anger, very similar to how Hitler behaved.

The Antichrist is the incarnation of temptation, luring you away from truth and promising you everything that the world has to offer. The Antichrist manifests when you turn all your attention to yourself, putting yourself first and foremost, so you feel you are independent from God and others in the web of life in all you do. Here you feel you have a separate will to the One and want to occupy for yourself what is yours. You feel you are a separate doer from God, independent in identity and authority, and above God. You feel that your unfolding is separate from everyone else's and that love is about being more focused on one or two people alone.

You try to manipulate others to make yourself feel better, acting and seeking to enhance your sense of self through deeds, interactions, and relationships with others. You try to make your ego self look bigger and feel better in your interactions with others, as that is where your self-worth arises from. You insistently defend your points of view, reacting to any perceived attack on your sense of self. You plan your life to detail and blame others when things go wrong.

The Antichrist has no basic trust in life, in others, and in being held, supported, and loved from the stages of early childhood and the womb. It is against love but really wants love, which is why it is the beast that puts down love. The Antichrist needs love when we are ready to do so.

The Antichrist is incarnated in many forms on earth. He comes directly to those who have the wisdom, power, light, and love to make a difference to the mass consciousness on this planet. Two notable examples are Christ Yeshua in his forty days of temptation, where he chose to meet and get to know the Antichrist so he could find out more about himself and the true nature of reality; and the Buddha's encounter with Mara just before his enlightenment.

The more love that arises on earth, the more the Antichrist is provoked as a form of hatred that has originated from the loss of this love. It is the force of resistance and opposition to love that wishes to annihilate and stop love flowering at all costs. It is death that constantly wants to keep you small, in fear, and denying reality. This beast can be felt as an ominous eye, a huge demon that is a cruel, cold, calculating force of destructive hatred and great pride.

Love heals all. Power is an essential aspect of love, and this power is distorted by the Antichrist force. This is why we have to claim our power from the darkness by traveling deep into it, learning the lessons from it, and reclaiming our sovereign power. In one sense the Antichrist is a guardian to your greatest power, and if you can meet this power and hatred with love, then you can reclaim this power. In this process one sees some of the deepest levels of why soul originally disconnected from love. Love illuminates these parts of self, relaxing and opening these aspects of psyche and soul to receive and embrace all parts of one's self. When we understand the Antichrist, we can then access the loving nature of reality through embracing being as it is.

The Antichrist is a part of God, created as part of the Divine Plan. Everything is God. In every program of consciousness, in every being lies the spark of God. Realizing this experientially when encountering the varied aspects of the Antichrist is to step more into your godhood.

## Five Guidelines to Working with the Shadow

As I witness people moving through the Nine Bodies, I have found that the shadow is one of the most challenging. Indeed, if enough people really integrated their shadows, they would quickly change, as would the world at large, as the integrating of one person's shadow below 15 percent affects the entire collective shadow. So here I share with you five simple ways to turn the shadow into a tool for balancing and integrating duality into unity.

These five simple ways work with the multiple aspects of the shadow as you travel through them. Remember, you have been working with these strands for many lifetimes. Now with clarity and a map to guide you, you can accelerate the process, yet you still have to do the inner work, contemplation, and investigation yourself.

When you encounter a shadow aspect, you can use any one of these five as a tool or way of perception. You will have to feel into which tool is appropriate for each situation. This differs from person to person, as each person is unique and has to find their own shadow pathway. Only when one is mature enough can one consciously work with the deeper aspects of the shadow, in effect when one is aware of, and no longer dominated by, the animal drive and grosser nature of the self and has the commitment to deepen in their investigation.

The five ways are:

1. Meeting and recognizing the shadow within you, and in your relationships. Finding your shadow myth and pillar.

2. Dissolving and using the sword to cut certain aspects away through ruthless compassion and dedication.

3. Embracing certain aspects of the shadow that need your love, attention, softness, and heart integration

4. Discerning and witnessing the true nature of need, desire, and attachment within.

5. Bringing your shadow into the earth's embrace.


These five tools work with the basic drives of the shadow: need, desire, and attachment.

## Need

Need is a hole in yourself that you look to "fill in" with something outside of yourself. In one sense it is a contraction that looks outside of itself for something to consume to fill the gap. This creates a myriad of beliefs, justifications, and denials around this hole that weave a web of illusion, sadness, and suffering as well as veils that cloak the real wound within. This leads to a need for validation of who you are from others, leading to the illusion that others can create you and drag you into their perception.

Relationship is an experience of connectedness between two people, each being an object of a need gratification to the other. Most human relationships are need-based. Our unconscious needs look for an object outside to manifest them in order to make them conscious. This is where opposites attract. Our natural instinct to be whole continuously motivates us to find a mirror to see the reflection of our potentials, which have been lying dormant in our (shadow) unconscious. Relationships are the crutches we use on our journey of growth, yet paradoxically through relationship we are able to endure some of the pain of transformation, although ultimately it is done alone.

## Desire

Desire is an outward movement from your hole of need, trying to ensnare and get, get, get for your own self. Greed, lust, and envy fuel this form of desire. Desire creates a hope of fulfilling this desire outside of yourself. Hope is the first and last illusion to disappear on the path to awakening, as within it lies the seed of this type of desire. Desire when made sacred is an evolutionary force, kindled in the art of making love and yearning for the divine, but otherwise let go of by the clear spotless mind into nonattachment.

## Attachment

Attachments are the cords that sustain needs and desires over time. As the shadow greedily finds its holes met in others who also temporarily find their holes plugged, attachment to external objects becomes solidified. As attachment grows and deepens because of time and habit strengthening these cords and bonds, it becomes like an ingrown toenail: only major surgery can undo it. While this can all be emotionally painful, in fact it is all governed by the mind and remedied by seeing it with the

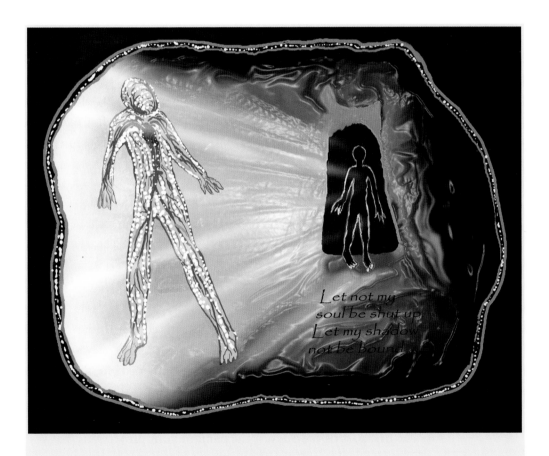

*Let not my soul be shut up
Let my shadow not be bound...*

**The true Shew.** (Amaya Du Bois)

higher mind, that aspect of us that is contemplative, reflective, discerning, and able to see life through the lens of the Ba soul.

Becoming enclosed within a relating, habit, or pattern, a way of being is different to being committed, which means you give something all your attention, love, and effort while remaining unattached to the outcome. Once attachment is illuminated it takes (the illusion of) free will to choose a course of action to free and cut that attachment and create something new. Ultimately, all the shadow constructs we create dissolve through laughter.

## The Essence of the Shew

The shadow is treated as a friend in the Egyptian texts, not as something to be feared, reviled, or hidden away. Shew is depicted in the *Book of the Dead* as a black, blank, featureless human form standing in a tomb doorway,[13] gazing at the sun Ra, accompanied by the falcon of the Ba soul. The text that accompanies this solemn facade is,

> Let not my soul be shut up. Let my shadow not be bound.
>
> Open the pathway for my soul and shadow that they may see the great god.

The Shew is the keeper and guardian of the Ba soul, and in this case is its reflex. By integrating Shew, one frees Ba to express its heart's desires and soul purpose. By hiding your Shew shadow, you shut Ba down. By Shew being freed of your projections (through the awareness of the Ba soul) and judgments, a pathway opens to take you into Hu, the immortal and universal body of light.

Another way to see this is understanding that the Ba is a clear mirror. The first part of the Shew is the paint of your projections that you

---

13. Normandi Ellis, *Dreams of Isis* (Chicago: Quest, 1997).

throw at the clear mirror, staining it until eventually you only get brief glimpses or clear reflections from the mirror from time to time. In clearing this mirror and dissolving the Shew into the mirror of the Ba, the Ba is no longer shut up, and the shadow is no longer bound as it has reunited with the Ba so it can return to the Hu, that which lies beyond any mirror.

In order to access this and to resolve any energetic issue, one must go to the next octave of energy to integrate it. In order to understand Shew, one must go beyond what you have projected it to be, what you have created it as, what you have overlaid your own perception onto it as. This requires connecting to the soul Ba and universal body of the Hu.

So there are two types of shadow: one that we have created, and one that is a sheath and layer around the atom. In the first aspect of the shadow, we project what we have created on top of the shadow, dumping and overlaying it on the shadow. The shadow absorbs this because it is the ultimate absorber, as it is blank and featureless, taking in anything, becoming anything that is projected on it like the ultimate chameleon. It is a blank screen that we fill with our own movies and perceptions; once we take away the projector of our own mind and unhealed shadow aspects, there are no images to see. All that is left is a blank screen.

Shew in this essence is formless, and once you truly rest in it, you are discombobulated; that is, you feel bodiless. Feeling bodiless can also be attributed to some of the other light bodies, but this is a different state, as the shadow is neither light nor dark. Initially this is a strange feeling, as you are now operating from a blank slate, a colorless, featureless perception. It is neither nothing nor something at the same time.

Consciousness as we know it is not in the shadow; it is a gateway into the experience of emptiness, as the Buddhists call it, but not the total experience of emptiness or *sunyata*. The wisdom of sunyata is not in the shadow, but an experience of voidness is. There is nothing there, no consciousness or its contents, no feeling, mental forms, spiritual forms, or anything of substance at all. It is blank, surrounded by light that has the merest glimmer of the beginnings of form in it yet is still formless. This is a type of bardo state, as mentioned in the Egyptian *Book of the Dead* and the *Tibetan Book of the Dead*.

Shew is essentially without form and life force. It is emptiness lying around the perception of form, and emptiness waiting to come into form, into perception. It is a gateway between both, the intermediate state, accessed through deep meditation. The shadow is an aspect of the atom that is blank and featureless, looking to the light in the atom but remaining in the shade.

Shadow contains that part of you that you do not see, which can then get interpreted as those parts of you not healed or nurtured. This blank part that you cannot see is always with you, and it can become anything and take on any form, shape, or guise. It can be manipulated to bring forth more images and perceptions, or it can be allowed to be its blank canvas self, found when one sits in the shade of light within the atom.

On a universal level, Shew is a type of antimatter formed when matter first formed in the Big Bang. This is found within each atom that contains a black hole, a zero point, similar to the black hole of the Galactic Center from where all creation arises and flows. We contain this within each of our atoms, and to access this requires we move through the many layers of the Shew to realize its innocence and our own. This, then, is how Shew becomes the gateway to Source.

Anaiya Aon Prakasha

David Andor

# ~4

# SEKHEM: POWER, LIFE FORCE, BLISS

I am the enflamer of truth—the enlivener of the living fire within all things. I am the never-ending stream of life force, sparking and igniting the spirals within each and every cell of your bodies. I am the divine breathing through your body-world. Breathe me in, sound me in, remember me. Pay heed, with attention and intention, discipline and dedication, to allow my continual pulse and flow to fuel and fire your life, burning away that which no longer serves, creating a fertile ground for birthing.[1]

The lion-headed Sekhmet, "The Great Powerful One," is the goddess of the power and flame within life, the third fiery eye of the sun god Ra, the spiritual warrior who creates, destroys, and regenerates. Sekhem flows throughout all our subtle bodies and channels, meridians, and *nadis* as the creative force of the universe in motion.

Sekhem, similar to Shakti, is the creative power and flow of life-force energy, the flow of life force that connects and flows through your body-mind and soul. It is the living power of the goddess, the creative force

---

1. Carol Orlick.

that manifests and creates. It is the zest, the passion for life; it is the dance and engagement with life; it takes life by the horns and rides with it. It can be sensual, rich, overflowing, and blissfully loving as well as powerfully transforming and ruthless in its destruction.

Sekhem is the creator and destroyer. It manifests in order to play; it destroys in order to play. Its dance is one of delight. When we are in delight, free-flowing, following our heart's desires and living them, when we are dancing in our full power and joy, we are in its flow. Accomplishing your soul's purpose comes through the flow of Sekhem merging with your heart-soul, the Ab Ba.

In Egypt and in India the fiery power of Sekhem emanates from the one-pointed third eye of both the goddess Sekhmet and the god Shiva. As legend tells us, Sekhmet was asked to destroy evil armies on earth but went on a killing spree, destroying everything in her path, so blood-drunk and berserk did she become. Her reign of terror stopped when she was forcibly reigned in by Ra and manipulated by Thoth to stop.

When focused, the one-pointed eye of Sekhem burns anything and everything to ashes. Sekhem can "see" and penetrate through any veil, any illusion, any covering that cloaks and hides the truth of a person or situation. It is developed by drawing up the kundalini from the base of the spine and the hara-womb into an intense one-pointed concentration of willpower focused at the third eye or *bindu* point that in turn develops immense firepower. This is most effectively achieved through the science of the Ren or mantra yoga, which then leads to various forms of psychic powers or *siddhis*.

When Sekhem is consciously directed and attuned to the other eight bodies of light, she flows fully, dissolving the attachment you have to ideas about who you feel you should be, or who you want to be, or who you might not be, all of which create a constant distraction for the mind and for your attention. Many of you are trying to play a role, trying to live up to some idea about who we think you should be. Sekhem dissolves these ideas and reveals who you really are without your ideas of who you think you are.

Sekhem manifests as pure joy and in its deepest state as pure loving bliss. It is joy that has no reason or cause to be joyful—just by its very nature, it is. This most powerful creative pulse of the universe is the wave of energy constantly humming behind all life, the throb and tremor that gives rise to all waves of life. It is bliss, bliss that has no reason to be blissful—it just *is* blissful.

When you live in this stream, you live according to your heart's desires, your innermost urging and true calling, following your inner voice. Listening to your body's natural rhythms as they harmonize with the earth, your loved ones, the cycles of time, and life itself. Living in this way keeps you connected to your core, which in turn leads to joy. Yet when you allow filters and conditionings to get in the way of this joy bubbling up from deep within your core, you lose your creative "spark," disconnecting from your own expression of vitality, your own unique expression of the pulse in all life.

Connecting with your bliss, your joy, is a step to living your heart's desires, the bridge into the now. Feeling this presence and pulse in your own body is when you most align with the natural synchronicity and spontaneity that creates nature's processes. This life spark within all of us pushes toward this movement.

These movements constantly go through you and the earth, and are made conscious when your emotional state is agile and you can easily emote, for emotion = energy in motion. For you to align to this wave requires that you become fluid. When you are fully fluid, you can experience any feeling whatsoever, at any time, at will.

Thus if you can, at will, produce equanimity, delight, love, anger, or tears without charge or attachment to them, you can be moved from within by the spirit that is always fluid and open. However, the less you can summon feelings, the more you are frightened of them, the more you are at their mercy. Conversely, the more you allow yourself to experience feelings, the less you can be enslaved by them. If you allow them to pass through you, you become transparent, without charge, without holding onto anything or anybody.

In this you learn to move the body, feelings, and mind so that spirit can move through you. In this fluid individuality, you can be any aspect of consciousness at any time, for you are able to feel and express whatever you are needed to be in any given moment to express all parts of yourself. In this flow, you feel you are in sync with everything within and around you. The world and your relation to it seems different—it is as if you are involved with the process of creation, instant by instant—you are creating it as it is creating you, for it is always there. You just are too busy to notice it.

Have you ever noticed when you ask for something, it magically appears within a day or an hour? This is living in the flow, for it is already happening; it is manifesting through you.

The main barrier to Sekhem is blocks in the womb and hara, sexual abuses and loss of connection to that area, and the strictures of our culture and upbringing and the way it expects you to act and behave. The straitjacketing of free expression, the distortions and manipulations around sexuality and what love is, what is considered right and acceptable in "polite society," in politically and spiritually correct circles, is what keeps your Sekhem under wraps, and in a "safe" place.

To express Sekhem is to freely be who you are and all that you can be in your highest potential. Sekhem is the fuel for this. The greatest achievements and greatest happiness come to those who do not let what others think about them stop or influence them. Rather they follow their hearts first and foremost, even if they get judged for it by a society that is too scared to let go of control and express their truth even if it goes beyond what is conventionally accepted.

Sekhem is the ultimate transformative force, the movement of the spiral. It flows best with no mind, no hope for the future, no reference to the past. It is the energy of the present moment in dynamic, powerful, joyful, and creative expression that becomes deep, loving bliss.

# Power

Sekhem is the transformative power that is much needed on the planet at this time, individually, collectively, and by Gaia herself. Sekhem harnesses the creative power of instinctual sexuality, the flow of vital dynamic life force, with love. When you bring this instinctual nature together with an awareness of the other eight bodies within you, the creative potential of God becomes expressed through you and magnified in your relationships with others.

Deep within all of you lies this power, an unstoppable primal force. Teeming with life and overflowing passion, this power hides in the darkness, from where all life pours in an inexhaustible torrent. This force can be as scary and as threatening to the control of the mind and small self as it is loving and nurturing to the soul's freedom. If you have resistance, then chaos and fear is what you will experience. If you have no resistance, you will experience its bliss, which enlivens and screams life to all your senses and soul.

When you encounter such power, you could respond to it in fear, the fear that it will have power and control over you, fearing it will destroy you. And it will: it will destroy the resistance to being free, it will wipe out part of who you think you are, the greatest fear of all. It threatens your very identity. It cares not for these boundaries, blasting through them. It is freedom, spontaneous, wild and free, and has no order, structure, or reason to it.

When you cut off from it, it consumes you in other ways, making you greedy or lust-driven for something you know you possess but have forgotten how to tap into. Denying this denies a vital part of your aliveness, your connection to the web of life. Denying the flow of Sekhem leads one to overindulge in the external instead of living fully what lies within. It leads to one destroying and devouring oneself, creating a wasteland, a desert of consciousness, instead of a rich, lush forest of fertile abundance. When you allow it to take you, pull you, you live in wild freedom, wild joy, loving this unpredictability, this uncertainty of living in the moment.

Sekhem shares her sensuality without shame, for to her it is natural. There are no taboos, no conventions to adhere to in "polite society" as there are no rules—just flow. This flow appears to be chaos to the mind that lies in resistance to the flow of life, afraid of the unknown that lies so vast beyond what the mind can ever try to understand. The energy or catharsis created by the mind's resistance has no form or rhyme to it, so it gets called "chaos." Yet all flow is the experience of life force in its essence.

Chaos and powerlessness, disorientation and fatigue are what the conditioned mind encounters when confronted by this energy. In the exhaustion and the giving-up of the mind, the giving-up of resistance to flow, one truly relaxes and flows into the most creative force. The mind releases into a seething ocean of infinite possibilities where anything becomes possible.

This is deep, deep nourishment, before words, ideas, and even emotions. It shows you how the world is fed and works. It shows you how we, throughout the ages, have tapped into the power that creates new realities.

The unformed, uncontrolled life force lies behind all appearances, all structures, all apparently ordered and reasonable things we do. It is always there as the substrata of life, waiting for us to tap into and break the rigidities of what we have self-created in order to live what true creating is, moment by naked, vital, pulsing, moment. Much philosophy and many ideas and spiritual systems—most of it is trying to hide away from this force, trying to rationalize, spiritualize, and make politically correct your most natural of impulses. All of this is done out of fear to create an ordered society that denies life and therefore denies love.

Sekhem is bliss wed with the heart-soul. It leads us to love through this fertile, uninhibited force, dissolving all the ideas, beliefs, and thoughts that stand in the way of the pulsing life force of wild joy, the expression of love untrammeled by convention. It says yes to love and connects all life forms once you have allowed it to flow through you unchecked, once you have allowed it to take you without reservation.

Sekhem is a radical force for change, for liberation, for freedom without boundaries, without rules, without ideas—just the pulsing vital flow of living love itself. Surrendering to this primal life force allows you to experience the love that creates all life. And this is vital for women and men to reclaim. To stand up and have full trust and confidence in who you are and what you instinctively and passionately feel means that the whole world can change in a single moment.

Sekhem generates energy, power, and strength. Her grit and determination allied with her exuberance, natural intuition, and sovereign authority enable you to break through any limitations or restrictions that bind. She is that quality within you that gives you the power to break through old patterns that keep your energy from flowing and manifesting new visions and following your heart's desires. She is vitality and empowerment. She leads to the breakdown that is the breakthrough.

She can manifest to the mind as dense irrational chaos that is danger, that is radical, that is the essence of risk itself. Without facing this danger, without going to the edge of your experience and beyond, you can never become who you truly are. You have to dive into the deep unknown to know who you truly are.

The new vision that births through you from this is focused and directed yet expansive. It encompasses and embraces many possibilities, never losing its direction in where it wishes to go. By opening up to all possibilities while remaining grounded, centered, and in your power, you can birth your soul purpose.

The shadow of Sekhem is lust and power out of control and addiction to seeking, to changing. It is important to remember here that Sekhem needs the heart-soul to be whole and in its right place, in harmony. The purpose of transformation is to become and be, rather than to eternally process or analyze. Its power, when unleashed, generates change, but to integrate this change requires rest. When Sekhem is balanced, we can simply rest in being. Passion goes out of control without the cool detachment of deep contemplation, and the unchanging knowing that the absolute truth does not, and never will, change.

## Life and Death

Sekhem reveals death as part of life, intimately interconnected. A simple law of nature is that for something new to be born, be it a new you, a new way of being, a new way of relating, or a new society, culture, or government, something has to die. Something has to die in you for you to truly grow. Something has to be destroyed on this planet for a new culture and a new planet to arise. When humanity learns this lesson, new forms of creating can arise that are in a natural grace with the cyclic flows of the feminine, and deaths of old forms can happen in a less traumatic and dramatic manner.

This power, which can be seen as magical, is what many fear and are also attracted to simultaneously. Sekhem brings forth the deepest polarities, the wildest extremities, in order to harmonize them into flow. The path of eternal life is very much one of death, progressive and successive deaths, which become subtler and subtler, more and more graceful, as one progresses.

Sekhem leads you to death, a good death, reminding you that you are mortal, reminding you to get up and experience life now as it is. With death on your shoulder, you cannot ignore life and what it presents you with any longer. Absence reminds you of the amazing potential for total presence, and this is what the best spiritual teachers do: reveal their absence to facilitate you into total presence, or bewilderment, as the case may be.

Sekhem holds life and death in each hand, as seen in the Hindu goddess Kali. She holds a space for life to reveal, create, and generate itself, and she holds a space for death to conceal, dismantle, and dissolve forms and ideas. You can experience this by holding your breath between your inhale and exhale for certain periods of time. When you do this for long enough, you experience this point between life and death and the fear that lies there also.

The inherent threat and thrill of the point where life meets death is dangerous, radical, scary, holy, and sacred; here, Sekhem acts as the bridge to your full empowerment. Those who dare to bridge life and death are the most radical of all, and it is these people who act as way-showers, as guides, for birthing into eternal life.

## Destroyer

Sekhem provokes and is provocative. She teases, tempts, triggers, and catalyzes in order to bring more true, grounded love into your human life here on earth now—not in the future, not in the past, but in the naked, searing intensity of the present moment where we are continually being born every nanosecond. Being born in every moment can take us to the brink, the edges of our being, the edges of light and dark, and ultimately into love.

Sekhem brings us to clarity amidst the chaos by taking us deep into the chaos to bring us clarity. As TA notes,

> I am the volcano waiting to burst, to burn, disintegrate, dissolve that which stands between humanity and god. I am ultimate compassion that knows that in order for the divine to truly arrive on this planet destruction has to happen. . . . The phoenix cannot be born until he burns to ashes. My service is not always easy, nice, or soft, but always giving, giving of truth.

This energy was demonized by patriarchal orders out of fear that this power could not be controlled, and therefore it became synonymous with all "demons" and the dark: that which men fear as it leads them out of the transcendent state and back into normal human life with its cares and concerns; back into matter, into form. As WC notes,

> When you can rest in the full flow of your Shakti you are in true presence. True presence has no mind: it is without barriers, preference, fear, and belief of any kind. Unencumbered by the weight of light and dark, right or wrong—my vision is clear. I aim to destroy your smallness. The full power of Shakti blasts through any resistance to being in the unlimited, unfathomable power of now. This can be dark. This can be hell. It is only your idea of hell. It is only your fear, your aversion to power, to death. Your attachment to your ideas keeps you bound. *Resistance* is your death. I've come to liberate. Be forewarned: your death will be your life; your darkness your deepest joy. Surrender to me. Surrender—and find your bliss.

In Egyptian thought, the twin goddesses of Wadjet and Sekhmet are two complimentary aspects of the one Sekhem. When both combine, transformation happens, resulting in a change in fortune by tearing down to create anew in harmony.

# The Four Locks

Sekhem starts in the womb and sacral-hara belly area. It then goes down into the yoni and lingam, then rises up the spine into the heart and brain when guided to do so. The womb is the key to Sekhem activation, and the womb is guarded by the womb lock. The womb-lock is part of your chakra system, which has three main energy locks, known as *granthis* in Sanskrit. These three energy locks are found in every human being and are a key part of yoga and meditation practices.

The first lock is in the root chakra, and it governs your grounding, money issues, survival, family issues, safety, and abundance. The second lock is in the solar plexus chakra, holding your empowerment, giving you the ability to be selfless, vital, and radiant. The third lock in the throat chakra governs your ability to fully express yourself and to surrender your fear and sense of separation to universal spirit.

The fourth lock is in the womb, guarding your connection to the heart and to the nurturing of the body with light. The womb is where you give birth from, not just to a physical baby but to your higher self. The womb is the light generator of the female body and the creator of joy. It is the place where the divine feminine and divine masculine are born and is the hidden power source of the divine feminine that was extensively used by the priestesses of Isis in Egypt and later in Palestine by Magdalene.[2]

In the release of this lock, abortions, old relationships, sexual abuses, and unhealthy connections to the collective womb of humanity can be released. When these centers are clear and they activate, you can connect with the full unbounded expression of life force, healing age-old wounds in both the male and female aspects of yourself.

---

2. For more, see Padma Aon Prakasha, *The Power of Shakti* (Rochester, VT: Inner Traditions, 2009).

Once the womb lock, which resembles a cage around the womb, is released, then what is known as the Sekhem rainbow arc can become activated. The Sekhem rainbow arc of light connects both ovaries into the womb in a fiery dance of rainbow-colored lights, creating an infinite loop between both ovaries (or a sideways figure eight). This infinite loop then activates another infinite loop from the womb up to the heart (a vertical figure eight).

As the locks release, you enter the unified chakra column, where all the chakras merge into a single pillar of light. This experience of stillness and light is where all chakras become one and where you feel whole, where the dualities of the chakras cease to exist, and where everything in your experience becomes graceful, natural, joyful, and abundant.

Sekhem, when aroused and ignited, can awaken all bodies as it flows through all life. When the Sekhem activates the Ba or heart-soul, then one's soul can come into direct contact with the universal body of Akhu, *if* guided by the spiritual bodies rather than just the psychic bodies. *Sekhem* means "the powers," the powers to connect God to human and the powers that you possess to create life and control your life force as well as others. Sekhem is the ultimate dynamic force emanating from the immortal bodies of Akhu and Sahu when we are in alignment with these forces.

Sekhem is a duality of male and female found in the left and right channels of the spine. In the harmonizing of these dualities we find the dance of creation and the rhythm of life. Desire for pleasure and sensory distractions as well as fear form the negative sides of these two channels, while holy desire and divine power form their positive sides.

What do you desire most? What do you fear most? Name five things for each polarity. When, or with whom, have you felt the most desire? When, or with whom, have you felt the most fear? These desires and fears are keys to your healing of them and are flowing up and down your left and right channels of your spine in red and white, like the caduceus, right now as you think about it.

These polarities form the basis of much of your experiences of life: good and bad, light and dark, painful and pleasurable, sad and joyful, depressed and blissful, loving and hateful, fearful and courageous. To harmonize them is to experience all polarities until you decide that the middle way leads to happiness. Once you choose this balance and become disciplined in your daily practices and how you use the life force, you can begin to witness the different extremes, swings, and shifts. Then things can start to change as you choose your heart's desires, the union of Ab and Ba, which leads you into the central channel of the spine, the middle way to happiness.

However, these two channels have their obstacles to union, namely through their opposing qualities, known in India as *tamas* and *rajas,* of dullness, laziness, sloth, and heaviness, contrasting with excessive passion, action, busyness, and talking. To fully come into Sekhem, we have to direct these two dualities, male and female, left and right, into the central channel of the spine through focus, central channel breathing (see "Central Channel Breathing" in Chapter 3), and the union of Sekhem with love.

Uniquely in this age, the technosphere also blocks Sekhem by redirecting this energy into the mind and into interfacing with technology. While we all use technology, the distortion of life force into interfacing with technology means that the rest of your body-mind does not receive it. As always, balance is the key.

## Ruthless Compassion

Sekhem wields the sword and power of discriminating wisdom that separates between beneficial and nonbeneficial actions that must be taken in your life. It is the power of wisdom and will in direct action that cuts away any illusion. This sword is the power to cut away all that is useless, destructive, and resistant to change. It simply says no to anything that blocks your evolution and cuts away the expected roles that you feel you have to live that only serve to keep you small or limited.

It cuts away all that keeps you locked into the small self, limiting the shining of your light. It cuts away all expectations that you place on yourself and all expectations you place on others. It cuts in order to reveal something new, a new possibility where once before there was deadwood or old baggage.

This sword vanquishes ignorance and creates discernment and detachment through the exercising of willpower. By cutting through illusions and leaving behind egoic actions that only lead to more unhappiness, you become clear. By exercising your willpower in this way, you strengthen your soul power, abilities, and purpose. Your soul grows each time you use the sword correctly, as you are validating this aspect of divine power as a part of the trinity of love, wisdom, and power.

The sword is the protector of the sanctity of the soul. It protects and chastises you when you forget what you are here for, your soul purpose. It transmits fire. With the eyes of an eagle the sword sees the bigger picture and can dissolve any ties that bind. The sword conquers and transmutes the darkness, and chaos, of the mind. It can be frightening, purifying, and transmuting.

Owning and using this power of the sword to radically transform is ruthless compassion. In this, anything that stands in the way of your growth is cut away: any attachment, any fear, any person of any sort that distracts from your goal is removed by the sword of ruthless compassion. It is the ruthless cutting-through of any and all illusions and ignorance to awaken the soul. It is death to the ego and total surrender to Self.

Ruthless compassion is compassion that is unmoved by worldly troubles, cares, or concerns. It is direct, clear movement that dissolves all obstacles in its way, cutting through the taproots of egoism, acting and dissolving no matter how its actions are perceived by others. It is compassion for the soul and the bigger picture; it is the lack of any concern for the ego. It is destructive force harnessed to divine will, and it has no remorse. Once started it can never be stopped until all obstacles and ignorance are destroyed.

This force provides rapidly accelerated evolution where no stone is left unturned, and it is for those who wish to be fully enlightened no matter what. In ruthless compassion, one is ready and willing to do absolutely anything to become a channel for divine will. Ruthless compassion can appear to be cruel as it usually involves giving you what you need to grow rather than what you want. Comfort comes last on the list of priorities for ruthless compassion. For this reason it is often not appreciated until well after it has been received, and it can be initially greeted by the ego with judgment, resentment, and anger.

Love without power dissolves into an astral, weak fairytale. Love without strength and depth crumbles into an ungrounded chaotic mess. Power without love becomes a game of control, fear, and tyranny. Discipline without joy becomes an intense self-defeating oppressive hell. Owning and using this power of the sword to radically transform is ruthless compassion.

This creates a heart of spaciousness that allows others to be in their pain and suffering so they may grow. It is relentless in that it is not affected by pain or suffering; it sees all without hiding, flinching, or avoiding. This is the heart of acceptance, accepting what must be, for the highest good of all. This requires great surrender and wisdom to flow with it and implement its actions and directions. Wisdom here is the ability to see beyond the appearance and see the true clinging, suffering, and need of a person, situation, or event. Acting on this directly arises from being objective, calm, and clear in understanding how and why the ego protects, hides, and cloaks itself. It will protect itself at all costs.

Ruthless compassion is not an emotion or feeling. It is a way of being that arises when we are fully dedicated and surrendered to Self in our self, and by extension, all others. It is being uncompromising, direct, and unflinching, which becomes a process of relentless surrender that grinds down anything that stands in the way between your larger Self and your smaller self. It witnesses what is happening in silence and being totally present. This leads to total harmlessness, as no reaction, no harm can affect you when you have no harm, no violence, no triggers left within you. Then these forces can be wielded in order to serve love most effectively, as and when it is required.

Sekhem illumines illusion in a direct, uncompromising manner. My friends, do not compromise with the seeing of illusion in yourself and others. Do not think that by not pointing something out to your brother or sister you are being loving. Be radically honest, for this serves love. Be frank, be directly engaging, and do not shirk your responsibility toward the growth of the soul.

The sword leads people into and through the dark night of the soul, or should I say the dark night of the ego. It builds people's character and dissolves their small self to lead them into joy and loving service, service that will have true impact as it is based on authentic, deep, lived experience of the darkest places that a human being can go into. Once you have lived through this experience, then anything is possible for you, as you have reclaimed your power from the darkness and can now wield it. Darkness forges the soul into a diamond by burning the dross away, leaving only that which is immortal.

Here there is no your truth or my truth; there is one truth that we both align to. The sword is not here to help you or your illusions, for in the dark night you come to realize that there is no self to help, just the one Self that needs no helping, just resting within and embracing.

# Tantra

The most common and easily accessible ways to awaken Sekhem power are through deep breath practices, dance, and the union of love in sacred sexuality: redirecting the life force between masculine and feminine, the two basic polarities, up the spine and through all the chakras to eventually reside in the heart and brain. These tantric practices were extensively practiced in Egypt, and there was a temple set aside for the cultivation of this loving sexuality where the root chakra and the heart chakra were united and healed between man and woman, priest and priestess to allow the free flow of kundalini safely into the brain and higher chakras. Once this was achieved, deep one-pointed meditation in the third eye could result in the full flowering of Sekhem into the Hu bodies.

In this process of merging between masculine and feminine, wounds, mistrusts, and barriers to this relating or divine marriage may occur as you are now connecting on the most profound level. You may find yourself losing yourself in your partner, you may find a deep aversion or attachment forming, you may feel angry, resentful, or invaded *if* you are not ready for this level of intimacy. It is at this point that a true relationship or sacred marriage occurs if these wounds can be met with sensitivity, responsibility, loving kindness, support, and compassion by both of you.

Because of its dual nature, Sekhem can be used for light and dark. A great deal of Sekhem can be generated and released without love, simply through focus, willpower, and one-pointed deep meditation. It is power, and power and will can be used for any purpose—for love and passion to help others, or into war, anger, and violence. Sekhem is, in the highest potential, the power to ignite, catalyze, and transform you, to radically change your reality. We only have this power if we exercise it, if we put it into action, and that takes becoming active in knowing what we want and what our soul purpose is. What do you love?

It can flow out of control or be directed to create and regenerate. It is like a river of celestial fire and light merging and combining, coursing through your veins and pathways, lighting up and igniting whatever comes in its way. It is passionate power merged with love refined into compassion; it holds all these qualities at any moment. It is pure loving bliss, rich and deep in its love.

Sekhem is often aligned to Heka, or magic, and Ren, words of power. Through the four stages of Ren we can access infinite Sekhem, which burns through and opens up the brain chakras. Together Ren and Sekhem are two of the most potent forces in the universe, and they lead to great power. With the union of them the Egyptians could create whatsoever they desired. And they did, both from the desires of the heart and from the desires of the shadow, which eventually led to the destruction of ancient Egypt. This is a warning to us all: when using willpower without heart, when using magic and words without love and the recognition of the soul, we destroy that which we value most dearly.

Sekhem is the fire of life within each of us. The highest form of Sekhem is the fire of pure being, the fire that creates, preserves, destroys, and transcends the entire universe. The deepest form of Sekhem is the flame of bliss, which is also a power that pervades all of nature, a power that can both create and destroy, nurture, and dissolve.

In the eyes of Sekhem, we are all flame walking around within form. The human soul is the result of the evolution of the animal soul, and of the plant, devic, and mineral realms as well. As human beings we are the intelligence of fire. While minerals represent the earth fire, plants the water fire, and animals the fire fire, humans can manifest the air fire, or the fire of the heart, air being the element of the heart. Through this cosmic air element, known as the Holy Spirit, the human fire can transcend form and enter into the cosmic spirit so that we can freely move through the entire universe.

The flame within us naturally seeks to return to its divine home. Our soul fire is the divine will within us to return to God. Spiritual practice can develop this fire on all levels of consciousness, opening up the many pathways in the body-mind and soul to allow the sacred fire to flow unimpeded throughout all parts of us, reuniting and reconnecting our differing energy flows into the heart fire, the sacred fire of the soul.

Refining and transmuting our animal and human desires, lusts, and passions requires the practices of fire alchemy. This involves living in nature in balance with the elements, eating well and simply, breathing deeply and with focus on these pathways, and meditation. One potent form of fire alchemy is chanting and meditating on the 1,008 Names and Mantras of Agni, the essence of the sound and light of the sacred soul fire that can open us up further to the highest potential of embodiment. These mantras are from the Sanskrit Rk Veda, the Hymn of Creation, and are rarely sounded outside of India in their fullness.

The deepest form of Sekhem is found in deep meditation, once the Sekhem channels are cleared, as Sekhem is what fuels the heart-soul, the Ab Ba, to go into Sahu, the universal body. As we evolve, it expands into this universal fire, unfolding both purity and compassion, destroying all ignorance, and bringing the heart-soul into the infinite unfolding of Sahu, the breath of God.

Anaiya Aon Prakasha

Amaya Du Bois

# ～5

## KA: YOUR DOUBLE

The Ka is the first form of the soul that we can readily access, and it is a vehicle for ascension or awakening once you connect it fully to the heart-soul, the Ab Ba.

We first connect to the Ka through our etheric or auric body, our energy double, which is similar in appearance to the physical body but is made of light and vibration. It is this energy double that holds the perfected templates for your physical body in energetic and holographic form, making it very desirable to connect to, as it holds the blueprint of emotional and physical well-being as well as psychic and intuitive abilities.

Ka is known as the inner controller and is where we find our personal power, vitality, auric presence, and the ability to sustain and regenerate our Self. Ka represents the smallest form that the universal soul of the Hu bodies can recognize and work with consciously and actively. It is the smallest, yet is connected to the infinite Hu. As Ka is the inner controller of the human mind and body, it is our most immediate stepping point into the infinite. It is for this reason that Ka is so important at this time and why it needs to be worked with consciously so we can evolve quickly.

Ka holds the first stage of human enlightenment and awareness connecting our different bodies through the third to the sixth dimensions. We fully access the Ka when we have learned and integrated our solar lessons or our astrological chart. When we do this, we expand beyond being ruled by our astrological or planetary lessons into the galactic realms of the Ba soul, or heliocentric-stellar astrology.

Ka is our holographic connector, connecting us across many dimensions into an embodied form on earth. It is a massive key to embodiment of your soul presence, the "I am" presence of the Ba soul. It is a holographic matrix of finely interwoven strands of light that stretch into and permeate the body-mind, emotions, and soul with the earth, the solar system, and with other life forms. It does this by efficiently connecting the holographic templates of our different bodies of light together into form, such as the holographic version of our nervous system. Ka is also connected to galactic timing cycles, as seen in the thirteen-moon calendar synchronization of the powers of time with the Galactic Center.

Today your Ka, and the collective Ka body of humanity, has become obscured through the technospheric matrix, the artificial sheath of signals and electromagnetic pollution that stifles and inhibits the Ka fields that are inextricably intertwined with Gaia and the biospheric field. Ka is a holographic web of light that connects into Gaia's web of life, and it can be used to access Gaia's memories and energy fields through the "Driving Your Ka" practice. Of course, there are many memories stored in Gaia, and some of them can be unpleasant, but if one experiences this, there is a lesson and healing for you in it.

The Ka has five faces: the first that we can readily access is our etheric field or energy double, which can often be ripped or damaged. This etheric body connects into our biophotonic field, the hologram of our cellular field and central nervous system that is our template for perfect health and well-being. This acts as an interface to connect with higher frequencies of light to bring into our physical body. It is here that the Ka connects to your sexual partners, creating a feeling of merging but also codependency or "Ka dependency."

Ka connects into your ancestral lineages and the lessons and gifts that your families hold for you. As you clear and heal these distortions and integrate their gifts and learning, you then come into contact with your divine Ka, which acts as an interface for the soul to be brought into the physical realms.

This divine Ka is an aspect of God, or a God form. In Egypt this was seen as one of the Neters, so your divine Ka could be Isis or Anubis, for example. Similarly, in Tibetan Buddhism and Hinduism, this is a visualized deity, Buddha, god, or goddess form, which you learned to merge with over time through meditation practices. This is a common practice but one that has been largely lost in the Egyptian lineage.

To realize and embody your divine Ka requires that you also look deep into your shadow and its faces and forms. The Ka and its power has its shadow sides that we learn to integrate over time so that it becomes an ally that serves us and our soul rather than dominating and running our lives. This is a massive key to fully embodying the Ka as an interface to the soul Ba, so we merge both into the Ka Ba.

Let us now explore these many facets of the Ka body in depth.

## Your Crystalline Double

The first face of the Ka is the etheric body image or hologram of the denser physical body. It is the harmonic pattern from which the physical body is formed, lying in your etheric fields. It is born with you and is your energetic double, the mirror of your physical body, the foundation of the physical body first created on the etheric level before it manifests on the physical level. Ka is the interface between the physical and all the other light bodies, providing the energetic blueprint for the physical from the third to sixth dimensions. Ka provides the infrastructure for the body, emotions, and mind to exist. "If you were to remove the Ka, all subtle bodies would dissolve."

Ka is a matrix both within the body and outside the body. When you have evolved enough, it integrates with the physical body, appearing as a network of fine golden lines, known today as the biophotonic network. Outside the body, the Ka can look like a clear quartz replica of the physical body, although the colors and hues may differ from person to person.

Feelings and thoughts are stored in the Ka. As the holographic information that enables reincarnation, Ka also holds information and memory about other lifetimes. Functioning as a vehicle for consciousness, it is both the small *i* and the connector to the "I am" presence of the Ab Ba, heart-soul. It is seen in the aura surrounding us, plants, animals, and all other sentient life forms. Ka asks us: How well are we able to live our realization? To what degree does our daily life express an integrated, full-bodied awakening that is rooted in the lower chakras?

Ka leads us to an integrated, full-bodied experience of awakening, one that not only includes but celebrates physical embodiment as not being separate from God but another expression of it. When Ka is well-nourished, we feel powerful, present, charismatic, alive, and delighted. We feel that we are able to achieve whatever we desire. Our motivation and clarity are high, and we have the power to move forward. We are actively engaged in the physical, and we enjoy life.

Life is good and satisfying for the strong and balanced Ka, and the Ba soul's soul desires manifest and unfold gracefully in the fullness of time. The ability to catalyze, create, and manifest more delight, more radiance, more power also emanates from the Ka, as well as the ability to desire and merge with another in conscious sexual practice.

A strong Ka leads to both intellectual and spiritual power, for Ka is the power that individualizes your soul or Ba. In other words, Ka is a spark of the flame of the soul that is the Ba, the bridge and interface between the spiritual self and the physical realm. It is the software program that communicates between your body-mind and the soul, Ba.

Ka merges more with the physical body when enough light comes into the physical, which is when Ka manifests in the spaces between the cells, the spaces between your thoughts, the spaciousness of the emotions and body. When this is all connected and unified, the physical body hologram and matter rises to a new frequency that is permeated by light.

Ka is a living hologram that provides the platform for all parts of our Self to coalesce and form into a coherent unity. Ka is the interface between light and matter, light and life force, wisdom and power. It is through the Ka that we receive and work with higher intelligence, for light is information that when combined with the free flow of life force results in enlightenment.

According to the Egyptians, after death you go to your Ka. Even though the physical body is lifeless, the soul still exists in the form of the Ka. In the funerary rites, it was protected and preserved following death in order to attain a successful afterlife journey through the Duat or underworld. In this journey, Ka needed to be kept energized and conscious in order for the individual soul to carry out the tasks and transformations needed after death, which involved remembering certain mantras and rules of navigation through these worlds, much as you would do when driving a car through a city. This energy was fueled by the attention of the priests and family, which fed the Ka in these after-death rites. By remembering the dead, their Ka is supported and energized.[1]

Ka is the imprint of that part of you that has a connection with the place that your physical body lives, with the objects you possess, and with the cords of connection and relationship you have with others. In the psychic realms, Ka imbues its imprint into its relationships and

---

1. Special Ka priests were able to contact the Kas of particular ancestors such as great kings or healers in order to seek advice.

objects it possesses. Each object and relationship we have holds an imprint of our Ka, which stays with it, much as a fingerprint stays on a glass. Psychics have the capacity to pick up these residual traces of Ka energy by touching the object. For example, just by picking up a coin, a psychic can know who else has touched it, how many hands it has been through, and even what some of those people looked like, as well as some of their characteristics. Equally, one could walk into a room where another person was a week before and be able to retrace their steps exactly in that room. Psychics with these abilities have been used by the police to find dead bodies and solve unsolved crimes, and there has been a rash of TV programs that highlight and explore this ability.

Our ancestors knew and understood this power of the Ka, and thus chose to own few objects or possessions so as not to fritter away precious Ka energy by spreading it randomly. When they died these Ka, or power objects, as they are known to shamans, were gathered together by family and friends and placed in the tomb with the mummified body so that the Ba and Ka on the journey through the Duat would be able to complete their journey with this extra power. It is also important to note that these Ka power objects were used extensively in life to boost the Ka energy of the user at certain times, like during rituals, important meetings, meditation, and lovemaking.

Ka is left when the Ba soul, or animating force, departs the physical body. It is the psychic imprint of your spirit. Many people see these Ka imprints as ghosts, wandering around supposedly haunting the living. They are not haunting you—they are the ones haunted themselves, as they could not depart with their Ba, or soul, when the soul left this world.

Why does this occur? Because the Ka still has lessons to learn from this plane of existence. In this separation, the Ka has the opportunity to learn from these mistakes, for as the soul leaves the body at the time of death, Ka can stay to complete its learning in its ghostly and disembodied world. This world, just outside our own, or in another overtone of the third dimension, is an illusory landscape that can be seen as heaven or hell.

In this scenario, as body or Khat dies, Ka relives or recapitulates its whole life, again and again and again into eternity. This ensures that Ka learns its lesson and purifies itself. One way to do this while alive is through the process of recapitulation, remembering all the most important or emotionally charged moments from your entire life, and bringing them into resolution, forgiveness, or healing through the process of negative cellular memory clearing.

All Ka practices were designed to boost your energy level in life and to stop the Ba soul from reincarnating. To do this it was necessary to stabilize the Ka in order to anchor the Ba so as to keep the vital umbilical link between them both.[2] If one was successful in accomplishing all these rituals, the Ba could be freed from reincarnation, able to pass into the Boat of Ra to become as one with the gods and to become a "light body," or a star in the heavens.

## Seeing Your Double

Sit down, and take a few deep breaths into your belly.

Center yourself and clear your mind. Close your eyes.

Directly in front of you, visualize your Ka double sitting opposite you. It looks exactly like you but is transparent and crystalline.

Look at it. What is it doing? What is it showing you?

Now look at it more closely. Zoom into it. There will be red lines on its body, showing you where it is wounded or where there are rips in

---

2. Certain rituals using the science of biogeometry, and the three main light rays or sources of creating sacred space in alignment with the light bodies, were designed to keep the Ka in alignment. The technology of these practices has been remembered and released back into the world again through the science of biogeometry, and it can accurately be applied into any space.

it. Notice where these are, and see if you can ask your Ka what they are connected to and how to heal them.

Dialoguing with the Ka is important, as it holds much information for you. By establishing this dialogue consciously, your Ka can become your own guide.

## The Biophotonic Field

Ka is the connector to the web of life. It is through the web of life that our Ka bodies receive replenishment, nourishment, and connection to the life force that connects all things. It is the vehicle through which we access the web of life and come into connection with the Ka bodies of all other sentient beings.

This is first experienced through your biophotonic field. Biophotons are weak photon or light emissions emanated and carried by our biological systems. They are weak electromagnetic waves of light. All living cells of plants, animals, and human beings emit biophotons that cannot be seen by the naked eye but that can be measured by special equipment and sensed by our intuitive minds. Energy practices like yoga, healing, tai chi, and acupuncture sensitize us to these flows of biophotons.

Biophotonic light communication is the cellular hologram equivalent of the nervous system. Using light for data transfer, it operates far more quickly than the nervous system, acting as a quantum biocomputer. In their resonance with the DNA and the unified grid of the earth's fields and ley lines, biophotons create an interface between our bodies, souls, and environments.

Our entire body-mind and soul is pervaded by this biophoton field. This web of biophotonic light connects cells, tissues, and organs within the body, serving as our main communication network, similar to the flows of our energy channels or meridians but deeper and more complex. One could say that the meridians are one aspect of the biophotonic network, which works with Axiatonal alignments.

Axiatonal alignments clear and heal all twelve primary meridian pathways of the body and relate to the healing of the organs, glands, and cells of the body. In these alignments you can shift the physical, mental, and emotional bodies of your own electromagnetic field, helping you to align more with the fields of Gaia, the solar system, and your Ka. Axiatonal alignments connect the Ka grids, making the flow of your energy clearer, connecting Ka into the physical body through the biophotonic fields.

As this occurs, the biophotonic fields become fluidly structured, geometric fields of information that connect many of our single parts together at the speed of light. Our entire cell metabolism works on an extremely rapid transfer of information that can only be achieved by light transmission. Each of our single cells communicates with others through the biophoton field by creating continuous waves. The high coherency or order of these waves transmits information clearly, effectively, and precisely.[3]

Biophotons order and regulate in order to bring us into balance, harmony, and into higher octaves of resonance, health, and expanded consciousness. In doing so, they elevate our body-minds and souls to a higher oscillation, which manifests as feelings of vitality and well-being, and which, when consciously worked with, can create spiritual growth and regeneration.

The biophoton field of the Ka is the mediator between body and soul, as light is the organizing principle of matter. As we know, matter is just light slowed down, so the biophotonic field organizes the physical body and helps repair it through regeneration when diseased. The Ka

---

3. In contrast, chaotic incoherent light simply transmits energy and can collapse within seconds, whereas biophotonic light retains its structure.

light body embodies and expresses itself fully when your cells recognize light as an energy source and metabolizes it like plants do in photosynthesis. This step in evolution increases metabolism, encouraging detoxification, rehydration, and ultimately regeneration. This ignites the liquid crystals of our cells, enabling them to evolve from standard hexagonal structures into other geometrical forms such as the tetrahedron and the octahedron. These other geometries hold more photonic energy that then forms the liquid crystalline matrix for the transformed blood and tissues.

Biophotons do this by modulating and communicating information throughout the body and into our extended environments through the DNA. Biophoton light is stored in the DNA, and it is through the DNA-RNA signals and transmissions that a dynamic web of light is constantly released and absorbed by the DNA. DNA has the ideal geometric form of a hollow resonator, which allows it to be the central storage depot for light in our bodies. Light emissions become strongest whenever DNA is reproduced, with the DNA emitting about 90 percent of the biophotons in the cell nucleus.

In this communication, light aims to counteract entropy, the loss of structure caused by different parts of you not being able to communicate. Some parts of you may be stagnant, shut off, and simply ignored, which is where the communication across the biophotonic network of light that holds your body-mind and soul together has disintegrated. Chaos and disease result. For example, cancer cells and healthy cells of the same type can be discriminated by differences in biophoton emission.

Any disease can be interpreted as a loss of information and communication between the body-mind and soul. A high level of geometric light order within the body enables an undisturbed flow of information and communication between all parts of you. Biophotons create this network of light, which is connected to nature and our environments through the DNA. DNA and RNA molecules act as a type of biological laser light, producing a hologram that resonates with the earth's fields and the Ka body as well as the artificial earth fields, or technosphere. They are the ultimate fiber-optic network found in our bodies, minds, and souls, connecting them all together at the speed of light and beyond.

As individuals we are networked with these DNA light emitters and receptors, and as a species all of humanity is connected and networked to each other through the Ka body. Much like our individual cells form our body, and just as each of our light bodies eventually coalesce to form and embody our entire being, the planetary body of Gaia works by connecting all of us together through the Ka. Through the conscious activation and connection of the Ka and the Ba, we then become a holographic biocomputer, a "biological Internet" linking all parts of us together, which then connects us to all human beings.

## The Ten Ka Memories

There are many layers of memory encoded within the Ka that prevent us from fully accessing it. These layers affect us deeply and inhibit our power from fully manifesting as well as blocking our Ka from merging with our soul Ba. In understanding, healing, and connecting these strands, which often coincide with our shadow body, or Shew, we open, release, and embody the Ka not only to enter more deeply into the physical body but also to expand its web of connection into the galactic sphere of the soul Ba through the web of life.

Ka can hold many illnesses and wounds because the Ka can be damaged and repressed by:

1. Traumas and destructive cellular memories that keep perpetuating themselves

2. Deep stress over time created by constant denial of the heart's desires and the delight that comes from this, as Ka is fed by loving nurturing of our soul purpose and the feeling of delight, fulfillment, and happiness that comes from this

3. Injuries from past lives, which can be carried over to the present lifetime, causing discomfort and halting your ability to access and hold higher light bodies

4. Earth memory and distorted spiritual lineage connections

5. Ancestral DNA distortions and inherited physical illnesses or weaknesses

6. Sexual or Ka dependency; unsupportive or draining sexual relationships

7. Crystalline and Devic disconnection

8. Psychic attack

9. Connection into the technospheric Matrix (see "The Technosphere" in Chapter 1)

10. Keeping yourself small and giving power away; Ka is sovereign authority of Self on earth

1. Repair, healing, and etheric surgery of the Ka is necessary in many of these cases, and in extreme cases it becomes necessary to replace the tainted Ka blueprint you have been using. When these etheric fields transform and are cleared, they become replaced by our monadic blueprint, the Ka in its fullness.

2. Ka is an interface between our pranic bodies and emotion, strengthened by breath and feelings of delight and love. This vital force energizes and informs our emotional body, opening the heart. As the Hathors

say, "the ability to feel deeply allows the Ka to vibrate at a faster rate." In order to feel deeply, we have to access our subconscious and the stored memories there that may be inaccessible by normal means as they lie deeply buried, out of conscious reach and awareness.

Ka is linked to your heart through the solar plexus. When it is fed and nurtured every day, it feeds the heart and vitality. When the heart is hurt, Ka too suffers. Ka focuses on life-giving and life-nourishing pro-creative activity. It needs nourishment and food to continue itself on the physical plane, but on the spiritual plane it needs the nourishment of spirit to survive. Ka nourishes your true Self by you actively putting love into action in your life and service to others. Service to others actually nourishes your Ka and other light bodies.

Ka holds your vital essence that empowers the heart's desires and opens the heart, enlivening and activating the outward expression of the heart. It is most commonly experienced in the auric field as someone's charisma, presence, and authority, their outward emanation. However, this emanation can be cloaked at will by people with strong Ka bodies and abilities, as sometimes it serves to be invisible rather than a magnet or beacon, which is what Ka can also do.

Even if the physical body dissolves, the Ka can remain if it is strong enough, even for many years. When united in service to the higher bodies, it is a powerful force for service, alchemy, and love. For the Ka is multiple in nature; it is not just one but many forms of the one Self. The idea of parallel realities mirrors this: there are many versions of ourselves in many different parallel realities, each of them pursuing their own life and also able to connect with the rest of their myriad selves throughout past and future.

I have met versions of myself, future and past, where this has occurred, and I have even remembered sending my Ka into the past to help me in difficult situations. To send one's Ka back in time to an event that has already happened, and in which you remember meeting your

Ka, connects all your timelines and different selves back into unity, regathering the different Kas into one time and space. This gives you more energy to be able to accomplish your heart's desire, the union of the Ab and the Ba.

As we are born, and as we die, there is a transference of energy that occurs through the breath. Our first breath connects us to this world and our unique place in it, and our last breath connects us to our spiritual light bodies, where we merge with the light. This all happens through the interface of the Ka. As God breathed life into humans, as a baby takes its first breath of life as it leaves the oceanic womb of the mother, so we can share our Ka with another through exchanging the breath. By finding our home in our breathing, the breath that connects to all life, and then sharing this with another, we connect and strengthen our Ka, healing and transforming the leaks, rips, and tears within it in order to fully embody our higher light bodies into the physical domain.

## Earth Memory and DNA

Ka is the psychic manifestation of the soul on earth. Like a footprint left in the sand, like a fingerprint left on a glass, Ka leaves an impression of the soul Ba essence behind.

Ka connects to your present-day family, your ancestors, and DNA. Your Ka is handed down to you from your ancestral bloodlines, so it also carries their resonance, gifts, and distortions. As you clear these distortions, the ancestors along your genetic line can get raised into a higher frequency, facilitating their return back to Source. This can also manifest in the spiritual lineages you have been initiated into that may not be clear of distortions, or are still plugged into the old paradigm or the old earth memory. This old earth memory, polluted by war, strife, and survival mechanisms, prevents a lineage or ancestral line from evolving.

Within these connections can be held your resonance with earth's memories. This can often be most felt in sacred sites or power spots, where your Ka entrains with the energy from this spot and the memory contained within this site. The memories held in earth's sacred sites can hold many gifts for you as well as traumatic or painful memories. To heal this and obtain the gifts from them allows the Ka to be free and to stabilize more fully within you.

There are a few ways to clear the Ka of old DNA distortions that prevent you from fully utilizing its power as an interface to your original DNA blueprint. These are all predicated on you acting as a vessel to clear your ancestral lineages so that you literally become a Christ figure to your ancestors so they can be released from their positions and suffering. In this age many of your lineages are crying to be healed and released, and for many of you reading this, this is your sacred task.

The ancestral DNA patterns within most human beings keep them stuck in the deepest traumas, pain, anger, sadness, and suffering. Genetic patterns are passed on from family to family, ancestor to ancestor. At each step along the way of this long genetic chain, each generation can add qualities or additional defects to the DNA pattern, passing this information down to the next generation, and so on. For example, the mother of a scientist friend of mine bent and broke her finger in her early twenties. When John was born this manifested in a curled-up finger, which then also manifested in his daughter, and so on. The cycle continues until one person resolves and heals the trauma on the genetic level, literally becoming a savior or a "Christ" for their bloodline.

The Ka and its connection to the womb-hara holds our DNA patterns past, present, and future. In the release of family and ancestral imprints, we can go into fever and catharsis as these deep imprints dissolve. For once we truly clear and heal our genetic distortions; our ancestors past, present, and future also receive the healing. This is a potent, visceral, physical, emotional, and spiritual experience. It can change the brain and body-mind, and you can feel it deeply in your bones and in the dissolution of the mind into vast empty space. This is not something you just receive; you have to give your all to receive it. As CO shares,

> All the mothers in my ancestral lines, back to the first, were present for this clearing. In love, gratitude, and support, they sounded with me, deepening the commitment and presence, which rippled out into the collective, whispering to those ready to hear from within; spiraling, shimmering strands of ancestral DNA, connecting us all, being cleared and cleansed in the golden infinity loops flowing between the ovaries, from the womb to the heart, between the nipples and from the heart to the third eye.

As TA recounts,

> In experiencing this mandala with the intention of clearing my DNA ancestral lineage back to the first ancestor, I was graced to feel and understand Christ's experience on the cross. He went through this clearing first on a grand scale for all of humanity. The first to journey so that others may follow always goes through the most difficult tests. I was filled with a comprehensive gratitude of new heights for his conscious gift to us, one that even makes it possible for us to follow his example. In turn, in our giving, we can make the way easier for those that follow us.
>
> In the healing of our own vessel and being willing to take into ourselves all the distortions and sufferings of our ancestors, we create great healing for all of humanity, including our future generations that won't carry these distortions forward any longer.
>
> The experience of all of these ancestors around you, as if they have been waiting to see if you could do it, knowing you were the one born to do so, and giving you support, is deeply moving. Feeling

the deep humility of this place, the purity of the healing in process, and the deep connectedness of it all to you as an "individual" and you as all things, is profound. . . .

## Coloring the Ka

Color carries information as part of our biophotonic network, or Ka body. Through color we connect different parts of our body-mind and soul together and become aware of feelings, interconnections, and information that we may be missing. Color is a language of communication and feeling, more feminine and relationship-oriented, as each color relates to another. Imagine creating a home where the colors are out of balance, where they do not match against each other. Similarly, take a look at the inside of your body and you may be able to see the imbalances and mismatches of color within you. It is here we find the connection between the Ka and the Shew, or the shadow.

For example, some color tones may be very well defined and strong. Others may be weak and patchy. We all have these imbalances, which manifest as physical and emotional pain, stagnancy, and stress. Some parts of us may be numbed and cut off from other parts of us, buried or suppressed. Color is the bridge of feeling that brings back communication between these parts of ourselves. These feelings may be tears, sadness, forgiveness, release, joy at feeling what you have forgotten, love, or peace. Color can return these emotions, reigniting them and bringing alive the forgotten and buried parts of ourselves.

Sometimes we may have too much of a mental color, which denies our feelings; sometimes we may gravitate toward purple, a more spiritual color, and leave out the reds and browns, the earthing colors. Sometimes we may enjoy the soft pastel hues and shy away from the strong orange or black. Sometimes we may enjoy the strong primary colors too much and miss out on the subtler, more sensitive shades of feeling. We have different moods at different times, and the trick is to stay in balance with it all, to have a whole spectrum rather than a limited one.

The favorite colors you have and wear in your clothes are the ones associated with the organs and emotions you are most confident with and dependent on. Name your three favorite colors right now. What is the positive and negative emotion connected to each of these three colors? Can you identify with that? When was the last time you used that emotion?

We are made of color, sound, and geometry, languages of vibration. All of the main twenty-four different organs of the body have different colors associated with them. Many of these organs are missing their essential health, which is coded by these twenty-four different color vibrations. When we work with these colors to ignite them in our bodies, we reach optimum health physically, emotionally, and spiritually.[4]

Each organ holds a positive and negative attribute. The kidneys are fear and clarity, with the color being sky blue on a cloudless day. When we heal the negative attribute, we harmonize with the positive and embody that color fully into our bodies, nervous systems, and Ka bodies. The nervous system and Ka systems unite and our overall frequency rises, resulting in more joy, better health, and an overall sense of harmonious well-being. When we are in balance and harmony with our innate twenty-four colors, an equilibrium of body, mind, and soul occurs. To be truly embodied requires that this process be completed so that all our colors are dancing together in harmony.

---

4. This science is held in the Tibetan medicine lineage and has been used for thousands of years to heal millions of people.

# Ka Dependency and Sexuality

Making love with another means you merge Ka bodies. While this can feel beautiful and pleasurable, sometimes we can stay connected to another's Ka body even when we do not want to. We may still think of that person, still long for him or her, and even though we have finished our relating with them, we may still feel a pull toward them. This happens through the Ka, so it is through the Ka that we must disconnect from that person.

There are many ways to share Ka energy, and it is easy to become enmeshed in another's Ka, especially if we are lacking certain colors or vibrational qualities within our own self. We can look outside of our self to another's Ka to support us and fill in our holes, to give us what we need, but this will never fulfill our self. To ground the Ka light body requires you clear up all the cords and unfinished residue and business of your relationships. Cleaning up the past and the mistakes you have created with people is a key here.

Although our Ka bodies are interconnected to all life, sometimes we can become too connected or enmeshed in another person's Ka. This is common in intimate relationships, where people sleep with each other for many years and share their Ka bodies indiscriminately with each other. This happens not just through sexual relating but through sharing a lot of creative time and space with another, doing business with another, signing contracts, fixing agreements, and so on. In essence, "getting into bed" with someone means you are connecting Ka bodies, yet sex does not necessarily have to be part of this Ka merging.

It is important for Ka to have its own space, its own room to breathe, its own connection to Source. Breath and meditation alone help to cement this connection. If you becomes too enmeshed with another's Ka, you can take on their issues and distort their connection to Source as well as your own. You can become too involved with their life and forget your own. You can give away your power and sovereign authority to someone you think knows better or has more power than you. The male and female sides of us can become unbalanced and lopsided.

This happens every day, if not with your intimate relationships, the media, TV, the Internet: all the time the Ka is operating, we can give away our power to something outside of our self at a subconscious level. Separating your Ka body from enmeshment is quite simple once you are aware of it. Reclaim your space. Meditate alone. Sleep alone sometimes. Become aware of how you are dependent on others, and how others are dependent on you. Observe whether this is healthy or not. You may choose to do the Ka clearing (see below) to sever any cords that connect your Ka body to another's Ka that is not healthy.

In relationship, codependency, or Ka dependency, is common. As Ka is an aspect of personal power, charisma, and presence, people are drawn and attracted to it and feed it through their attention. Attention is what feeds the Ka, which is why sportspeople, politicians, and media figures seem to have a presence. This presence gets fed by people giving it attention. Have you ever noticed when you walk into a room that all the people look at you? How do you feel? You feel pumped up, fueled, enlivened—with a strange aura around you. Suddenly more people come up to you and are interested, magnetized by the extra power in your Ka.

Many people live for this rush of energy to their Ka, as do rock stars on stage, some of whom cannot live without this "food." All of these instances are people feeding the Ka. You can harvest this energy and use it for your own purposes to feed the soul or the shadow of the ego. Of course, the Egyptians extensively used the Ka after death, with groups of Ka priests giving attention, energy, and focus to the Ka of the deceased so it could wend its way through the afterlife.

There are many magical ways to expand the Ka, which are used by black and white magicians alike, yet they all involve manipulation of one kind or another. The most reliable and loving way to expand your

Ka is through your own inner work, for the Ka is expanded most through love and integrity so it can connect with and serve the Ba, the soul. Not the ego or shadow.

To do this, take the attention and energy you receive and focus it into your heart with humility. It's that simple. Be humble when you receive the attention, and internalize it into the heart, feeling it as the humble power of joy. Then share that joy with others. More energy is created as they get lit up from the positive heart energy you are sharing with them, and they too start to share the joy with you and others, and so on. A positive Ka chain reaction is started that can touch many.

Ka dependency occurs when we become overreliant on external sources of energy and attention and do not refuel alone. We become hooked on this energy and forget our own source of it. Ka dependency, or codependency, is pulling energy from other people in various ways. It stems from our own lack of self-love, from failing to give worth, love, and empowerment to our selves. Hence, needing the approval of someone else, needing their love to prove your own self-worth, becomes an imprisoning game of extracting love and approval from them. This can apply to partners but also to parents, teachers, religions, and authority figures.

On another level it is as if someone else is responsible for your happiness. The subconscious feels this as a loss of personal power, so controlling the person who is responsible for this false happiness generates a lot of drama. A soul is very tired from these cycles. We start to realize that we are completely powerless over other people and that we may even live in fear of them by constantly trying to look good in various ways.

In Ka dependency, or codependency, behaviors arise from this voice:

My good feelings about who I am stem from being liked by you and receiving approval from you. Your struggles affect my serenity. My mental attention focuses on solving your problems, relieving your pain, or pleasing you. My fear of rejection and your anger determine what I say and do. I use giving as a way of feeling safe in our relationship. I put my values aside in order to connect with you. I value your opinion and way of doing things more than I do my own.

As we realize our Ka dependency, we can then become free from struggling to try to get control and approval from others. We focus on loving ourselves. We regain our own Ka bodies, our link to our soul, the fountain of loving wisdom and true power. Projection, expectation, need, and desire are the underpinning threads that create the tapestry in which one's Ka can become enmeshed with another's, becoming Ka dependent. This will inevitably unfold into an experience of rejection, which can then, with conscious awareness, trigger and clearly reveal your own shadow.

Self-responsibility creates the clear view of the patterns in your shadow, and with the Ka present with the heart, the true purpose of a relationship and its lessons can be seen. Once the purpose and intent of both souls in the relating are clearly known, then clearings can happen on multiple levels, once you let go and cut the Ka cords, which is where the attachment starts.

## Ka Clearing Practice

This is an easy four-step process to disconnect any cords or Ka dependency between you and another. Ka body cutting is much more effective than other forms of cutting cords as it deals directly with the essence of the energy, speaking directly to the subtle body that can get entangled and connected to others. Cutting these cords in the Ka reclaims energy and empowers your Ka, allowing it to connect deeper with all your different bodies, making all your eyes clearer. Ka is power, so reclaiming your own Ka means you bolster your power.

1. Breathe deeply into your womb-hara. Now visualize the crystalline double of your Ka in front of you. See the colors and geometries within your Ka. Observe it: its colors, any rips or tears, any discolorations or unusual additions, or even any missing pieces.

2. In front of your Ka, see the crystalline Ka of the person with whom you intend to sever the cord connection. See deeply into their Ka. Observe its colors, any rips or tears, any discolorations or unusual additions, or even any missing pieces. Now see the colors and geometries within the other individual's Ka and in the cords.

3. See where the cords and tentacles are connecting in the chakras between each of your Ka bodies. Ask what emotion the cord is holding. Breathe rapidly and deeply into your womb-hara to generate fire and heat. Build your own personal power.

4. See the cord between you clearly. Raise your hands into a V or sword shape and use them as a sword's blade to sever the connecting cord while firmly stating, either in silence or aloud, "I command the disconnection of X to me, now, now, now, and forever more."

Repeat this whole action three times.

Now place your hands on your heart and breathe in the liberated energy to nurture yourself. Feel it in your heart.

According to Moikeha,[5] the trinity of crystals green calcite, diamond, and malachite help in letting go, removing life force from a person or situation, and cutting cords. These crystals can be used either in liquid crystal or rock form. Simply charge them with your intent as you do this cutting.

---

5. www.theliquidcrystals.com.

## Money

Another way the Ka can get bogged down is through money, which acts in this age as a form of exchange of energy. When this is unbalanced, or when one person is dependent on another for money, Ka bodies get enmeshed. In many long-term relationships, money can be handed over as a subtle form of power and authority to the principal earner, so it is wise to have your own bank account and money inflows. Too much receiving of money from another without having to do anything for it can weaken your base. In India, the illustrious sage Swami Vivekananda used to warn people about receiving gifts for precisely this reason. It meant you lost your own sovereign connection to Source if it became a habit or something you relied on.

Begging also connects into this. However, many holy people in India are reliant on others for food to live as they spend their time in meditation, fully dedicated to Source in this manner. Their Ka bodies are fully connected to and reliant on Source for nourishment, and it is through various spiritual practices that this connection is established. They then see the god in each person giving them their food and drink for the day, so there is no duality or Ka dependency on another.

Ka dependency can also be applied to inheritances, stock market dealings, and other ways of getting without giving. In fact, receiving like this ties you to those people. For example, receiving a large inheritance can mean you get entangled in the family lineage and ancestral lessons and healings. The money can be an exchange for you to become the receptacle and healer of your entire ancestral healings and karmas. Perhaps this is one of your soul contracts and part of your path to help your ancestors heal, as Ka also holds the DNA of your ancestral lineages within it. With the stock market, you are not strengthening your Ka by giving; you are playing in a world to get for yourself. Your Ka becomes dependent on the financial system, which is a living entity by itself, as many a trader will tell you. What they do not tell you is that Ka gets weaker as you spend more time in your mind.

## Crystalline and Devic Disconnection

The crystalline and devic kingdoms contain the minerals and energetic frequencies that allow the Ka to fully settle into the physical body, changing our identification from the physical body, from being identified with matter, into becoming identified and at one with light. Our disconnection from the Ka, which serves as the resonant interface between light and matter, is now being healed through the reintroduction of crystals and their properties back into human consciousness.

Working with these sentient life forms, known as devas, and the crystals they are associated with, allows the Ka, the earth body, the physical body, and the biophotonic networks and grids to merge, healing the distortions that block us from these pathways. The crystalline kingdom was extensively used in Egypt to facilitate precise states of consciousness and the healings and lessons associated with them. The more we work with specific crystals, the more we can heal and create the right balance of minerals within us that allows embodiment of the Ka and soul Ba. To heal this requires we delve deep into the crystalline matrix of light and uncover our own unique lessons and healings associated with each crystal, as well as reconnecting to the spirit of the earth and the earth's voice and wisdom. (See "Life Viewed through the Nine Eyes of Light" in Chapter 1.)

## Psychic and Magical Attack

In Egypt, and even today, the Ka body of an individual could be imprisoned or cut off from the other bodies of light if that individual was seen as a threat. In these ceremonies, magical spells were placed around the individual, separating their Ka from them. This was often done if the individual was misusing the power of the Ka for black magic or manipulative purposes. However, as the civilization and noble ideals of the Egyptians crumbled, this ritual was done to imprison well-meaning white wizards and priestesses whom the corrupt ruling elites wished to control and limit for their own purposes. Some of these rituals involved burying the person alive inside a sarcophagus with spells, magical seals, and incantations designed to seal the person's Ka body inside the tomb, separating them from their power source and connector. These magical seals and spells, which can last many lifetimes, can be released through a priest or priestess initiated to do this work.

## Strengthening the Ka

The Ka is strengthened through how you live your life. Every thought, word, and deed, every interaction, judgment, and impulse that occurs in your life has a small part of your Ka involved in it. As every sacred tradition knows, our growth and evolution continues even after the death of the body, so that whatever happens on earth in your life now would be recorded and possibly continued in the afterlife *if* we have not learned our lessons. In India this is known as karma.

All sacred traditions thus were careful with how and with whom they spent their Ka energy: what friends and lovers they had, what general company they kept, what contracts they signed, how much time they spent with certain people, what types of boundaries they had, and so on.

Ka grows through living in honor, integrity, and emotional purity coupled with vital power and expression of your truth. It manifests as joy and dynamic engagement with life as well as love. The key is to keep your Ka continually clear in all your interactions and relatings. The laws for keeping the Ka clear and connected to the heart were held by Ma'at, goddess of harmony, truth, justice, and order, found in the heart's wisdom, or the Ab.

The heart, Ab, the center of your being, was called the Ka in your body: "For you are the Ka that was in my body, the protector who made my members hale."[6] This link between the Ka and heart is strengthened by the purity, joy, and bliss that the heart feels as well as the power of the solar plexus to serve the heart. Ka is further strengthened by meditation and contemplation, breath, bliss, joy, delight, loving kindness, tantric lovemaking and ritual, and increasing and harnessing your personal power to align with the selfless nature of Self.

## The Ka Clock: 13:20

A powerful way to embody Ka into physical form comes through the opening and connection of the thirteen joints or articulations of the physical body into the Ka body of light. As we saw in the Khat, the thirteen joints are part of the network that creates the flows of the physical body, interrelating to the blood, lymph, and nervous system. These thirteen physical aspects are known and mapped in the Mayan *tzolk'in* or thirteen-moon calendar that was originally a wisdom piece of the Atlantean civilization. As the legends recount, priests and priestesses fled Atlantis before its fall to take wisdom teachings to modern-day Belize, Guatemala, and Central America, with a part of these teachings being the knowledge of the thirteen-moon calendar and its resonance with the thirteen joints.

The connecting of the thirteen joints to the Ka body aligns both with the energies of time. Time is synchronized to the Galactic Center and the waves of energy emanating from it, which are mapped by

---

6. Carol Andrews, ed., Raymond Oliver Faulkner, trans., *The Ancient Egyptian Book of the Dead* (New York: MacMillan, 1985), Chapter 30b.

the thirteen-moon calendar, tzolk'in, or wave spell. This map allows us to work directly with the energies and wisdoms of the Galactic Center, the Source of our galaxy, as seen in the Mayan calendar today. In this understanding, one could embody the direct resonance and alignment with the Galactic Center through the thirteen joints of the body and the twenty digits or measuring units of the fingers and toes. These thirteen major articulations in the body are: the ankles, knees, hips, wrists, elbows, shoulders, and the atlas bone in the neck. The twenty fingers and toes are digits with which to express and embody this energy into form.

This frequency of thirteen and twenty enables one to access the Galactic Center through measuring the different waves emanating from it and then connecting these waves into your physical body through the interface of the Ka body. When you add twenty and thirteen, you arrive at the master number of thirty-three, which is the number of vertebrae in the spine, the basis of the nervous system and the pillar of the body. According to the Egyptian master Thoth, the time-space continuum is attached to the spine. Indeed, the spine, the digits, and the joints have been the focus of many sacred traditions; the Egyptians used the hands to create mudras to create light body fields; the Hebrew culture bases its language on the hand; the Nordic culture used the hands as the basis for the runes and runic mudras; the Tibetan and Indian cultures use mudras to connect different electrical circuits together within the body-mind system, and even saw the thumb as the measure of the soul.

The joints are reservoirs of energy that can be harnessed and utilized through spiritual practices found in Egyptian yoga, tai chi, qigong, and Tibetan energy practices. In massaging and opening the thirteen joints, we release the crystalline deposits, stresses, and armoring around the joints, allowing more space into them. It is in this space "in between" that the Ka resides within the body, and it is in this space that Ka can harmonize and connect to all the other light bodies, bringing them into physical connection and raising the frequency of the body and matter itself. As space opens up in the physical body, the Ka expands and integrates; with the opening of each articulation, agreement is made between the physical body and Ka to allow light into form. As each articulation is opened, one becomes a walking part of the one that is in the flow of, and serves, divine timing and the Divine Plan.

In this measurement of the thirteen, you become a human timepiece that helps to open up the DNA like tumblers clicking into place. As each cycle of time connects into the physical body and the Ka, different sequences of DNA come "online." As these wheels and spins "click in" on all these different levels, your DNA spirals and threads into the Galactic Center. This means that you become a patterned part of infinite time, resonantly entraining to natural harmony.

The thirteen are a DNA map between the physical body and the Ka. It is how Ka understands and communicates in harmonic geometry to the physical body, connecting our physical geometric structure to the geometric structures of the other bodies of light through movement and measure. As Ka sees these patterns, it recognizes how to work in interface with the body; it sees the map and knows where to go. In effect, the tzolk'in is an overlay on the Ka body that is used to alter DNA patterning in alignment with the waves of light and radiation emanating from the Galactic Center.

As we open the thirteen joints and synchronize our physical bodies and Ka bodies to the thirteen-moon cycle, we walk in divine timing, for the thirteen are a map of your form and flows. Vast amounts of information and energy are stored in the meeting of the Ka and the thirteen joints, and with each turning of the thirteen-moon cycle, different parts of your physical body spin into resonance with your other bodies of light. When these are harmonized, a multidimensional and creative perspective arises within your consciousness, your relation to your environments, and your physical body.

Opening the thirteen articulations brings deep grounding, vitality, and empowerment to you. Each articulation is aligned in pairs, so two ankles, two wrists, and so on are massaged and resonated with over a two-hour period. Any conscious, talented deep tissue bodyworker can work with this template so you can embody Ka more. Simply by both of you attuning with conscious awareness to your Ka bodies before receiving the deep joint massage, the physical body can open up more into galactic forces.

## Meeting the Ka

As one journeys into meeting the Ka, one sees the first face of the Ka body form and begins to merge with it. The first meeting with the Ka is like seeing a replica of yourself. This changes the deeper one travels into and uses their Ka until the Ka starts to take on the appearance of one of the Neters, or archetypal god-goddess powers of creation. However, this replica of yourself can take on many hues according to where and when you last used your Ka consciously. The Ka also has wounds and tears in it, which can be repaired in the Ka practice. As RD describes,

> It was like first seeing a mirror image of myself clothed in red robes. When the circulation of light began I received a huge amount of physical energy—a completion of a loop that had started and had never been finished. Ka is the bridge between the physical and non-physical realms. It needs daily attention and is fed and nurtured by taking attention *away* from Ka-draining sources—talking too much, listening too much, looking at things too much. Interestingly, my experience is that it takes going into the Ka and experiencing it for it to tell you what its needs are and what is draining it in your life (relationships, personal activities, etc). The Ka is a continual area of exploration and limitless possibilities for communication on different levels.

According to SMC, "As I sat with my Ka and first looked in to *her* eyes, she had such a big smile on her face and so much love in her eyes and heart for me. I felt her gentle albeit powerful wisdom shoot from her third eye as a ruby red light into my third eye. She embraced me, and I could feel the love build in my being."

MT also shares that she

> was pleased to see her again and thankful to observe her healthy robust form. Unlike me, the losses of significant others over the last two years had not seemed to change her appearance. I immediately wished to be in her place, not mine, and by that desire, she sat down in front of me and we wrapped our legs around each other, placing our yonis and foreheads together. At that moment I felt my physical body retreat, and I became her, looking at me, seeing through her eyes.

## The Divine Ka of the Egyptians

In hieroglyphics, Ka is represented as a pair of upraised arms mirroring each other in front of a horizon. As sacred languages hold seven levels of meaning to them, this hieroglyph means, in ascending order of consciousness:

- a greeting
- an act of worship
- a yearning and strong desire for the divine
- pulling down the light of the divine into form
- creating a pillar of light between heaven and earth
- an embrace of the divine within and without
- the union of light and form on earth

Where are you on this scale of the Ka?

In Egypt, the god of the Ka body is a winged serpent god called Neheb Kau, whose name means:

- uniter of the Ka, implying the connecting of the many different aspects of the Ka
- allotter of the Ka, implying there is a distinct giving or soul contract involved in each person's individual Ka from your ancestral lineages
- creator of Ka in its seven-headed cobra aspect, or the seven rays and stars connected to the seven vertebrae of the neck, especially the atlas and C1
- former of the Ka from the primeval waters, implying that the individual Ka of each sentient being comes from the void, or zero-point energy; Ka is our first connection to that zero point or universal field
- Ouroboros serpent or circle of continual creating, bringing the world into being through substances or experiences
- holder of all potential: this serpent-power of Neheb Kau has the Ka bodies of all beings held within it. As creation unfolds, all Ka bodies become embodied into beings alive on earth through divine breath, or the air element.
- the emanating force of the Ka from the void itself

Which stage of the Ka do you still need to work on?

## The Ka of Asar Osiris

Ka is your double on the etheric plane, and the double of your Neter or god-goddess form, the god or goddess you feel most aligned to. When you truly connect to this, you can see which Neter you embody and what aspect of the divine pattern you work with and embody. To embrace this is to receive this divinity through your Ka, animating you with that individual vital essence.

In Egypt, there are fourteen aspects to the Ka body of Asar, or Osiris, corresponding to the fourteen parts of his body that were cut up and deposited in various locations around Egypt before he was resurrected through the love and magic of Ast, or Isis.

The fourteen aspects of the Ka of Asar are:

- the ability to sustain the body-mind and soul by knowing one's self, its processes, and what it needs. To sustain takes endurance, stamina, and the ability to see something through until its end, which takes nurturing, attention, and discipline.
- the ability to nurture the body-mind and soul through right relationships, healthy internal and external environments, true speech, right conduct, and integrity.
- the creative power of food and greenness. Being in touch with the spirit of the earth and its voice, living with nature, recycling, being zero-waste, eating organic living foods and herbs that activate and nurture the body along with the pleasure derived from eating well for your body and blood type. Greenness is an energetic quality found in your Ka field that means you have a living link to the fertile living processes of nature, its voice, and the web of life and interconnection. The Ka holds these abilities and powers and also works with the primal and biological drives that drive sustenance, biological reproduction, and preservation.
- the ability to penetrate a situation, person, or thought process with clarity and insight, to reveal the inherent truth in it, and to cut through any veils of illusion. This could also be called deconstructing thought processes and ideas with a penetrating or diamond mind that then serves growth through the shedding of old beliefs and ways of being.

- the ability to cut through illusion with power and sever connections or create connections. Penetration is also a sexual act; in penetrating a woman, healing and spiritual experiences occur because of Ka power.
- the capacity to sit in a holy state of consciousness, to command respect through your presence and accomplishments. This may not be just in the spiritual arena, as many people who have achieved a lot through age or material accomplishments also have a certain aura about them in their Ka, as they have created a resilient and enduring Ka body.
- the ability to use power to get something done when the time is right. The ability to be a leader and take charge. The ability to break down and break through any and all obstacles.
- the ability to consider all aspects of a situation and then act decisively and accordingly.
- the ability to consider others and their feelings, seeing other points of view; the power to be patient and kind.
- the power to be honorable, to tell the truth and be honest and humble as a form of empowerment. The power to stick with honesty, honor, and integrity when everyone else is not. The ability to be strong in this no matter what temptations are presented, and the ability to live in Ma'at or truthful integrity, as seen in the forty-two Laws of Ma'at, which connect the Ka to the Ab or heart.
- the power to know your own worth and the worth of others. Self-worth and self-esteem are a key part of the Ka; without these qualities the Ka is weak. Self-worth means loving, nurturing, and valuing one's Self and being centered in sovereign Self authority, knowing, and leadership of the other parts of your self.
- the power of radiance is the ability to radiate light and knowing to others through the power of the Ka and heart combined.

- the power of illumination is the ability to illuminate any shadow, any darkness, any confusion in self or others; to light up, move, inspire, and catalyze others and yourself into action, clarity, and well-being.
- the power of splendor, to be the royal being that you are, to sit in your presence that is naturally royal and the ruler of the lower aspects of your self. To be majestic and not be ashamed of it; to be splendid without egoic attachment or concern; to sit naturally in your queenly or kingly self, the royal self that serves others; to be the center of your queendom or kingdom, for self to be the center of your universe around which everything else revolves.
- the power to wield magic; the ability to change, alchemize, and manifest situations, people, and abilities. The ability to make the impossible possible and the ability to wield the power of the Ka for any number of purposes seen as miraculous or incredible by others.

Each of these fourteen attributes of the Ka are created by the Ka's ability to create, harness, and build vital essence to the heart. Vital essence is connected to the breath. The first breath is what the Egyptians called the Ka, your first individual breath of life, your first gasp of individual life away from the nurturing envelope of your mother's womb and placenta. Ka creates and sustains the movement of energies that occur during birthing and dying, the beginning and the ending of something, be it life itself or a project, relationship, or move of some kind. It is wise to consciously evoke the Ka when starting or ending anything of any significance to you, as birth, completion, or renewal can happen by connecting with or disconnecting from people or things through the Ka body.

# Driving Your Ka
## The Ka Body Vehicle

The earth's Ka aligns to your own Ka as they share the same geometries, which become a living, breathing, spinning geometric form when activated. We have always shared the same body; we have just forgotten what that was. Earth itself becomes our vehicle for ascension, for growth, as we are its vehicle for growth and ascension. You can experience this through the merging of the sphere, the diamond octahedron, and the cube. These geometries help to create the Ka body, and by harnessing them we can learn how to drive our Ka body.

The physical geometries of the earth and the physical geometries of the body are held within the cells that become permeated with Ka light. As this process deepens the more we drive our Ka, negative cellular memories and the shadow held within the cells arise to be cleared. By creating this space within the cells, our DNA becomes antennae to receive more light from incoming solar flares, radiation, and galactic waves, which in turn activate the DNA further. This constant feedback loop, once activated, perpetually feeds us with light through our biophotonic networks.

In December 2008, NASA announced the discovery of a huge breach in the earth's magnetic field that is allowing, right now, large amounts of solar plasma to enter the earth's magnetosphere. As we will see in detail, the Ka is attuned to and affected by solar plasma. An increase in the flow of solar energy, of the Ra energy, charges and activates our Ka bodies *if* we can align to it through sacred geometry.

The Ka body serves to transmute this radiation and light into a usable form for our bodies to work with and to accelerate our evolution. Gregg Braden states that the incoming solar waves, flares, and galactic radiation create a new synthesis of amino acids in our DNA, mutating our DNA. Without the right geometries to guide these high frequency waves, the ride can be rough. However, with the Egyptian sciences these energies can be harnessed, directly bringing these energies into our bodies of light and the physical body DNA to work with them in a powerful and accelerated way.

In order to be able to handle this increased frequency, as well as the increase in information that this brings to our consciousness (which is amplified by the amount of information available to us, now doubling every year), we need to strengthen our Ka bodies and nervous systems and install the right "decoder software" into ourselves: the sacred geometry of the Ka body of light.

There are three geometries to the Ka body: the cube, the octahedron or diamond shape, and the sphere. Each one is created around the human form in sequence to create a powerful resonating field. The cube brings the light body into the physical through the base of the spine and the Ka's biophotonic network; the octahedron or diamond balances and translates the incoming solar radiation into our bodies and the devic kingdoms; the sphere resonates and holds it all in perfect integrity with the soul Ba.

Driving your Ka empowers, enlightens, and opens the physical form to connect to five of the nine light bodies. The more you drive your Ka, the more centered you become, and the more you are able to use and create with these five. The Ab and the Ba, the heart and soul, were aligned before one even started to drive the Ka through the purifying of the heart through the laws of Ma'at. This ensures that each person who drives the Ka body is able to generate the feelings of love and gratitude as an integral part of the practice.

## The Three Levels of Consciousness

The Egyptians saw that there are three levels of consciousness, or three different ways to interpret the one reality, which are represented geometrically as a cube, an octahedral diamond, and a sphere, all of which sit around and within our physical form. These three levels of consciousness represent the primordial human or aboriginal state of consciousness, the human collective consciousness, and awakened consciousness.

Each level of consciousness rises in frequency, and as humans we need the second step or geometry to help us ascend into the third, Christed Consciousness. This second level of the collective human consciousness is of the human heart, the Ab, that is the gateway into the third level of the Ba or soul. This understanding of consciousness is seen clearly in the progression of the Nine Bodies, which when combined leads one into Christ Consciousness. Nine is the number of Christ in this view, with three being its harmonic.

Each of these three levels and pathways can lead to Christ Consciousness, and different people will have different inclinations based on these pathways. For example, you may be more drawn to working with the earth, to communicating with devas, crystals, flowers, and herbs, and indigenous wisdom and shamanic practices. Similarly, if you are more on the human or second level, you are drawn more to simple human ways of being and self-development. If you are more drawn to the third level, you are more drawn to starry knowledge and wisdom and these forms of communication and ascension into the stars.

Each level of consciousness ultimately blends one into the other to create an integrated and unified being: a cube with a diamond inside surrounded by a sphere. Each person will feel more drawn to one pathway, which you are already predominantly on. Which pathway are you most drawn to?[7]

---

7. For more detailed information, see Drunvalo Melchizedek, *The Ancient Secret of the Flower of Life* Vol. 2 (Flagstaff, AZ: Light Technology, 2000).

# The Cube

The Cube is a matrix of light in the body of form, the principle of earth. The cube unifies all things to make them equal, bringing light into your body in equilibrium and balance. This is normally associated with the number four. The central core of the cube is where all forces unite. Our foundation on earth connects to our foundation in heaven: as above, so below.

The size of the earth and its geometry of the cube are in harmonic proportion to our human energy fields and geometries. It can be said that within us lies all the measurements of our universe, if we know how to use them through sacred geometry. Through knowing all our energy fields we can know everything in creation.

# The Octahedron

The cube is the brother of the octahedron, another balancing and translator geometry. Together they modulate and bring in cosmic forces to be used by you in your embodiment process.

The octahedron assists us in maintaining balance as we increase our vibration, helping us to modulate, absorb, and handle the increases in solar and galactic radiation that are changing our world, our bodies, and our DNA as well as the subsequent ascension symptoms and challenges we are being faced with. In order to fully experience the Ka and the Ba, it is important to build our crucibles, containers or energy vessels to accommodate these higher frequencies. The octahedral diamond shape helps to refine and work with much higher frequencies, as it is the geometrical shape of the new unity or Christ Consciousness grids. It helps to attune to the new frequencies and grids and to focus and direct these energies into our physical bodies through the other bodies of light, raising our frequency to embody our "I am" soul Ba presence.

The octahedron balances energy, especially the male and female aspects of consciousness. The octahedron is the shape that is able to contain the greatest density of energy for the volume of space within it, more than a cube, sphere, tetrahedron, or any other platonic solid. It helps us to adjust to holding greater electromagnetic charge.

Diamond is the crystal connected to our bodies of light and to bringing light into matter. Diamond brings light into the physical and makes physical the light body. It blends and unites all the nine different bodies into the high-frequency speed of the united light force. It is the hardest substance known to people and carries the highest amount of light, purifying, accelerating, and speeding up light-bearing processes once we have established the other bodies in alignment with the physical.

On a galactic level, the galaxies in our universe arrange themselves in superclusters that are octahedral in shape, and the molecule that is responsible for transporting oxygen around your body is four octahedrons of iron surrounded by chains of enzymes. These superclusters may contain billions of galaxies inside of them.

Doctors E. Battaner and E. Florido, in a paper titled "The Egg-carton Universe," write,

> The distribution of superclusters in the local supercluster neighborhood presents such a remarkable periodicity [i.e. ordered pattern] that some kind of network must fit the observed large-scale structure. A three-dimension chessboard has been suggested. The existence of this network is really a challenge for currently suggested theoretical models. . . . In this case, however, the identification of real octahedrons is so clear and the network is so noticeably well-defined that a direct inspection is straightforward.[8]

8. E. Battaner and E. Florido, "Magnetic Fields and Large Scale Structure in a Hot Universe IV: The Egg-carton Universe," *Astronomy and Astrophysics* 338 (1998): 383–385.

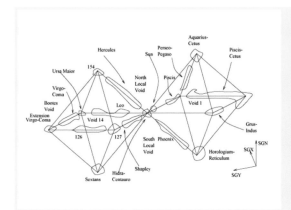

**The two large octahedrons closer to the Milky Way.** (E. Battaner and E. Florido, "Magnetic Fields and Large Scale Structure in a Hot Universe IV: The Egg-carton Universe," *Astronomy and Astrophysics 338,* 1998)

The octahedron is directly connected to the crystals of selenite and its brother the cube of diamond, and can link one to the Arcturian energy. Selenite is an activator of the soul-star chakra or Ba just above the head, and it directly increases the amount of light quotient within you. It is intimately associated with sacred geometry as a geometric translator of the Egyptian light body and is connected to Thoth. Selenite also helps you to access earthly and devic wisdom directly by traveling in the octahedron to connect into the earth.

Selenite increases the amount of liquid light in the flow of water in our bodies, helping to bring spirit into the body through the soul-star chakra. It is important today because of the increased influx of solar and galactic radiation that is bombarding our planet, which is modulated by our soul-star chakra and brought into our bodies through water and light flows.

The octahedron is a gateway for solar energies and is an interdimensional gateway for the spiritual-physical system. The octahedron goes beyond the three physical dimensions into the fourth and can be used as a vehicle of time travel. As we build our own octahedral or diamond grids, we connect more strongly with the grids of our planet and the Ka body.

# The Sphere

*The Nature of God is a circle, center everywhere,*
*circumference nowhere.*

— Empedocles

Modern physics states that the universe was created in a highly symmetrical state, but these symmetries are hidden or "broken" in our everyday world, hidden from the senses, until we reach higher levels of consciousness. Beings living at such higher energies would see a highly symmetrical universe with a single underlying force made up of waves and particles with "notes" of mass. To such a being, our own world of electrons and protons would be but a ripple of energy on the surface of a sphere. If we continue on these levels of scale, nature is seen to be a series of spheres of influence, each sphere being an adjustment to the next. All of our perceptions are modulated by these filters on consciousness.

In the sphere, all life interconnects. Through its membrane, one gains a multidimensional perspective on everything that is viewed through it. Both modern science and the world's sacred traditions agree: the universe is but countless spheres within spheres within spheres, the "bubbles" of material creation, as the Buddha said. Each of these spheres are created like when a pebble is dropped into a still pond—each ripple, each undulation, each concentric circle created is a different vibration, a different frequency, a different world. It could be said that each one is a different sound, holding a different meaning. We are at the center of all of these ripples, these lenses or shells, looking out at the waves and effects our thoughts, feelings, and intuitions have in all directions.

## Spherical Shells

Each of us lives simultaneously in multiple spheres of consciousness. Our ability to relate to each sphere deepens our ability to feel and communicate in states of highly enriched experience. Experiencing consciousness as spherical allows for multiple dimensions, states of consciousness, and multiple movements of time to coexist as fine membrane "shells," each shell vibrating at a different rate containing a different level of consciousness.

These shells are always moving and changing, cyclically rotating all polarities, for nothing stands still in the sea of vibration we live, feel, and think in. When we experience all these polarities, we can become totally feminine or masculine at different moments in order to experience the full range of creation's possibilities and dance. This helps us to live in a field of infinite possibility by being able to move fluidly between one and the other, and sometimes to be neither.

## The Fluid Center

At the center of the sphere, our core, the life spark within us pushes toward movement. This spark manifests and aligns all other levels of creation to its innate nature: movement. These vibratory movements constantly go through us and the earth, and are made conscious when our emotional state is agile and we can easily emote, for emotion = energy in motion. For us to align to this our Individual core, which is free, without charge and attachment, requires that we become fluid.

When we are fluid, we can experience feelings at any time. If we can, at will, produce equanimity, delight, love, anger, or tears without charge or attachment to them, then we can be moved from within by the spirit that is always fluid and open. However, the less we can summon feelings, the more we are frightened of them, the more we are at their mercy. Conversely, the more we allow ourselves to experience feelings, the less we can be enslaved by them. If we allow them to pass through us, we become transparent, without charge, without holding onto anything or anybody.

Thus we learn to move the body, feelings, and mind so that spirit can move us. In this fluid individuality, we can be any aspect of consciousness at any time, for in the sphere we are able to feel and express whatever we are needed to be in any given moment, to express all parts of our universal character; in effect we become "all things to all men."[9]

## The Sphere of Ma'at: The Forty-two Notes on the Scale of Creation

> Do you not know that Egypt is an image of heaven ... in Egypt all the operations of the powers which rule and work in heaven have been transferred to the earth below ... the whole Cosmos dwells in our land as its sanctuary.[10]

The Egyptian Edfu Temple Texts state that Egypt was mapped and created as a celestial kingdom: the kingdom in the stars was mapped out on the earth through the land of Egypt itself. This measuring and creation of heaven on earth, as above, so below, was carried out by seven sages or builder gods, presumably from Sirius, known as the Sirian Lords of Light.

This map was created using the forty-two harmonics of the Sphere of Ma'at, the divine principle of order, harmony, coherency, and divine alignment. These forty-two harmonics were created in the land of Egypt through Lower Egypt, the Kingdom of Set in the dry infertile desert

---

9. 1 Corinthians 9:22.
10. Walter Scott, *Hermetica* (Boston: Shambhala, 1985), 341.

regions, and Upper Egypt, the land of fertility, greenness, and Horus. Each kingdom was separated into different regions or nomes, with their own rulers or nomarchs. Each nomarch was seen as an embodied god-goddess or Neter, wielding the specific influence of that Neter's power and function.

Each nome and kingdom reveals a particular state of consciousness and a particular measuring of the creative process reflected in the making of stars down to the creation of the sense organs and the elements in our bodies, from the manifestation of spiral galaxies down to our reproductive systems. Each nome maps out this spiraling process of creation, from the largest to the smallest. Perhaps the most important of the nomes was the twenty-third nome, the first nome in the Kingdom of Horus and the site of the Giza pyramids, the Sphinx, and the Temple of On.[11] This nome is where Upper and Lower Egypt became united into a single kingdom, and according to Cox, this nome "symbolizes the visible form of the galaxy as a whole."[12]

These forty-two harmonic kingdoms together created the forty-third harmonic of wholeness that was the sum total of all its parts: Egypt as a galactic kingdom and portal to universal consciousness. The significance of forty-two is seen in the weighing of the Ab or heart in the Hall of Ma'at, where forty-two judges came to judge the heart to ascertain whether it was pure and light as a feather to enable it to pass through into the Kingdom of Osiris and to become a liberated soul free of the wheel of reincarnation. Emotional purity, integrity, and honor were the gateways through which the unified heart-soul could manifest, flying freely into the heavens as a liberated soul.

Forty-two is also the number of Sanskrit syllables that map out the creation and the creative process of manifestation from formless into

---

11. The twenty-third nome is also the site of the cosmic egg at Heliopolis, and where Horus defeated Set to become the ruler of all Egypt. The seventeenth nome is Anubis.

12. Robert E. Cox, *Creating the Soul Body* (Rochester, VT: Inner Traditions, 2008).

form, as seen in the Maheshwara Sutra, one of India's key texts on sacred sound and creation given to humanity by Shiva Himself. The main role of this Sutra or "Thread of the One" shows a single Awareness creating the fabric of time and space through the movements and meanings of the Sanskrit alphabet, from the beginning of the Big Bang through to the formation of our galaxy, planets, chakra systems, minds, and bodies.

In this process the forty-two sounds paint a sonic picture of the harmonious unfolding of vibration that creates our universe and our minds. These movements of creation and holographic language are depicted in the fourteen classes of sound (similar to the fourteen body parts of Osiris and the fourteen Stations of the Cross found in Christ's crucifixion journey), from which the forty-two syllables of the Maheshwara Sutra derive. Forty-two is also the number of angles found in the Sri Yantra, the Hindu map of creation. Coincidence?

This scale of forty-two harmonics is the harmonics of the scale of creation. These harmonics are precise, with certain syllables occurring at certain frequencies that continually rise and fall. This continual rising and falling becomes an infinite wave of sound, with thoughts, feelings, and spiritual-physical emanations arising from these harmonics, which are continually playing all the time. We are just not aware of them and are only tuning into and consciously resonating with a portion of this scale.

To resonate with the whole scale requires that we create a crystalline bridge through our bodies, blood, bones, and DNA to our bodies of light. These bodies of light connect to and resonate into form through these harmonics that span the full spectrum of creation. We first come into conscious awareness of this scale through the Ka body, and as we deepen into the Ka we can clear our many "stuck" notes on the scale as our physical form rises to a new frequency able to play these higher harmonics. The whole scale becomes knowable when the

Ka merges with the Ba soul, and the Ab or the heart of Ma'at: truth and harmonic order.

## Spheres of Sound

Both sound and electromagnetic energy travel spherically. If you could see the sound made by your vocal folds, it would be about the size of a pearl, only a few hundredths of an inch in diameter. This beautiful pearl of sound expands in size as it passes through your throat and leaves your open mouth as a small bubble, perhaps an inch in diameter, less than a millisecond later. There it is joined by a second bubble that leaves your nostrils, which helps to give your voice its unique character.

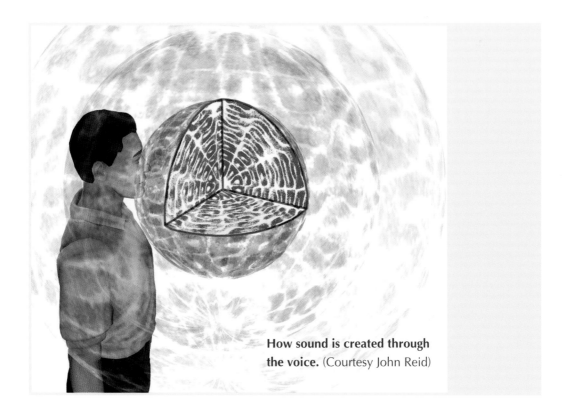

**How sound is created through the voice.** (Courtesy John Reid)

The combined sonic bubble is at its highest intensity just at the point where it leaves your mouth, and it propagates rapidly away from you at around seven hundred miles per hour. This intensity falls off by the inverse-square law, so that as the bubble's distance from you doubles, its amplitude quarters. When the sonic bubble leaves your mouth and begins its rapid expansion, it can only do so by jostling air molecules. This jostling causes friction at the atomic level, which in turn causes a release of infrared electromagnetic energy. The sonic energy has actually been converted to electromagnetic energy.

Now, the wonderful thing about electromagnetic energy is that it travels through air and through space without being unduly converted or absorbed. (Witness radio waves, which are simply a lower frequency version of the same type of energy. They travel from their transmitters through the atmosphere, and some frequencies even circumscribe the globe by bouncing off the ionosphere). So, when we speak or sing outdoors, at the very place where our sonic bubble is at its highest intensity, that is, right in front of our lips, a powerful electromagnetic bubble is formed. That electromagnetic bubble expands away from us at 186,000 miles per second, and it never stops or falters; it goes on forever unless it meets some dense matter.

An example of this in reverse is the light energy that leaves a distant star. Say a star is one million light-years away from earth. Imagine that, one million years ago, a tiny packet of light energy leaves that star on its journey toward earth. It travels through an unimaginable void of space for a million years, never needing to replenish its energy. All it had was the energy it was given when it was created, and that was more than enough.

Now, imagine you are standing in your garden one night and you raise your head to look at this star. A millisecond before you look, the little light packet finally arrives at the outer limits of our atmosphere after a journey lasting a million years. Does the atmosphere stop it? No.

If the sky was hazy that night it might have absorbed a little of its energy, but tonight it's a crystal-clear sky. The little light packet speeds its way through the air to earth where you are looking up. It enters your eye at a speed of 186,000 miles per second, and there in that moment its progress is finally halted, never to go any further. You stopped it. What happened to it in your eye? Molecules in your retina were vibrated infinitesimally and the light energy was extinguished in that moment, converted into a minute movement of a retinal molecule.

The point I am making is that that tiny packet of light energy traveled for a million years, and that is precisely what the packets of infrared energy that leave your mouth will do. So, when you wish upon a star, your message will, quite literally, one day arrive at that star.

As with all energetic systems, there is scope for good and evil. If we are indeed immersed in an ocean of spheres, some will contain energy of good intent, but sadly some will be of evil. When someone compliments you, those loving vibrations are usually received with grace, but when someone shouts abuse at you, the vibrations are usually received with pain. However, in light of this hypothesis, it now seems likely that those good and bad energy fields do not stay local to us. While they will not travel through walls, they will travel, theoretically, to the horizon, if we are talking outdoors. On their way, the bubbles may pass countless people (especially if we live in an urban area) and each person it passes will absorb a little of that energy. That is a nice thought if the energy is loving, but if it is abusive, it is a very uncomfortable thought.

This discovery may forever change the way we think about our vocal exchanges with others. Perhaps this is why the Buddha placed so much emphasis on right speech, and why the Egyptian culture also placed such great importance in their temples about the right use of sound. Everywhere there are spheres, and on their surface are beautiful patterns. We are surrounded by this beauty, yet our senses do not allow us to see it. Imagine two people singing together, and as they harmonize their spheres of sound literally merge together, creating glorious and beautiful sonic bubbles. This is an ancient Egyptian practice that was used to train the priests and priestesses into the true nature and use of sound.

Thanks to John Reid for this article; see www.Cymascope.com for more.

## Driving Your Ka: The Practice

Sound travels spherically. Egypt was created as a kingdom of heaven on earth using a harmonic scale of forty-two harmonics based on galactic wisdom encoded by the founders of Egypt in the Zep Tepi, or golden age. Through using the three geometries of the Ka Ba body, we can access this wisdom, light, and power to rapidly accelerate our evolution and strengthen the Ka to hold the increased frequencies coming to earth now.

Now that we understand how and why the Egyptians used the three key geometries of the Ka body, we can actually learn how to drive the Ka ourselves. This is a powerful experience that can be done every day, leading to the increased ability to hold higher frequency in five of your light bodies as well as rises in consciousness.

The longer you do it, the deeper you will go. It is up to you to feel into how long and with what length of time you do it. If it feels too intense, then only do it for twenty minutes. If you feel you can handle it, do it for longer. Everyone is unique, and the experiences you may have in driving your Ka may range from the mild and gentle to the dramatic and intense, depending on what you need and are ready for at the time you do drive your Ka.

For this practice to work most effectively, you must be dedicated and committed to evolve. This is an advanced practice that works when your Ba soul and your Ka are ready and able to connect in order to create a gateway to Source. The spinning motions found in each of the three geometries creates a vortex in the light bodies, which moves the soul energies of the soul Ba into the Ka vehicle, and then into the physical body, Khat, to help heal and integrate the shadow Shew. In effect, the meditation of driving your Ka clears, opens, and connects five light bodies at the same time, which, when you are prepared, can lead you to enter the universal light body of Sahu.

Driving your Ka involves three aspects: breath, creating sacred geometries, and the emotions of gratitude and appreciation allied with the conscious directing of the Ka and Ba energy flows through the spine.

## Creating the Cube

Sit up comfortably, spine straight. Take a few deep breaths and center yourself.

Visualize your energy-double Ka in front of you.

Now imagine a cube around both your physical body and your Ka body, spinning and rotating around you, clockwise. Watch it as it spins around you, slowly getting faster and faster. You may see it as diamond, white, or the color that comes to you most readily.

Command the cube three times to spin at nine-tenths the speed of light clockwise around you.

## Creating the Octahedron

Imagine a pyramid with its point facing downward at your Ba or soul-star chakra above your head. Direct feelings of real appreciation and gratitude to the Ba soul. Really feel these feelings: bring back memories of when you have felt them before if you cannot feel them easily.

As you continue to send appreciation and gratitude to the Ba, you will feel a downward movement of energy from the Ba in response. As this occurs, breathe the pyramid down, allowing it to come and rest gently at your heart.

Now imagine and gently breathe another pyramid, its point facing upward, ascending from below your feet and the earth-star chakra.

Both pyramids meet and slot in together at your heart, with the bases of both pyramids forming a straight line at the heart. This then creates a diamond or octahedral figure that encases your whole body, from the Ba above the head to just below your feet, with the axis of the octahedron extending through the center of your spine.

Visualize yourself surrounded by this crystalline three-dimensional octahedral field of light.

Now command the octahedron three times to spin at 1.3 times the speed of light counterclockwise around you.

Each pyramid will spin faster and faster and may even assume the form of a gyroscope rotating around you. Rest in this for a moment.

## Connecting the Octahedron into the Spine: Central Channel Breathing

Now focus on your Ba or soul-star chakra and connect this to the thin white line of light that runs through the center of your spine, which is the middle of the octahedron.

Purse your lips like you were going to blow out a candle. In this position, inhale light down from the Ba into the spine, then down into the earth-star chakra for seven seconds.

Repeat this six times up and down the spine. It is now anchored into your central nervous system. Visualize yourself surrounded by this crystalline three-dimensional octahedral field of light.

Rest. Now command the octahedron three times to spin at 1.3 times the speed of light counter clockwise around you.

## Creating the Sphere

Now imagine a disc extending out around the cube and diamond octahedron. This disc can be as large as you feel it needs to be. Of course, a disc is a sphere if you look at it from top or bottom.

Command the sphere three times to resonate at the harmonics of zero, twenty-three, and forty-two. As you do, the cube is rotating around you clockwise, the diamond octahedron is rotating counterclockwise, and the sphere holds both spinning geometries together in harmony.

If thoughts start to come and disrupt you here, simply bring your attention back to the sphere and the other spinning geometries and their connections. You can also simply breathe up and down the spine, which is a great way to center yourself or feel the emotions of appreciation and gratitude again.

## Driving the Ka Body: The Experience

When you activate the triple geometries of cube, diamond octahedron, and sphere, the whole fluid resonating structure becomes alive like a gyroscope, serving as a bridge for conducting, transmitting, and receiving higher frequencies of light. Many different things can happen, depending on what you are ready for. When you drive the Ka correctly, the sphere becomes a resonator connecting the Ka body with the sun, Sirius, Arcturus, and the Pleiades.

Sometimes driving your Ka is gentle, and at other times vast amounts of vibration course through you. Reactions can occur, such as headaches, nausea, even passing out. All of these are spiritual and physical detoxification symptoms, or ascension symptoms, as your bodies adjust to the incoming higher frequencies and purge whatever is unnecessary to allow in these frequencies. As SA shares,

When I activated the cube, the pyramidal octahedron, and the sphere, I was projected straight in a space of peaceful presence. I was home on the other side of the life-death veil. It was a space so well known yet so long kept unconscious. From that space I saw myself sitting in front of me, appearing in a pure crystalline light body. This body appeared so pure to me, a pure reflection of my light. More and more I feel I'm away and here at the same time; the border between the spaces becomes so narrow that I come back here in a flash at the end of a meditation.

As MT shares,

As the cube spun faster and faster, I became one with my Ka. I became encased in a breathing, spinning globe of pearlized light, like that of the moon veiled by clouds. The walls of the spinning cube became transparent, and . . . I viewed the earth beneath me resting peacefully in space. Upon seeing it I became infused with a sensation of overwhelming love and desire for the planet—a great longing. The bottom part of the octahedron detached, and its pyramidal form rose toward me. As it drew closer, its point peeled back like a banana, and a cruciform image emerged. . . . I saw before me a large gold scarab beetle, and it entered my brain. At that instant I became the star within the octahedron spinning around at near light speed within the whirling sphere and cube. All sounds and images faded away to darkness. There was nothingness and everythingness.

As SM shares,

The smaller diamond cube in the base of my spine generates a grounding. The larger diamond cube surrounding me generates a foundation. The embracing of my Ka body strengthens my energy. I feel more complete. Commanding the larger diamond cube to spin has the feeling of opening a door. The experience of the octahedron feels like I am en route to my true "home." The central channel breathing, both in the front and back of the body, feels like I am resonating with the energy of my true "home." Anchoring the octahedron into the cube is just that, putting down roots in my true "home."

The sphere feels like I am claiming my true "home" and residing there. After that, I usually travel . . . I am not sure where. Random pictures pop into my head. Overall, I feel a sense of heightened energy, vibration, and peace. I have a vague recollection of being surrounded

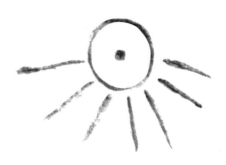

**The meeting of the Ab and Ba.**
(Photo taken by Padma Aon in Central Coast, Australia, and edited to highlight features)

by a circle of beings smiling at me. One being that represented the group was communicating with me telepathically (with symbols that represented big blocks of information) and something was placed on my shoulders. I was taken somewhere and shown energy moving, undulating, transforming. My outward experience of the inside is crumbling, dissolving. I have no thoughts in my head—I don't think—to use my brain the way I used to. These days I feel more and more that life is living me, breathing me, animating me.

To MR, "The cube represents Gaia, the earth; the descending and ascending pyramids represent the fires of creation, as above, so below, connecting in the heart of humanity and Gaia; the undulating sphere shimmering in a vast spectrum of rainbow essence."

## The Five Faces of Anubis

We as humans call forth extremes of experience throughout the many lifetimes we live in order to learn. Whatever extreme lessons of hardship or pleasure we have received in this lifetime and learned about are ones that we have dished out to others also. While this could be called karma, it is actually a game you have created in order to learn about true compassion and right action. By experiencing both sides of the coin, being both the giver and the receiver of a lesson, light and dark, we unite all the polarities into the middle way of peace, acceptance, gratitude, and equanimity—the middle way of compassion.

Compassion for another and one's self is most deeply generated by experiencing that suffering, which oftentimes is what we have given before. For example, if one is suffering from cancer, one may have done something grievous to body-mind and soul previously and is now rebalancing and learning the opposite side of the lesson in order to complete that cycle of learning. If one is poor in this lifetime, one may have been fabulously wealthy in a previous life and has now chosen to experience the other side of the polarity in order to complete that cycle of learning.

This is something we choose to learn about compassion, about human experience, about the deepest nature of duality and unity, and about our true Self. This type of learning, which we all undergo, helps us to let go of any judgment, and this in turn fosters peace and nonattachment. It is this bridge that unites the Ka with the Ba into the physical body of the Khat.

When the human Ka unites with the galactic soul Ba, it enters the vastness of inner spaciousness or intergalactic space: the Hu body of Sahu and Akhu. The foundation and receptacle of this is Khat, the transfigured physical body containing light. The whole purpose of Egyptian spirituality was to merge Ka and Ba to realize and embody Sahu and Akhu.

Anubis or Anpu is a gateway into embodying the Ka Ba because of his ability to stand equally in light and dark as guardian of the Ab heart: the gateway to the Ba soul. His wife is Neheb Kau, the creator of the Ka body, and he is her visible representative and agent. His energy is starting to become more noticeable again in the world as we race into 2012 and beyond, for with the return of Ma'at, (whom he serves), the truth of harmony and justice, comes the return of Anubis and nonduality.

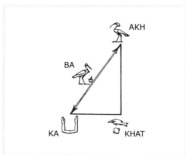

The goal of Egyptian alchemy: the uniting of Ka Ba and Akhu through the Khat.

Anpu is seen as a jackal-headed Neter but is actually a wolf from the dog or wolf-star Sirius. His main temple is found at the Sphinx, which stands directly in front of the middle or Mother Isis Pyramid in Giza. Recent excavations have uncovered many of his artifacts from there, and

Robert Temple reveals, through scriptural and photographic evidence, ancient sluice-gate traces that demonstrate that during the Old Kingdom the Sphinx as Anubis sat surrounded by a moat filled with water.[13] This moat was called Jackal Lake in the ancient Pyramid Texts, and it was where many sacred and religious ceremonies were held.

The Isis Pyramid is the portal into the Womb of the World, the space of Isis, the primordial creative and feminine space, which connects into the Galactic Center, the womb of this galaxy. The Egyptians used this space for potently transformative actions and to birth new realities that were to come into manifestation on a larger scale for their entire community and the world at large. This womb was used extensively by the priestesses of Isis and by the Djedhi priests and was where they did collective ceremonies together.

Anpu is intimately connected to working in partnership with the divine feminine, through Ma'at as guardian of the heart, with Isis as her pyramid guardian and with her being his adoptive mother, and with Neheb Kau, the goddess creator of the Ka. Anpu is starting to make himself known again as the resurfacing of truth returns to earth, revealing much of the ancient wisdom to provide humanity with the tools and awareness to make the next leap in awareness. As he is the protector and helper of both Isis and Ma'at, the goddess principle of truth, justice, fairness, and order, he stands as a gateway to truth. As Jesus said, "No one comes to the Father except through me,"[14] so Anpu says, "No one comes to the Mother except through me."

He is the gateway or crossing point between light and dark, standing simultaneously in both worlds, not judging either but retrieving the gifts of each to help embody and connect our Ka to our Ba, or soul

---

13. Robert Temple, *The Sphinx Mystery: The Forgotten Origins of the Sanctuary of Anubis* (Rochester, VT: Inner Traditions, 2009).
14. John 14:6.

essence. Anpu is the bridge between your true Self and the self that you have buried your truth behind. He holds a great key to the Ka Ba, as it is through your physical body that you will ascend as we come into 2012. It is vital that we prepare and clear the Ka and our physical body so they can raise their frequency into the Ka Ba hologram.

As the earth's frequency rises so too do the obstacles to this arise. Instead of going into fear or judgment, we too have to straddle the divide between the old earth's frequency and teachings and the new earth's frequency and behaviors that resonate with humanity's collective ascension into a new paradigm. Anpu is the bridge between both, which is why he is making himself known again *now*. We increase our frequency by connecting to and embodying the Ka connection to the Ba. Gaia does this too through her Ka body, replacing the old outworn earth with the "new" templates. As matter, which is simply frozen light vibrating at a slower frequency than the Ka, speeds up its frequency, so too will these outmoded and restricting ways of being be separated from the new frequency.

All it takes is willingness and an open heart to begin to tune into and work with these new frequencies and incorporate them into the Ka. This is done through the meditation of driving the Ka, which helps us to embody more of our Ka and Ba. Embodiment means bringing all of your soul into the present, into your body, onto earth now. This is how the earth can transform and how a new civilization can be created. Embodiment is the most rewarding act a human can do, as to embody is to live your highest potential. It is an experiential living in the present designed to bring every part of you back together again, to reweave all parts of yourself into the fabric of life.

The direct reclaiming of power from the shadow, which Anpu stands in between, means one can embody all of your bodies of light into physical form. Each of these bodies has a specific function, and the more we embody each one, the more light we hold in our physical bodies.

This also means that you develop more spiritual abilities and have deeper intuition and communion with all life. As all parts of your soul recongregate and coalesce into your body and conscious awareness, you realize your unity with all life precisely because all parts of you are now woven back together again in one living tapestry. You become one. The feminine holds and provides the platform for embodiment, which is why Anpu guards the feminine mysteries as the loyal protector of Isis.

As you move through the Duat, the underworld of your suffering and spiritual pathway, he is the final guide who walks with you, hand in hand, as you step out of the Duat and into the light of day, the light of awareness. For me, whenever he arrives or appears, he does so suddenly and without warning, as Christ said, "like a thief in the night."[15] The first time I met Anpu was when I was meditating the day before I was leading a group to Egypt on an initiatory pilgrimage to several temples. Midway through the meditation, without warning, Anpu appeared. I was surprised, to say the least, as I was not calling him and had never even met him before; but I did recognize him.

We were both standing in a dark tunnel, and he was on my left side, holding my hand. I felt comfort, like he was my friend. I instantly trusted him. We started to walk together, side by side, out of this tunnel, which I was later to cognize as the Duat. I could see light in front of me while being aware of the darkness all around me. As I walked toward the light, I felt to turn around, still with Anpu's hand in mine.

As I did, a huge wave of black sludge cascaded toward me, stopping just before my feet. As I watched it calmly, it solidified into a black wall and froze. I turned to Anpu, and he simply nodded to me. We continued to walk, and to my surprise we walked out of this tunnel into a blazing yellow light, a clear and brilliant sunlight. I looked down and could see the Giza pyramid complex below with all three pyramids

---

15. Thessalonians 5:2.

clearly laid out. The light was blazing yellow, reflecting the sands into light that was all around me. I looked up and could see the whole structure of the Duat clearly visible. It was like a huge black serpent, clearly a self-enclosed loop that stretched all the way out into the galaxy, through Sirius, but which clearly ended right above the pyramids. I looked to my left, and Anpu was gone.

## The First Face of Anpu

Anpu has five different faces that we can journey into. The first of Anpu's five faces is clearing. When we are ungrounded, we can be scattered, inefficient, moody, and exhausted. It can seem like we never have enough time to get what we want done, and the things we want always seem just out of reach. We can be reactive, unable to step back from people, events, and relationship experiences to allow appropriate action. We feel that life is too fast, that it is passing by too quickly, and that we cannot quite catch up to it.

The First Face of Anpu is a gateway to bring in light into the body and nervous system. The cutting away of negative energies in the aura and the body and of any and all things in your life that do not serve your growth are activated here. Cutting cords in toxic or stagnant relationships and all body-related illnesses and massage work will also help to move old energies out of you.

As you enter into the pathway of opening and embodying the light bodies, you have to clear the obstacles out of the way to carve more space for light to reside in your physical body. As this occurs, your body becomes lighter and more fluid as your identification is with light rather than matter. Paradoxically, by going more into matter and seeing its restrictions and holding patterns, we spiritualize the body by honoring it. As we honor it for providing us with certain lessons, we begin to identify more and more with the light inherent in the body rather than the slower vibration of matter.

All matter is empty, and essentially we are empty space with a sheath of water, skin, and bones around us. We are space, seemingly in a body. The First Face of Anpu allows us to see this as we let go and clear that which keep us stuck in the lowest and densest frequencies: guilt, fear, body pain, negative and destructive cellular memories, and attachments to people and objects.

You may feel you have done this, that you have cleared all these things and are far more evolved than this. You may think you have, but as you bring more and more light into your awareness and body, remember that you are on a spiral path. With each turn of the ascending spiral there can be an equal turn on the descending spiral. This is a continual process, so the more we evolve, the more we have to tune into and use the First Face of Anpu to keep us grounded and in holistic harmony. This is a spatial process that is always happening. The First Face of Anpu balances, clears, and opens the doorway to this process happening in harmony without becoming too earthy or too crown-heavy.

Lightness arises through traveling through the First Face of Anpu. Every evolutionary spurt we go through is a gateway to hold and embody more light in our physical forms. Anpu is the gateway on multiple different levels of consciousness, and it is up to us to keep these gateways open rather than forget about them as we ascend.

As more light comes in, more darkness can arise. This first step is a physical step. Old pains and physical ailments reappear or get accentuated so we can see them fully and inquire into their deeper purpose in our lives. We see the role that these physical pains have in our lives and why we have created them on our soul's path. It is a great reminder that you cannot run away from or pretend it is not there, as it is constantly very present in your body.

These pains are connected to our emotional bodies. As we clear them to open up more space for our souls to emerge, we release the burdens and density of the physical world. Anpu here is an earth-centered love, a physical nurturing and opening that attracts to itself all fear that is stuck on the physical and emotional level and dissolves it. As these blocks are held so deeply, they suppress deeper courage and place limits on ourselves that we ourselves have created. As we start to clear these obstacles, commitment and dedication to our healing arises: we are ready to do whatever it takes to grow and shed these limiting beliefs. Even if we think we are beyond certain healing, we reenter them in order to fully embody our highest potential.

Anpu, through the use of one of his stones, malachite, draws out radiation and absorbs energy from painful, diseased, or inflamed areas, bringing forth the underlying causes and therefore a real pathway of healing. Malachite helps vision at the third eye and restores breath in respiratory illnesses, releasing and balancing the area of the solar plexus and loosening tension at the diaphragm. If you feel any of these symptoms, use this stone either in solid or liquid form.[16]

## The Second Face of Anpu

The Second Face of Anpu connects the light bodies into the Ka and into the physical body. This face is subtle in its harmonizing aspects but powerful in providing a foundation for higher energies to anchor and settle into form. This second aspect of the Ka is gentle and subtle in how it works. In its subtlety it cleans and clears you, taking the sting and charge out of your emotional wounds and holes, enabling you to respond rather than react. As the volume and charge of the emotions becomes stilled, right actions can occur. Rest and spaciousness allow this to happen and integrate.

---

16. www.theliquidcrystals.com.

You become more present in the heart, grounded and in control of the physical-emotional process, rather than it controlling you. Errant emotions become neutralized, and polarities merge. This neutralization calms and unifies the physical, emotional, and mental bodies together. Experiencing this neutralization of charge allows the creation of a strong vessel capable of going deeper into the silence that neutralization affords us. This graceful transmutation of energies allows one to go deeper into true self-reflection to anchor the Ka body.

True self-reflection arises from the mind adhering to spiritual principles in the face of fear, both others and your own. This mental focus and concentration brings order to chaotic situations, and with this aspect of Ka activated, can draw tension out of the body, neutralizing negativity and releasing anger, calming the mental state. This then allows the anchoring of the higher light bodies in balance to the physical.

The stone of the Ka here is hematite, which is protective and shielding and reflects any negativity with its polished mirror surface.[17] Protection here is not about others. It protects you from negative energies within you, transmuting these energies and neutralizing them. In truth, there is no need for protection. Love needs no protection—only fear does. Medallions, spells, fields, devices: all are manifestations of fear protecting you from yourself. The need for protection in energy work is one of the biggest perpetuators of fear. If you start a healing session by having to protect yourself, you are starting the session with fear. If you end a session by protecting yourself, you are ending the session with fear. Anything else in between is greatly reduced as you are feeding duality by your actions. The greatest protection is love, and any need to protect yourself in any way is cutting yourself off from love's truth, which is the highest truth.

---

17. This stone is also able to activate the earth-star chakra below the feet.

Love needs no protection. True protection is transmuting your negative energies within yourself so you can be more harmonious and loving with all parts of Self, in others and within your own self. This is the lesson of the Second Face of Anubis. All negative projections are your own lessons to grow, discern, and neutralize into unity. Again, each face of the Ka body may reappear at different times for you to look at and immerse in. There is a sequence to the grounding and healing of the Ka, yet the sequence can be done at different times along your journey.

The Second Face of Anubis is the scarab beetle. Scarab amulets made of hematite were often placed over the heart of the mummified deceased. These "heart scarabs" were weighed against the feather of truth during the judgment in the Duat before Ma'at and Osiris. The amulets were often inscribed with part of the Confession to Ma'at (from the *Book of Coming Forth by Day;* see Chapter 6 on the Ab), which asks the heart, "Do not stand as a witness against me." This meant that the scarab was there to assist the purifying of the heart from guilt and shame because if you ask someone not to stand against you as a witness, you are automatically assuming you have done something wrong, and you do not wish to be seen or corrected for your misdemeanors.

These hematite scarab amulets were worn not just in death but also in life. The priests and priestesses of Anubis would wear them when they performed the confession and opening of the heart before Ma'at so they could live in harmony and truth with the heart and body united, not separate.

The scarab grounds the heart and shadow, balancing the process of descent into darkness, and renews the tired heart so it may be present. It allows the heart to come into the body, grounding the higher light bodies through the heart. If one focuses on the heart, everything else becomes clear, as Jesus said.

So, ask yourself: What is weighing heavily on my heart? What keeps bugging me and will not go away? What do I have to do to heal and clear whatever is weighing me down?

## The Third Face of Anpu

Every journey of soul consequence begins at a doorway, face to face with a guardian or a test. Sacred vows as a sincere commitment to truth are needed before you can enter this doorway. During these times of transition we are forced to look beyond everyday experience for answers. It is almost as if the outer disruption forces us to look internally.

Once we make the commitment to pass through the doorway, to go through the fire, to have the bravery to step into the unknown, even though it may be frightening, we start to encounter a deeper intuitive knowing about something else that lies beyond the world of appearances. This bridge into a vaster reality is what Anpu provides.

Wrathful guardians are guardians of truth, knowledge, bliss, and power. They hold keys to secret wisdom that in turn holds keys for humanity's ascension and awakening. They guard these treasures of knowledge fiercely. Some of these guardians today are best known from Tibet (although they were also used and practiced with in Egypt), where they protect those who practice dharma meditations. These guardians were originally demons who were converted from their ignorant and self-serving ways into becoming selfless supporters of those who wished to attain enlightenment and serve all beings in this process.

When you encounter the wrathful guardian deity aspect of Anpu, you can run away or embrace the lesson and find joy and great laughter. Wrathful guardians guard the truth about your self—the truth you may not wish to see, but the truth nonetheless. They highlight these areas of fear and bring them into light in a direct way. If you have fear,

fear will arise. If you are fearless, joy will arise, as you can then dance with them and see their true nature of love and bliss.

They are uncompromising in their fierce compassion to show you what you have hidden away, and unrelenting in their power to serve you until you have learned the lesson and healed the obstacles within you to standing in true love, power, and wisdom. The wisdom they guard serves to transmute ignorance, dissolve evil, assist in the development of the good, and share compassionate wisdom.

In the Third Face of Anpu, one encounters the wrathful guardian aspect that guards the hidden treasures and powers of the Ka body. Only when one is situated in a degree of loving empowerment united by wisdom can one enter the deeper aspects of the Ka. Any fear or lack of clarity will block the door opening; any self-serving agenda will keep this door shut. Any idea of smallness, that you are not good enough, will be highlighted. Any dishonesty and masking of the self, any place where you do not love and accept yourself, any place where you are unaware of a need for change, will arise. This can be a tough journey, but it does eventually lead to joy and a powerfully loving and content state of resolution and centering.

Courage, honesty, and vulnerability allow the Third Face of Anpu to reveal itself through self-love and nurturing. This is not just a passive state but rather a state based on positive grounded action. In the Third Face of Anpu you find the pathway through the shadow self, which you can only walk through by total dedication to Self with the ability to give all you have in your search, without hesitation, without holding back. You have to give all to receive all. This is true loyalty to Self and to divine will.

As one travels down this road deeper into the Ka, one sees clearly any remaining polarities that one is still holding onto, especially between male and female, matriarchy and patriarchy. These cycles throughout time, where one dominates the other in different time cycles, is held in the Ka bodies of many people and in the earth's memory itself. In reconnecting the Ka, one learns how to transmute energy and dispel negativity, and even how to bring hidden physical disease and obstructions or shadow into light.

The Third Face of Anpu is where you can enter a deep inner space of silence, the middle road that lies between polarities. Anpu is your inner friend or guide through the underworlds you walk in every day. He manifests as the voice of the soul and the feelings of unrest that exist in us and that force us into the unknown, leading to self-destruction or self-discovery.

Anpu lives between spirit and matter as a messenger, inhabiting the place where light and dark meet. He is beyond the duality of good and evil and can lead you to both positive and negative outcomes as he uses either polarity at any time in order to make you whole. He lives in the space between angels and demons and holds the gateway to the rich mine of spiritual wealth known as the golden shadow—where our highest potential lies.

He not only soothes us but provokes our egos, breaking our boundaries and limiting belief systems that subtly control our lives in order to liberate us into our highest potential. The demands of Anpu upon you can be unorthodox, as it is not only a guiding energy but a transforming one. It completes the maturation of your soul through the unification of opposing forces within the self.

Anpu has no qualms or ideas of good and bad as he sees them both as coming from the same source: the power of our highest human potential. The five faces are not fixed but unfold in relation to our own spiritual development, changing over time as we too develop, transform, and evolve. Anpu is the portal to the One, accessed when one is at the threshold, the gates of a big breakthrough. Anpu teaches us not to be seeking a cure for our suffering but rather to seek a use for it, a channel to direct this force into, to create something out of it.

## The Fourth Face of Anpu

The Fourth Face grounds spirit into the body and allows for a deeper dissipation of negative thought-forms and emotions to be taken into conscious awareness and let go of. The Fourth Face activates and changes the root chakra significantly in order to anchor the light bodies into the physical body, anchoring expanded awareness at the base of the spine. The spine itself becomes more open, able to fluidly transmit and conduct more light in a subtle way. The challenges that you may feel become internalized, able to be seen for what they are, and then healed. Trust in yourself, your guidance, and your light become anchored in a physical way, allowing more light to enter the body, raising your frequency.

It is here that the most negative and densest energies can be seen and transmuted. You can hold yourself in this space and not collect the negative ideas or thoughts of others, not taking on the issues of others. You deepen into trust and feel secure in your own self. You rise above the negative electromagnetic radiation of the technospheric modern world that limits, disconnects, and stifles the Ka body from fully connecting into the other light bodies.

As we deepen into the Fourth Face, a whole realm of energies and relatings drops away. We feel protected because we are connected to our Ka, nurtured by our own light and Ka connection. As we become more connected we become more invisible to negative energies. It is almost like a cloak of invisibility is placed over you if you choose to harness this consciously; you can turn this on and off at will. When it is time to be seen you can turn yourself on; when it is time to not be seen, you can become invisible. This is one of the attributes of the Ka. When it becomes integrated you can become seamless and invisible at will, and all negative energies from within and without glide off you as you are centered in your core.

As the physical comes into harmony, a deeper meditative state of clarity can happen. Resting in this consistently allows an unfolding of love and peaceful centeredness to occur—a love that is situated between light and dark and deals with both. The integration of honesty and self-inquiry in the Fourth Face of Anpu allows the deepest humility to arise: the humility that leads to your greatest growth and uncovers the deepest shadows as you admit your weaknesses and simultaneously infuse them with light.

These are the ascending and descending spirals occurring at the same time. The deeper you go, the more light manifests. This veritable Jacob's ladder allows us to simultaneously ascend into our crystalline bodies of light while plunging into the depths of the shadow and our own hidden wounds and agendas to merge both into the physical body. This is how we embody: by riding and uniting both currents into where they both meet—physical form. We are made in the image of God, and this is how God manifests.

## The Fifth Face of Anpu

The Fifth Face is when you actively enter a unified state with your Ka. The disparate streams and strands of disconnection, veils, disempowerment, and negative memories all heal and integrate. The Ka body anchors into your physical body, and you are in full control of driving your Ka as your connection to Gaia, the noosphere, and all life heightens. You are empowered, residing in your sovereign Self authority, and have the power and drive to be able to manifest and achieve your heart's desires once you are established in your soul purpose.

You are the leader of the different parts of yourself. The ego is subdued and used as a servant of the soul. Your physical body brims with light, and you are radiant, able to turn on and use your light whenever it is necessary. You are aware of how your subtle intuition and energy works and moves, how it works on others, and how you can influence others; you are then able to correct it and use it to achieve what you wish. Nothing can stop you. You become a manifesting generator.

As you deepen in driving your Ka, you integrate much dark and light through the triple geometry vibrating in the forty-two-note scale of Ma'at. Ka can connect and engage in telepathic communication with other life forms. Ka engages in DNA healing in the individual, in the planetary biosphere, and in the earth's memory. As Ka integrates, rips and wounds get healed. Body becomes a voice to be used. Kinesthetic merges with light to form a kinesthetic hologram of light.

You become a self-contained authority of your own self, plugged into your guidance and putting your feelings into grounded action with power and precision. Ka manifests here as the voice within that will protect you, but only the "you" who serves its plan for your true Self. You will be guided by Self, and as Self is grounded in the impersonal ground of being itself, you will inevitably be guided into the One.

The meeting of the Ka and Ba occurs when your heart becomes renewed, revitalized, and restored in connection to your power. In Egyptian legend, Anpu is the remover of the heart, replacing the heart with a new one once you are ready for it. Your new heart of Ab Ba is then fully connected to the power of the Ka. The result: heart-soul power, the Ka Ba, the union of power and loving wisdom.

Anaiya Aon Prakasha

Amaya Du Bois

# ~ 6

# AB: THE HUMAN HEART

The Ab is the human heart, the foundational seat of the soul. It is the seat of your moral, ethical, and human values, the heart that is the highest human expression of love. Together, the Ab and Ba create the heart-soul: your center.

Ab manifests in every human heart as the impulse to feel others, to give, to share, and to help others who are less fortunate than us. This acts out in our wishing to help the poor, the homeless, the children who are suffering, the orphans, and the desperately unfair unjust situations in corrupt war-torn places such as Africa.

In the giving, sharing, and reaching out from your human heart, you feel the suffering of others and want to do something about it just for the sake of doing it, because you feel, you empathize, you care, and something stirs, moves, and touches you deep in your heart, stirring you into action.[1] The giving that arises from this movement in your heart serves to open and purify your heart, as there is nothing greater that purifies the heart than selflessly thinking and giving to others. This is known as karma yoga; helping others to purify yourself, to get you out of your self-absorbed and narcissistic life that only thinks about its own needs and wants.

---

1. Many charitable organizations act and give from the Ab.

In times of disaster and strife, such as the recent tsunami and earthquake natural disasters, people naturally respond and feel the suffering of others and give anything they can to help others who have lost their basic human necessities: home, food, and family. Ab is the connection between our root and our heart, and it unites both as the foundation for the soul, the mirror of the Ab known as the Ba, to manifest.

To purify your heart through selfless service for others helps you to feel. Feeling the pain and suffering of others in your own heart deepens and creates more compassion, strengthening your dedication to become a good human being. Mother Teresa exemplified the Ab heart in action, but we all do whenever we reach out and help another in distress, when we feel their pain and wish to do something about it.

It is also true that by experiencing, going through, and allowing yourself to feel your own deep inner pains in life, you breed more compassion and open the heart further. There is nothing quite like having a broken heart to open the heart, and nothing quite like feeling your own pain, loneliness, sadness, and isolation to soften and crack the shell around your heart.

The Ab human heart feels inequality and imbalance and naturally wishes to rebalance the injustices and disparities of our modern world, where the divide between rich and poor grows every day. Ab feels these injustices strongly, and heart actualizes within you when you put these feelings into concrete action. Some of the foundations of the Ab are found in moral codes the world over, like the Ten Commandments and the Indian *yamas* and *niyamas,* which form the ethical basis of yoga. Perhaps the foundations of all these moral and human values are found in the forty-two laws of Ma'at, the Egyptian goddess of harmony, justice, and the balanced human heart, which when lived into every day shows how to be a good human being.

Ab opens by living as a good human being. These values are universal and recognized in every culture and tradition as coming from the heart. Whatever street you walk on, a simple smile and an offering of some kind opens the doorway to meeting in the heart. Try this today, even in your local neighborhood. Does it not feel good? As this foundation of the human heart is set and anchored in your life every day, your soul can manifest more in your life as it has more space to breathe in.

## Purifying the Heart

> We must learn to tap the power of our hearts in order to align them with the desire of the universe so that what comes through us is spiritually correct—the Ma'at of the Egyptians or the Tao of the Taoists. When we tap the true nature of the Ab, what we can manifest is the Will of God . . . the light that shines through men and women and sets in motion the divine order of things.[2]

Within yourself, the heart's voice or conscience connects and opens up your shadow in moments of radical honesty, which is inevitably humbling. Forgiveness, acceptance, and embrace emanate from the heart once we connect to it and express it in vulnerability and self-effacing honesty. This opens the doorway to the soul Ba, which is the opening to the universal soul.

Peace can only prevail by speaking to a person's conscience, because their conscience knows that they want to find an end to their suffering. Through your conscience, and the guilt and shame that arises once you know you have done something "wrong," you recognize the truth of your negative acts through honesty and humility, and then clean up the mess you have created and the people you have offended.

---

2. Normandi Ellis, *Dreams of Isis* (Chicago: Quest, 1997).

Self-effacing honesty allows you to reveal your darkness, your failings, and your deepest darkest secrets. This is the last act the shadow wants to do, as it then means it is brought into light to be seen, learned from, and integrated. It can no longer hide. By announcing or admitting your hurts, angers, and dark side in moments of honest insight and confession, you can release stored guilt, anger, hurt, and shame to transform the shadow reality. In this release one can find much joy and freedom, as the dark secrets you have held deep within release into the light of the heart's awareness. This then allows more space for the heart and soul to expand and breathe.

The Ab is the human heart, simply accepting, warts and all, all that comes before it. Ab can be naive as it cares and feels, sometimes to the exclusion of the other bodies and their wisdom. Ab can get hurt, as it is your humanity. Yet in its true state it never hurts another and lives in a state of harmlessness. Harmlessness is much more than not harming another, eating vegetarian, and not killing flies and insects. Harmlessness is not reacting or harming under any provocation, occurring when there is no aversion or attachment, push or pull, to or from anything or anyone. Harmlessness is a nondual state of being, and it is felt and opened into firstly through the Ab, which knows the inter-connectedness of all beings. If I harm you, I harm myself. The closer you are to embodying harmlessness, the quicker you notice and feel the effects of your harmful actions, until it becomes an instantaneous knowing and witnessing within you.

This knowing is felt as the still, small voice of your heart that guides you to speak and act at the right time and that will not create any harm, conflict, or misunderstanding, but rather promotes harmony. The heart bides its time until it is ready to express in harmony, and until it can be received in harmony. The voice of the heart that you know, deep within you, reminds you there is more to life that you deserve to be living and that you have felt, perhaps fleetingly, but have pushed to the side or relegated to a dream, a fantasy, an illusion that there is not enough time for. And now you have settled for stability, security, and the known and have left out part of your humanity.

At any time you can notice this voice that has been running like a thread in your life. It can manifest as a whispered thought, an unusual feeling, a hope, a dream, a longing in the heart, a resonant conversation with someone you just happen to bump into. It is a reminder that keeps coming back to you at different times in your life.

If something comes from the heart, all it can lead to is more of the heart. This journey may not be quite what you expect, need, or want it to be, as it will lead you through your own wounded heart to its ultimate healing and love. Your heart is waiting for you patiently to notice and follow it. All it needs is for you to listen and act upon it to fulfill yourself, to complete yourself, for the good of all. Follow it, act on it, do something radical, and enjoy the adventure into the unknown.

Each person's heart voice and conscience knows what it needs to fully connect with the soul. For some, it may be to serve others, raise money for others, create art and music, orto be in nature to have an intimate relationship with one's own self; for others it may be to be able to make love consciously with another and to meditate. If one has passion and a soul purpose, their soul family and friends, and is living in a resonant place with the right partner, then this is a good recipe for the health of the heart.

The human heart makes mistakes, feels lonely, reacts, plays with your friends, judges, forgives, and is humble to its mistakes. It is what makes us human and what we collectively identify with as what it means to be a human being. The heart desires to love and be loved and to live joyfully in the way it wishes. It notices the discrepancies between what your heart wants and how you are living right now and whether they are in harmony. It never pushes, just gently reminds you, until one day you act on it and value your heart's voice, giving it support and strengthening it further through this act.

It is on this journey of the heart, of vulnerability, that mortals can eventually become immortal.

Think of all the times in your life that you have not listened to your heart's conscience, and what happened. All the times you went against the voice of your intuition and failed to act on it. Write down all these times, starting with today and going backward to your childhood. Think about your relationships, your sexual encounters, the little lies and exaggerations that you tell every day in order to feel more special, more appreciated, and less ordinary.

When you are humble, open, and honest, the heart speaks clearly and openly on a regular basis. Its voice resonates and reveals many things. Its clarity and honesty illuminate those parts of your self that need forgiveness. It will illuminate your doubts and fears, and center you in following your heart's desires, no matter how fantastic or far away they may seem to be to your mind. It will tell you what you have been hiding or trying to escape from, no matter how insignificant the shadow makes it seem. In the smallest of things lie the deepest of truths.

When you change your heart about something, the whole course of your life and destiny can change also. All the things you have seen and envisioned for yourself can change as the heart too changes its focus, its course, and its direction, changing your soul's destiny, forever impacting this life and every other life you may have. The heart is key: it is what binds you together, what can separate parts of you, and what fires your deepest desires.

What is your heart's desire?
What enflames and excites your heart?
What does your heart want most of all?

Following your heart is the bravest act you can do, as it often bucks conventions, both your own and those of others in society. Following your heart only leads to more love, and may upset others if it does not fit in with their agenda or view for you. While this can be dealt with compassionately and with wisdom, it should not deter you from your heart's desire. There is always a way to deal with the circumstances and barriers surrounding your heart's desires that only act as problem-solvers and motivators on the heart's path.

Fire and passion are what fuel the heart. When the human heart is clear and anchored in honor, integrity, clarity, and giving, when you are heart-centered, then the merge between heart and soul occurs in joy, love, and peace. The opposite of this, which may arise for healing, is bitterness, the inability to be alone, and the tendency to distract and fill life up with meaningless activities to shy away from the pain felt in the heart.

Follow your heart and only more heart will reveal. It may not turn out the way you hoped, but more love will result eventually.

# Space

The Egyptians placed particular importance on the connection between brain, heart, and body, for once the brain reunites with the heart and body, all the Nine Bodies coalesce together. The body, known well by the heart, becomes the vehicle of evolution. As a species, our deepest trans-formations and awakenings become a neurobiological phenomenon, which is evidenced in the changing of body, brain, heart, and DNA.

This evolution arises by creating space and spaciousness for all Nine Bodies to breathe, for all Nine Eyes to see clearly. Space is a quality of the heart. Creating space within yourself and in your relationships allows more unconditioned love to be present. This creating of space works in the physical body through rest, massage, and exercise; in your feelings by allowing them time to breathe and be expressed at the right time; and by meditating in the space between your thoughts. Create this space by dropping gently in between your thoughts and resting there; create more space in your relationships by being centered and whole within your own self; create more space in your environment by being closer to nature; allow more spaciousness to be more fluid with emotions, beliefs, and concepts and more fluid with sharing, giving, and being present.

The energy of the heart lives in the spaces between the cells, the spaces between the thoughts, the spaciousness of peace that can also crackle with vitality and creativity. The heart is also connected on a biological level to your blood, involving the elements of fire and water. To have clean high-frequency alkalized blood helps the higher heart systems to open, and the more open your heart is, the more your blood too can change, becoming more spacious. As the spaces between your cells magnify to allow in more light, aligning to the inherent spaciousness or void-ness of the physical form, more unconditioned, accepting, and peaceful Ab heart presence can also simply be present. It is all interconnected.

As you evolve, your blood will change into these "new" patterns of different geometric structures that involve octahedrons and tetrahedrons. Creating more space in the blood allows the changing of the geometry of your blood cells into more electrified blood, better energy flow around and into the bones, healthier reproductive organs that are fluid, flexible, and free of stress and that in turn produce better life flow and power, or Sekhem. Creating space between the joints and muscles in the physical body, Khat, and the flesh and blood, Aufu, allows more of the Ka and Ab-Ba to awaken in the body. Creating more space in between your cells through loving meditation then creates more space in your spine by clearing its channels, allowing more space in the brain for more light.

Creating space allows the light bodies to permeate, penetrate, and live in you. Spaciousness allows presence to be. In this presence the body and heart Ab can allow itself to let go and relax, allowing the soul light and consciousness of the Ba to inform you. The paradox with space is that boundaries are needed to maintain this spaciousness in the human heart as it merges with the Ba of the soul. This boundary comes from knowing yourself, knowing your desires and needs, knowing the essence of the desire nature, and knowing how to love yourself, or self-love.

# Holy Desire

Holy Desire is the desires of the heart combined with sexual energy raised into unconditional love and giving, not just in lovemaking but in the desire for the divine in all parts of your life and relationships. Through this complete vulnerability you find yourself as love begins to master you. You give in order to give, not give in order to receive.

Holy desire is an emptying of all your desires that need another to make your self whole. It is more of a wanting, an inner burning that propels you, fuels you to keep moving and growing. Holy desire is passion, passion for the soul, passion to fulfill the soul's deepest urge and yearning, passion to be all that you can be. This passion comes from the Ab, which then marries the soul Ba in the bridal chamber of your own heart.

Holy desire makes you give your all. Desire is the energy that makes all things grow, flower, and bloom. It enables the heart to expand and reach for the infinite and to surrender to the infinite, despite the fears that may arise. Holy desire is the beating pulse of the heart Ab; it is the life force and flowing blood of the heart. Without this blood flowing through the soul's veins, you are lifeless, hollow. When this flow of desire is blocked, you start to die. When you forget your passions, and allow them to fall by the wayside, then you lose a part of yourself. Death of desire and passion is the death of the heart Ab, a death that only a profound shake-up can then reignite.

Holy desire is like a golden thread that connects your heart to your soul. The more you amplify the voltage going through this thread, the more the immortal and universal Hu bodies will sit up and take notice, and actually send you more through this thread. Holy desire can be an intense force, sensual, powerful, passionate, and overwhelming. This is why many fear it, the fear being that once it is released you will not be able to control it as it leads to the overflowing of life through you.

When you live in holy desire you cannot be controlled, for you flow in life itself. You can, however, choose when you allow the tap of desire to open, what effects and manifestations it will have, or how you act on any wave of desire flowing through you.

Desire grows through intimacy; intimacy grows through desire. The more intimately you know yourself, explore yourself and your desires, and see what lies there, what is true and what is false, what leads to illusion and what leads to heart and soul, the more you refine your desire natures and want to know more.

## Giving

Giving feels good. Giving and serving others is only you giving to yourself. To give is to receive, and it always leads to more joy, for giving *is* your heart's desire. Reaching out to others leads you to your highest potential. The act of giving to and serving another actually opens your heart-soul; when this is merged with appreciation and gratitude the soul responds and wishes to reveal more fully into your heart. In giving we receive, and in receiving we are also giving if we are conscious and aware of this circuit.

Giving is a graceful flow from the heart that enjoys the love that bubbles forth and naturally wishes to share this with anyone and everyone. When you feel more joy and more beauty from what you give out, all you want to do is share even more of it. And so the spiral rises ever higher.

The more you give, the more will be given through you. The more you extend this to others in everything you do, with everyone you meet, as a way of life, the more love flows through you. Service is glory, glorifying the Self in all beings, drawing the divine out of people into their experience of life. There is no greater joy than seeing another transform in front of you and feeling that peace and Self-satisfaction.

When you are living in mastery, in reality, giving is what you do in every situation. You have unlimited energy to do so as this is what you live for. God is never on holiday. Time becomes more important as you master it and choose not to waste it, instead maximizing it in order to be an open vessel for the sharing and extending of loving transformation. The more you are situated in this flow, the more is given to manifest through you. Those who live in the highest spheres of service in the world are busy constantly serving others and have little time for anything else—save their own meditations, of course.

It is here that the very word *service* itself becomes a misnomer. Service is our most natural, effortless way of being. It is the very flow of life itself, and when we are in this flow anything else becomes unnatural, contracting, and experienced as a form of fearful heavy resistance, a drain and block to your full expression. You no longer keep anything for yourself, as there is the recognition that there is no separate self to keep anything for.

If you think you are in service and are not enjoying it, then it is not your true service. Service is never a burden; it is lightness. Service is never a duty; it is a voluntary willingness. Service includes all of your self in it and does not leave anything out. Service is not something to do. It is a way of life, a way of being. It is God's lifestyle.

It is our nature, our birthright, and our completion into love. Just as atoms whirl around each other in harmony, keeping each other in existence through their whirling, simply being what they are created to be, so can we realign ourselves to the way that we have been created to be, which gives us the most joy. Try it now; give to a stranger today, even if it is only a smile.

Giving continually realigns us to the constant flow of change, growth, and newness that life is. To tune into life, tune into giving; to tune into what your service is, tune into the passion of the life force, what ignites the most passion within you. Then you will be guided on the most magical journey back to your true joyful Self in harmony with the rhythms of life. And so it is.

## The Open Heart of Harmony: Ma'at

> You move in Ma'at; you live in Ma'at. She fills your body, she rests in your head, she makes her seat upon your brow; the breath of your body is of Ma'at, your heart does live in Ma'at. All that you eat, all that you drink, all that you breathe is of Ma'at.[3]

Ma'at is the goddess whom all the Egyptian gods served and the guardian of the human heart. In Egypt she was seen to be the balancer and weigher of the heart, holding the keys to the open pure heart and to living in the fifth dimension, grounded in a state of love, honor, and integrity. She is the law of harmony through which you can access truth, peace, emotional purity, and balance. She is the goddess Neter principle of balance, and balance with all parts of your self, all Nine Bodies, leads to wholeness.

---

3. Kerry Wisner, Akhet Hwt-Hrw, www.hwt-hrw.com.

Ma'at means truth, balance, and justice lived through the open heart. Ma'at is known as the "straight line," the underlying truth of reality. This underlying truth is accessed by the purified heart that is clear and living in harmony with itself and with all other people. All reality is held within the sacred space of the heart. All reality is dreamed from within your heart, which then gets projected outward to create your reality that you live in every day. Ma'at holds great keys to access your heart and to continuously live in your heart each and every day.

Her mantra is to treat another as you would like to be treated.

Ma'at is the foundation of an enlightened civilization on earth and was the foundation of the Egyptian civilization at its height. Without this harmony of the heart, there is no basis for an awakened civilization, as the heart is the foundation of peace, incorruptibility, honor, and equality. She is the key to the mysteries of Egypt, as each pharaoh and every Neter serves Ma'at. Indeed, the name Hapshepshut, the only female pharaoh, means "the soul of Ra is Ma'at."

Ma'at's laws never change. Although humanity may forget about it, it resurfaces when ignorance becomes too overwhelming in order to restore balance, justice, and order. All ignorance is caused by the absence of Ma'at.

In Egyptian sacred initiations, when your physical body dies your heart-soul Ab Ba travels to the Duat or underworld into the Hall of Ma'at, the Hall of Two Truths. In this Hall you see a record of your life and its actions from the perspective of the heart so that you can have an opportunity to review, learn from, and forgive every judgment you have committed on yourself and others while here on earth. In this review, one's heart gets weighed on the scales and balances of Ma'at, of justice, to see whether it is light enough to be allowed entrance into the realms of the Neters, the archetypal qualities of the open, clear heart-soul found within you.

This process is called the "Declaration of Innocence," and comes from the *Book of Coming Forth by Day,* commonly called the *Book of the Dead.* This Declaration of Innocence is said in front of forty-two judges in the imposing Hall of Two Truths of Ma'at in order for the heart to be purified and for the soul to be allowed rebirth, or for the perfected soul to no longer reincarnate. These forty-two judges each have a confession to be shared with them, from your heart to theirs, and these are known as the Forty-two Negative Confessions.

## The Hall of Two Truths

As your heart-soul walks into the darkness of this enormous Hall of the Two Truths, vast columns on either side of you stretch upward into infinite blackness. Flickering torches light your way. As you continue to press on through the hall, you see a blaze of light in the distance and a large pool of water with three figures silently standing on the other side. As you stand poolside, you look down and see your own reflection gazing back at you.

What do you look like?

As you look up, the three figures step forward and reveal themselves to you. Anubis, the original wolf and shamanic guide, the epitome of the surrendered heart, gazes back at you with chocolate eyes. His figure changes color as you look at him, morphing from black to gold, white to red, and then to gleaming silver.

He stands next to Ma'at, who wears two large feathers in her imposing and ornate headdress. She is regal, majestic, and dignified, wearing sapphire blue. She holds herself with royal poise. You cannot see her face, as it is just a blaze of light. Even as you try to look closer, all you can see is your reflection becoming clearer and clearer in her blazing light. All you can see is you, and the many facets of your life and your heart's experiences.

Next to Ma'at is the divine scribe Thoth, sitting calmly, looking at you with penetrating eyes. Yet there is such innocence in his gaze, even as it searches your heart and soul. Behind him is an imposing flight of wide, ornate stairs, thirty feet across, that leads high, high upward into the inky blackness. As your eyes strain to see what lies at the top, you can make out a dimly lit throne, upon which sits the shadowy figure of the Neter of the underworld and regeneration, Osiris, presiding over proceedings.

The forty-two judges surround you to hear the story of your actions in this life. Each wears a feather on his or her head of a different color, shade, and texture. Thoth, scribe of the gods, begins to record their verdicts as Anubis places your heart on the scales. Ma'at places a feather on the other scale. What happens?

There are two ways to understand the weighing and balancing of the heart. The first is that if your heart is heavier than Ma'at's feather, the heart is still burdened, needing the nourishment, peace, silence, and open giving that the heart thrives on. Then your heart-soul needs more lessons and experiences in order to grow, and it becomes reincarnated. This cycle of life-death-rebirth continues until your soul is perfected by living into and fulfilling the forty-two confessions during your life on earth, which occurs by living in the giving and living in harmony.

The second way is understanding that the two scales measure the mortal human heart against the immortal divine soul heart. In balancing these two, by including both in your life, the immortal soul guides the mortal human heart while honoring and listening to it. When you are successful in this, then your heart becomes light and free as a feather, and your Ka and Ba walk into the immortal and universal bodies of Hu, the abode of Osiris,[4] where you live among the Neters as one of them,

---

4. Some Egyptian traditions also state that Thoth is the final, forty-third judge on the path of wisdom, while Osiris is the final judge on the path of power. In reality, we have to embody both.

"becoming a star that joins the company of Ra, and sails with him across the sky in his boat of millions of years."

The forty-two judges represents acts you have committed against the innocence and truth of the open, honorable, and clear heart. Each judge represents a specific "sin" or fault and the truth of the lesson of the pure heart that each sin cloaks. *Sin* here means "missing the target," originally derived from Roman archery schools. The only "punishment" for sin was to try again until you did hit the target.

Each judge embodies these two truths, the double-edged sword. Each judge will make it known to your heart-soul what you have done *if* you are humble, honest, and open. You will feel this in your heart as you journey through the forty-two. In truth, each of these forty-two judges lies deep within you as living archetypes of your own judgments and the essential qualities of forgiveness of your self. As you progress into Ma'at, you begin to live and embody all these forty-two in your daily life.

This judging is an event that occurs continuously at every moment in your life because judgment is the beating heart of duality. Once you become aware of the straight line that cuts through duality, the heart of Ma'at, then these laws can become embedded in you. Each time you forget, your heart of Ma'at can gently remind you, and your heart can then realign to natural order and open.

When you ask for justice, balance, truth, and harmony in your life, then Ma'at can appear.

Her feather weighs how clear, pure, and consistent your heart is in its openness. Through the presence of Ma'at, your heart Ab can connect to your soul Ba. When her feather lands in your heart and remains there, this is when your Ab and Ba unite, and you are situated in the humility and honesty that makes all shadows reveal and balance through the heart.

The ceremonies of Ma'at have been remembered and given back to humanity so that the harmony of the heart can resurface. These ceremonies, enacted in the same way as they were in ancient Egypt, are performed in retreats over eight days to cleanse, open, and anchor the open heart. Anyone who is not already enlightened can benefit from them. For more information on these retreats, see www.christ-blueprint.com/events.

## The Journey of Balancing the Heart

"Ma'at is consciousness itself, and also the individual consciousness that each person carries in his heart, for she is both the motivating force and the goal of life."[5] The journey of Ma'at, the truth of the open Ab heart, begins with Anubis, the surrendered heart as the gateway to Source, and the guide into and out of the underworld or shadow. Thoth, the divine architect, then helps lead you to your rebirth or resurrection into Osiris-Isis, galactic awakening. This is an important archetypal meeting of four different parts of you. Your Ab and Ba, your heart-soul, meets with your Ka, your pure energy double and connection to the higher light bodies. These then connect with your Sahu (Thoth), the immortal part of you.

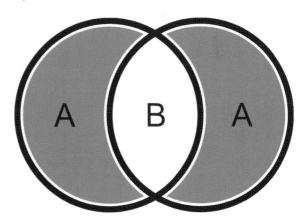

Padma Aon Prakasha

The whole point of this ceremony and unification of the different parts of yourself was to do it when you were alive in order to open your heart and develop. The reason why it is described as being done while you were dead is that you had to die to your old ways of narcissistic self-centered being to even step onto this journey of humility, for-

---

5. Normandi Ellis, *Dreams of Isis* (Chicago: Quest, 1997).

giveness, honesty, and authenticity. A part of you has to let go, die, and step onto the true soul path to attempt to learn and embody higher consciousness.

The Hall of Two Truths is a holographic vision of all forty-two parts of Self coming to sit and be with you. As all parts of you congregate and coalesce in this family of the Self or the Grail Family, you become whole because now you can see all parts of yourself, light and dark. This wholeness and doorway into the larger spherical reality is accessed by the mortal heart of the Ab becoming balanced with the immortal soul of the Ba on the scales of Ma'at. If the mortal human and immortal divine are unbalanced, then you will fail the judgment because you are still judging a part of yourself. We are both human and divine. The balance is staying in the two truths, realizing that the two truths mean not being attached to either version of reality but rather being in equanimity with them both, having neither attachment nor aversion to light and dark but being grounded in the world but not of it.

This journey of Ma'at and the forty-two openers of the heart were practiced daily by priests in Egypt both to purify themselves and to keep the flame of truth and loving harmony burning in their temples and communities. This return of Ma'at arising again in the world is a sign of love and truth resurging again through the hearts of people. Once you pass through the hall, Ma'at grounds your soul Ba into the consciousness of the heart Ab, revealing your shadow Shew and bringing it into the heart-soul's light and lens. This then serves to anchor you into the fifth dimension through a constant, heartful remembering that then becomes a completely natural way of being.

However, as you begin your journey through the Halls of Ma'at, you meet your greatest fears, your greatest hidden secrets, your deepest unresolved guilt and shame, all those parts of yourself that are the heaviest and most fragmented. The journey of Ma'at reclaims and reconnects these fragments of your soul by bringing them to the light of the heart, forgiveness, and embrace. All forty-two judges are parts of you needing to be recognized, felt, and then lived into. They ask: can you love and accept yourself as you are right now?

The journey begins with discomfort, heaviness, resistance, and mind chatter arising from your own lack of loving the hidden parts of yourself. In order to love, one has to love oneself fully. As this process accelerates, the body-mind ego relinquishes its hold over you. This initial opening of the heart's doors leads into a deep questioning of your values, the things that you have swept under the carpet, ignored, and forgotten about.

Buried deep in the subconscious, these things can arise to hit you hard in the face, asking for deep self-reflection as to why you have betrayed your own heart. Penetrating deep into the subconscious mind, the forty-two weave a lifeline of truth throughout the murky eddies of the dark depths of your unexplored mind and heart, opening the heart through the mystery.

You look deeper at your life and your path. Judgment rears its head—all the self-judgments you have had throughout your life, as well as guilt at what you have done and shame for letting yourself down. Your lack of humility, honesty, self-responsibility, and authenticity becomes rapidly highlighted. Your dedication and commitment to become all that you can be through these qualities of the humble honest heart becomes anchored.

The possibility of true self-love and acceptance becomes a living reality, a new experience as you excavate the depths to places you have never gone before. Filtering and examining your life with the lens of the heart brings one back to harmony. With sincerity, a deep purification occurs, leading you into authentic grounded presence in the human heart.

The mirror of the heart-soul reveals itself. As you look at truth through the lens of the heart, your reflection becomes clear as you see all parts, all facets of yourself clearly. Becoming softer and more compassionate as you forgive yourself for the experiences you have engaged in strengthens the heart's resolve to always stay open no matter what. You bring all of yourself into the heart and start to act and listen from here.

The witness situated in the heart starts to become heard, not just as a still small voice but as a guiding insistent flame burning ever more brightly in your soul. No longer having to hide anything means you can feel free and allow more Sekhem or life force to flow. Your boredom, resistance, and fatigue transforms to joy and delight; the tendencies and insecurities you cherished transform into peace; your physical attachments dissolve into the soul's longings and the reliance on the mind shifts to the soul, so the mind resumes its rightful position as servant of the soul.

You realize all parts of yourself, divine and human, are to be cherished and treated as a whole. You begin to truly "know thyself" and love all parts of yourself, meaning that now you can love all parts of others too without judgment. You become heart-centered and grounded in authentic presence, an emotionally and spiritually mature adult that has grown into the open heart, living in a balance of power and love. You now know how to maintain your life path clearly. You purge and let go of that which is unnecessary to hold onto so you can flow in the original harmony and voice of the heart.

Through the journey of Ma'at, you can receive your greatest gifts: to love and accept yourself completely, leading to true love for all. *Aloha mai ke akua ipo*—you love yourself as you love God. Integrating this opening, Ma'at and the forty-two master you as you live into them each and every day, serving as constant reminders, a constant bridge and reference code for the free flow of joy, love, and life.[6]

---

6. This chapter is based on the journeys of many people who have experienced the Ceremony of Ma'at, with the pattern of the heart opening being generally the same as one progresses through the journey.

## Confession

Confession or repentance is the key to opening the heart in humility, honesty, and forgiveness. Confession is not what Catholic dogma would have you believe it is, as it originally came from Egypt and the rituals of Ma'at. Confession is not thinking you are flawed and imperfect, born in sin and needing a priest to make you feel validated and to forgive you for your sins.

Confession and repentance are sounding a call to your self to hear the voice of the heart-soul and to regather all the scattered and fragmented parts of you back into wholeness. It recollects and reunites all parts of you around the one original voice of the heart-soul. In this gathering, you return back to your original source, your original wholeness, your original innocence.

Repentance gives you an opportunity, a crack in the veils that allows you to hear the call of your own true nature to return back to the still small voice within that always and already knows. This voice, which is always present, has the power to follow its guidance, the original memory of your unique soul blueprint, in all situations.

Confession allows you to let go, to expose your darkest secrets, to relieve yourself of the burdens you have been carrying. It is easier to tell the truth than to keep living a lie and to continue covering up for this lie. Once your darkest secrets have been brought into the light of conscious awareness, once you have opened the doorways to the subconscious, you can truly enter joy and peace. This is not something you do casually, as to truly clear the heart requires the ability to look long and hard at yourself honestly so that your heart can open. It is an act of deep self-responsibility and self-inquiry.

This leads to a surrendering and a forgetting about who and what you were before in order to step into a whole new you, sloughing off the old skin of the separated self just like a butterfly does out of its chrysalis. When you truly and heartfully repent, you emerge out of the cocoon of the ego, opening your eyes to enter the expanded heart of light where you become a light unto others by shining your own light brightly—a light that shines brightly because it is open and surrendered to the flow of love and life force.

## Judgment

Judgment is what blocks life force from flowing and your heart from fully opening. To actually observe what judgment does on a cellular level is to see the contraction of *all* your cells shrinking, twisting, and distorting their natural shapes and forms. Judgment is a cellular signal to cut off love from the rest of your being, keeping you disconnected. Judgment creates and keeps in place negative cellular memories, memories that weigh you down and keep you heavy. As you release these cellular memories, your cells open to receive and give.

Judgment is the beating heart of duality, fed by guilt, shame, and pain. It reveals the unexplored parts of yourself that you sweep under the carpet. Whether it is judging yourself or another, the illusion and idea are the same: "I am separate from a part of myself, and therefore you are separate from me."

Judgment arises through a denial of love. Each link in the chain of judgment is part of the other; each link goes hand in hand with the other and informs the other. They need each other to continue the chain of sadness. Judgment is a blessing for us to see, as it shows you where you are still hiding and what parts of you still need your nurturing. Recognizing judgment can bring to light your greatest pains and sadness, illuminating and freeing you into peace. It can enable and empower you to truly value in action, thought, and words that love is truth.

# A Few Foundations of Judgment

Assumption. From your own value system you have an idea and project that what is true for you must be true for another. "What is right for me must be right for another." This is very connected to your culture and family conditioning: peer pressure, peer agreements, cultural stereotypes that validate your own perceptions. You often seek validation for your illusions from your friends, who will comfort you and assure you that you are right and safe. This is largely unconscious, conforming to yours and others expectations; you put your desires on another person and expect them to fulfill them. This is all based on fear because you do not feel worthy of what you desire most.

In this cage of experience and false perception, you interpret others through your own lens, your own parental and childhood experiences, wounds, and beliefs. In adulthood this can continue through your own spiritual pathway, which may negate others' learning experiences as bad or good. To overcome this you learn to become Self-aware: to be vulnerable. This implies knowledge of the fact that you have developed unconscious defenses in order to survive, to feel secure and safe. Self-awareness is having the ability to become conscious of your own habitual defenses, which block intimacy.

Judgment increases because of a lack of clear communication. You interpret another through what you think is true and then do not communicate that to another in honesty and openness. Perceptions and gossip abound, and the veil of illusion grows tighter within your own mind. What is not expressed gets suppressed and turns into dense rigid thought-forms, destroying good intentions.

Projection. This is the effect of all judgment. What you do not like or own in your own self you judge, mock, condemn, or put down in others. You choose to project your shadow lessons onto others, be they partners, friends, lovers, countries, or governments. You choose to look outside of yourself and not learn your own lessons. You stay hard instead of softening, staying in the past instead of the present, investing your energy in the past image of others or yourself instead of being present to how you are today or how others are today. We judge others who have what we want and try to pull them down to our level.

Victim consciousness. Most people do not like others who have stepped out of the box and dare to live their heart's desire. As victims, these people feel they are inadequate and think they are not creators of their experience. They believe things around us just "happen to us." Victims try to make other people victims, or even victimize others, because they lack power in themselves. It is easy to be a victim, as it involves blaming others, blaming your "karma," and abandoning your self-responsibility to create change. It is the "Why me?" and the "poor me" syndrome.

Fear of difference and understanding. Be it racial, religious, or cultural, if you are different, you can be a threat. Why? Because you do not understand where another is "coming from," because it is different to where I am coming from, where my friends are coming from, and what has brought me so far in life to my "happiness." The real fear is not feeling safe because one does not feel we share common ground, so one cannot predict others' behaviors. It is the unknown, and the unknown creates the most fear and judgment.

Not taking self-responsibility. If you feel judged, or are judging another, then you are judging part of yourself. There is an aspect of yourself not recognized, owned, or embraced. Judgment is a mirror, pointing the finger at another instead of turning the finger around and looking at your own actions. Not taking self-responsibility for your actions or involvement in hurt or judgment is a denial of your lesson. Healthy adults take responsibility for their actions, needs, and wants. They recognize that if someone is pushing their buttons that make them react, there is an aspect of themselves they are not at peace with, and therefore it is a blessing in disguise to learn something. Self-responsibility means not taking responsibility for other people but rather taking responsibility toward your feelings in relationship.

Putting ideas before feelings. When you put the forms, ideas, and expectations of society before your own feelings, you betray yourself. When you do put your intuitions first, you may also be judged by society as not doing what is right or "acceptable." Your only barometer is your own heart and trusting it, rather than judging it, or listening to the judgments of others.

## Healing Judgment: Forgiveness

You can only forgive others when you have learned to forgive yourself. You can only totally love others, being in unconditional love, when you totally love yourself. To forgive is to be healed from the fear and judgment you have been projecting on self, others, and world. Something very deep relaxes. As you forgive you go deeper into innocence, as you see how you have been distorting your relationships through the power of projection and you see how the mind has such power to shape, and limit, your life.

To forgive means to choose to release another from the perceptions that your mind has been projecting upon them. It is an act of forgiving one's self of one's own projections. In projection everything is outside, and it is justified to blame another and the world for all the decisions that you seemingly have been forced to enact in order to survive in this world. Projection colors another with the very energies you are denying and judging within your very own self.

You create the veils through which you view creation and create your reality. Projection occurs when you deny a part of yourself, when you try to sweep into the basement what you do not wish to see or own as part of your own self. Projection owns nothing and blames everything; it is the ultimate victim consciousness, for in projection your ego states that everything is outside of you and that you have created nothing—the complete opposite to the eternal truth that you create and manifest everything in your life. Forgiveness chooses to surrender every perception that you have, that then leads to the truth of who you are.

In forgiving you become fully self-responsible for everything that happens to you, as you realize that you have created everything that happens in your life in order to learn and grow. This is a big step to take; to own everything in your life, all relationships, all actions, all wounds, all ideas of victimhood, to see everything as self-created, and self-perpetuated. To forgive and humbly learn your own lessons, not worry about others' lessons and perceived shortcomings, and embrace yourself and all others who have assisted you in this play of learning, is acceptance.

The opposite of forgiveness is judgment. In judging another you judge yourself. Judgment is the core of the shadow, and the greatest obstacle to opening the heart. Judgment is a moral that only *you* have decided to give value to, believe in, and think to be true. It is because of a lack of forgiveness, of judgment, in the world that there are wars and conflicts, inequality, and separation. Forgiveness allows you to let go of the certainty that you are right, allowing the possibility for something unknown to happen, something else, something new. If something has not been working one way, you have to try another way.

Judgment is an accumulation of all the knowledge you believe you need to make you safe, supported, recognized, successful, and loved in the world. In judgment you compare yourself to others, with this comparison based on determining worth or value; that is, who is better or worse. This means that if you are different from another, then one of you must be better than the other and therefore more worthy. As soon as the ego puts something outside of itself, it is not in control of it. When the ego is not in control of something, then it feels threatened and fearful, needing to create comparison and value in order to feel safe.

Withdrawing value from the experiences you have that do not lead to love is the action of forgiving. Forgiving creates harmony, humility, openness; it is the bridge between peoples, and union between seemingly separate peoples, forgiving your self for ever allowing the perception of being separate. Through forgiving you return all objects, all things back to their innate neutral state, a state that has no power over you.

All events are neutral. You make it good or bad through your own perception.

Value love; see the lesson behind it. All things lead to love with this attitude.

In forgiving lies the end of all judging. In not judging how things are, you free yourself from perceptions of fear. In this, you start to see what is actually present behind the appearance. Everything becomes new, fresh, and vital as there is no labeling, no box, no rigid naming of form. Forgiving is the establishing of love. Until forgiving is genuine you cannot fully embrace others, life, and God. And this embracing is the action of love.

Judgment places a moral value on someone dependent on your expectation of that person. Forgiveness never compares, contrasts, attacks, labels, or puts anyone down. There is no higher or lower in forgiveness. Forgiveness holds a space for all beings as a state of mind free from judgments in acceptance, the ultimate initiation, a deep cellular letting go. A space is carved open for humility, self-responsibility, and softness to simply be. In forgiveness you rest in the natural ability to see divinity in all people, no matter what. You see innocence; you see God in everyone you meet as well as their own illusions, but you choose to relate to the part of them that is God. You identify with the soul Ba that is the gateway to God.

Forgiveness sees perfection and all of our roles in the whole. Perfection is not to be without flaws but to live in the revealing of truth in each and every moment. You step out of truth the moment you judge, attack, defend; the moment you stop living in for-giving, the moment you stop giving.

## Guilt and Shame

You all have a strength, a body that you most identify with, be it the physical, the heart, the soul, or the immortal or universal bodies. Each one of you will feel most drawn to, and comfortable with, one of the Nine Bodies in particular. Which one do you feel most drawn to and resonate with? Which one do you feel least sure of, and have the most work to do on?

For those who identify most readily with the Ab, guilt, shame, judgment, and fear are what dog and haunt you most. In judgment you instantly separate yourself from embracing reality. This elicits guilt because there is a core place within all heart-souls that recognizes the perfect purity of all things. Forgiving is the healing from this guilt, which is a denial of one's essence. When you judge you move out of alignment with your essence, deciding that the innocent are not innocent, and therefore declaring this about yourself.

When you deny truth you can feel guilt. Forgiving is the primary antidote to the ideas of guilt and shame, two of the primary controllers of the human mind-set, and the mainstay of Catholic Church doctrine, as seen in the idea of original sin and Adam and Eve. Guilt and shame are the core shadows of forgiveness—guilt at having betrayed one's own self and others, and shame at not having done anything about it. When these are seen, forgiving becomes a tool for self-empowerment and is then let go of in order to enable one to truly enter Self.

As Saint Thomas said, "When you have trampled underfoot the sins of guilt and shame then you can enter the Kingdom of Heaven."[7] Shame is the idea or belief that you are unlovable, unloved, flawed, wrong, and dirty. Shame is an inward implosion, like light disappearing into a black hole, a denial of life force; an unworthiness to exist linked to a vague, unconscious feeling that something has happened to you that shows your lack of a right to life. It brings on depression, self-sabotage, self-destructive patterns, and even life-threatening diseases as the implosion robs the body-mind of life force.

Guilt is the mother of fear, a deep fusion to a form of identity as being inherently bad, a sense you have committed "sin." Guilt is an effect of shame, perpetuating a primal belief that part of you is worthless, lacking, and undeserving of love. Remorse is typical, even though you may not really know why, or for what, you are feeling remorse. Guilt is when you feel you owe something and that you have taken more than your capacity to return. It can also manifest as a resistance to, or even hatred of, having to be in the world. A constant sense of self-judgment "proves" the guilt is deserved, that when projected outward finds guilt in others, the world, and life, resulting in a sense of being crippled and ungrounded as well as attempts to numb feeling through drug use, alcohol, or similar addictions.

Guilt in its positive sense is morality, reminding you to treat others as you would like to be treated, keeping your ethical, moral, and spiritual senses intact in the harmony of Ma'at. Yet when guilt pervades the

---

7. *The Gospel According to Thomas.*

body-mind, it eats away at you, closing you down to what lies in the present as your energy is marooned in what could have been or what should have been, dragging you down and keeping you away from the possibilities of living life as it is presented to you right now.

In innocence, you can never know where another person is at on their path, good or bad. It changes in every moment: the murderer you condemn today may be Christ tomorrow; the person judging may have been abused and become very wounded; the violent rapist may have been abused in his childhood; the beggar homeless in the street may have been a king; the domineering woman may have been abused. Each of them is choosing another experience at any time: *one never knows.* Some of the greatest beings in history have been murderers, thieves, and black magicians—beings such as Valmiki, author of the *Ramayana;* Milarepa, one of Tibet's greatest saints; and many other awakened beings who have experienced and learned through the laws of love, not the laws of the world, which are of judgment.

Treat others like you would like to be treated is the answer. Talk to others. Share with them openly, honestly, and in respect. See their essence. Everything changes. That is a universal law, and everything can change in one moment.

One secret to compassion is knowing that love is expressing itself in all acts, all parts of your life and others' lives, to move you beyond the surface of things, what things appear to be. To know that love is in all things, even in the most painful of actions, even the most apparently unkind or unpleasant acts, frees you. Things are never quite what they seem. Fearful or immoral actions you consider to be wrong or bad are the surface ripple, the appearance; what lies underneath them? The heart opens in both sorrow and joy.

How has this happened in your life? What relationships, events, and people have triggered this in you? What lesson in opening your heart do they hold? How is the apparent duality serving you?

We all take on guilt to earn our redemption. If we say we have not felt guilt, we are escaping our own humanity and are hiding from what lurks deep within us, not wanting to see the light of day, not wanting to be exposed. We live in denial of our pain-body, buried within our subconscious. To fully feel this takes courage and surrender, to feel your deepest wound, your deepest separation, the darkest downward spiral you can travel on, a spiral so dark that we can lose ourselves plumbing its depths.

When you feel your pain, guilt, and judgment fully, you surrender and bow to love. You become humble and allow love to penetrate you to then guide you more and more. You belong not to yourself but to the divine and give to that fully without hesitation, doubt, or fear of not getting for your self. And you become free.

## Embrace

The hieroglyph for the Ab heart is a red pot in the shape of the heart-womb. The Egyptians viewed the heart as feminine, perhaps because it brings balance to both the higher bodies and the lower bodies, as it sits in between them as the mediator. The hieroglyph points toward this connection, as the heart and womb united create a circuit or infinity loop of love within the feminine form that embraces all that it is presented with. This hieroglyph was the basis of many of the Isis teachings about the loving power of the heart-womb, which perhaps is as important for women as the heart-soul Ab Ba connection. For women, the heart and womb are how the divine child is nourished, and when unified leads to the embodiment of Ab and Ba.[8]

---

8. For more information on this, see Padma Aon Prakasha, *The Power of Shakti* (Rochester, VT: Inner Traditions, 2009).

As soft as it is strong, love allows you to let go completely in even the most impossible circumstances. As you allow this to happen more and more by embracing all before and within you, then you yourself will start to feel embraced by all of existence, provided for, supported, and loved.

This is the fundamental loving presence that existence *is,* that supports you unconditionally, that gives you trust in the unfolding of life, that reassures you that everything is OK and that everything will work out if you but trust the unfolding. While our faults, our anger, and our blocks to love are seen, there is no condemnation of them. Rather, draw near to be enfolded in the gentle tenderness within your own heart.

In allowance you come to see the truth about yourself and allow the pain, the sadness, the anger, the grief, and the unworthiness to bubble up and be in you, simply allowing it to be present. In allowance you open the shutters of your heart, allowing it to be touched by something far greater than you, and in a felt sense "give way" to this feeling of love, melting all that is rigid within more and more readily the more you practice it.

Allowance is the open expression, the radically honest acknowledgment of what you feel may make you look small or weak, knowing that this allowance, this sense of humility will free you and open you to love ever more deeply. And this, my friends, leads to acceptance. Acceptance is the ultimate initiation. It melts and softens all hardness into the truth of what you are and can be. And it speaks only truth, for acceptance knows the nature of reality as open.

Allowance leads to acceptance, and acceptance opens the heart to embrace whatever is presented to you, thus transforming it and yourself. Embrace is enfolding what is presented to you, bringing it in, and then extending this enfolding out toward the person, idea, event, or situation. Embracing takes whatever you feel is unacceptable, makes it transparent, and then goes one step further. It makes you bring that vibration of the unacceptable inside your heart and then moves your heart to envelop, embrace, and extend itself into that vibration. And this is love, as Isis, Magdalene, Mother Mary, Mother Teresa, and countless other mothers and lovers throughout history have shown.

What can you not stand? What do you find totally unacceptable in the world, in your relationships, and in yourself? What turns you off, what repels you, what makes you run away from it? What do you hate? What is the last thing you would do in the world? What is the most unacceptable action, thought, or words that you would ever say, think, or do?

Name five things. Write them down, in detail, and place the paper in front of you. If you have more than five, then write them down also; in fact, write down as many as you can think of. Now look at the first of your list of what you find unacceptable. Evoke the feeling of what this brings up in you. Go into the feeling qualities in the body. Does it evoke anger, resentment, a sense of righteousness or injustice? Just *be* with whatever arises. Pay attention to what thoughts are ignited. Then return to the feeling of it. Observe what is happening within, perhaps tightness, constriction, pain, tears, sadness; simply let it be. Stay with it and breathe deeply and consciously into your heart.

Do this five times. No matter what resistance you feel, breathe it deeply into your heart five times and hold it there.

Now embrace it. No matter how unacceptable, horrific, wrong, or cruel it may seem. Just embrace it. Just allow the feeling to be there, and yet still breathe into the heart and allow the heart to embrace it. What happens within you? Now repeat it for all five or more; this should take about twenty minutes if you do it properly and with care and attention. Repeat this practice whenever and wherever these feelings arise, be it in the car, at dinner, or at home.

Another way to do this practice of conscious embrace is to actually meet the person you find most unacceptable. Go up to this person and hug them. While hugging them, focus on your heart and breathe in the quality you find most unacceptable about them, which is in fact one of your greatest teachers on love. See this quality as innocent and a part of you also. Embracing it in them also allows you to embrace it in yourself.

The master embraces and accepts what is happening in any moment totally. In embrace, one brings others into their own heart, feels the truth of who they are, and then gives them what they need in that exact moment. In the deepest embrace, one brings the planet and the sufferings of all humans into the heart. There is nothing that is singled out as wrong, unacceptable, or unworthy of embrace.

Feel this.

## The Dance of Ma'at

"According to the ancient coffin texts, the primeval sea instructs Ra to 'Inhale your daughter Ma'at and raise her to your nostril so that your heart may live.'"[9] The dance of creation is the harmony of creation. Throughout all of nature, throughout our bodies, throughout the universe, there is an innate order of perfection and harmony described in sacred geometry, rhythm, order, and intertwined harmonious relationships that keep us in balance, aligned, and clear. In life, Ma'at is the balance we keep between body, spirit, and mind, mediated through the heart.

All our sacred traditions were aware of this implicit order underlying the apparent randomness and chaos of our everyday lives, and in their wisdom devised means and ways to stay in tune with this underlying

---

9. Dimitri Meeks and Christine Meeks-Favard, *Daily Life of the Egyptian Gods,* trans. G. M. Goshgarian (Ithaca, NY: Cornell University Press, 1996), 14.

music of harmony and beauty. Over time we have forgotten this order and harmony and have left this harmony in order to step out of rhythm, out of tune, to enter chaos, disorder, disease, and moral decay. As a society we have entered disorder.

Ma'at is harmony, the rhythm of the cosmos, the rhythm and sound of all parts of our selves in communication and agreement with each other. This music underlies the world; it is always playing, just neglected, unheard, and forgotten. Ma'at is this wave of purity and balance that existed at Zep Tepi, the golden age frequency that many believe is set to come to earth by 2013.

What we may not understand is that Ma'at is a wave of energy that is already here. It does not arrive at any one time as it is the structure of all life everywhere. Ma'at is this underlying order behind all the harmonics of creation, all the notes of creation, in a perfect symphony. She is the underlying resonance of the golden age, the frequency of equality, harmony, and the balance of love, wisdom, and power that is available at any time to anyone. She is an actual force that you can live in constantly and that nourishes you as you nourish it.

Ma'at is the power that is the weaving of right relationship. If you live in Ma'at, the relationships between the different parts of you and the Nine Bodies are balanced and in harmony. If you are out of Ma'at, your relationships, both internally and externally, are conflicted and maladjusted.

Ma'at is the small voice within that prompts and reminds you when you are about to lie or when you are about to step out of harmony in any thought, word, or deed you are about to entertain. This voice is cultivated over time, and in Egypt was installed within you through the Ma'at ceremony and forty-two declarations (see the end of this chapter) where Ma'at and the Neters are evoked in a ceremony to ensure you do live by these guidelines of harmony.

Ma'at is often depicted as a regal, majestic queen with wings and wearing an ostrich feather[10] on her head. Her face can never be seen as such, for her role is to reflect truth to you through the mirrors that surround her. Truth has no face. She does not want you to worship her; she wants you to see your own truth reflected through her so you may live it. In this living, one connects to your heart-soul, Ab Ba, as the gateway to this.

Living in truth means you see who you are, and you see all the aspects of your Self in the Nine Bodies. Ma'at plays an important role in this as she serves you throughout the journey of all Nine Bodies to see where you are at and what your reflection is along the journey at any given time.

Ma'at grows steadily and consistently every day. She is tuned into through living her laws in integrity, purity, and giving each and every day. It is through these qualities that you live and move in harmony with Ma'at and are able to commune with and integrate the Ab Ba, the heart-soul, which leads to you eventually embodying your greatest potentials. This then gives meaning to existence, answering the question, "Who am I, and what am I here to do?"

## Divine Selfishness

"The reward of one who does something lies in something being done for him. This is considered by the Neteru as Ma'at."[11] This is divine selfishness. When one is living in a giving state, in Ma'at, then all one does is good for the whole. All the actions that serve you also serve

---

10. Her ostrich feather may be bent and folded without breaking. When folded, it returns to its original form. So, too, is truth. Kerry Wisner, Akhet Hwt-Hrw, www.hwt-hrw.com.

11. A royal text from the Thirteenth Dynasty as quoted in Jan Assmann, *The Mind of Egypt: History and Meaning in the Time of the Pharaohs,* trans. Andrew Jenkins (Cambridge, MA: Harvard University Press, 2003), 128.

others and the greater whole as you are living this relationship. All that benefits you benefits all. In giving one receives, and in receiving one gives.

Divine selfishness means that when you give selflessly, without expectation, then something is automatically given back to you, even though you may not realize it at the time. This is the universal circuit of giving and receiving. In the giving, you receive. This can manifest when you give by you also learning in that moment. Some new piece of information may reveal itself as you share with another that you never consciously knew before; you may feel a deeper opening of the heart as you share love with another. There are many ways this can manifest, and sometimes this may happen years later. But the cycle does complete: in giving we receive.

In offering and giving of yourself you enter the universal circuit, where everything is constantly coming into your heart and leaving, going back into the universe. Visualize this for a moment: a stream of light is entering your heart through your crown, and then going back out into the universe, and then returning, creating an infinite loop.

We can tune into this circuit of perpetual giving and receiving, or we can receive and no longer give out. Most people are stuck on one polarity or the other: some people find it harder to give, and some people find it harder to receive. Which one are you?

This polarity can be seen in intimate relationships and in your relationship to the earth. This is particularly true of many sacred sites, where people come to receive, but not to give, or give as an afterthought. The giving, the offering, comes first—then you can receive and give it back out again. If you do not offer and give out what is coming into you, you can get stuck, and the heart closes. If you just take and take from the earth, from others, from life, your heart gets smaller and smaller and contracts. The healing happens when both are balanced; then you can enter Ma'at and begin to live in her in the universal circuit of giving and receiving. This then transforms into "in giving we receive, and in receiving we give." There becomes no difference at all.

## The Forty-Two Doorways to the Open Heart

"I present Ma'at to you. Chanting to your Ka, the lie is abolished."[12] The Ceremony of the Forty-two Doorways to the Heart, the forty-two judges of the self, is a powerful ritual of experiential heart-healing and Self-inquiry that can be used every day. In Egypt, one accessed the Ka body and cleansed it before this ceremony, allowing it to stand before one so it could connect to and fully empower the heart Ab into the other bodies of light.

The following ceremony can be done alone but was traditionally done with four high priests and priestesses holding the energy of Thoth, Anubis, Ma'at, and Osiris in front of the assembled initiates. The initial invocations (not included) and mantras of Anubis are sounded in Egyptian, which ensures the Neters and forty-two judges are present. This is a powerful vibrational experience, as ancient Egyptian mantra holds a deeply transforming resonance more powerful than many other sacred languages such as Sanskrit. These mantras ensure that everyone present in the ceremony is in integrity and deeply enters the process of Ma'at as a living experience of the Duat, or underworld.

For the individual reader, you can prepare yourself by lighting a candle and creating a sacred space, preferably at twilight or at dawn. Sit silently, and invite the Neters of Thoth, Anubis, Ma'at, and Osiris to be present. Breathe into your heart and allow it to soften. Make a vow to

---

12. Sylvie Cauville, *Le temple de Dendara: Les chapelles osiriennes* (Cairo: Institut Français d'Archéologie Orientale, 1998), 33, trans. Kerry Wisner, Akhet Hwt-Hrw, www.hwt-hrw.com.

yourself to be humble, open, honest, and receptive to the real truth of your life and the actions in your life.

Maybe some images and memories from your past will already start to arise; maybe you will feel the energies of the Neters with you. This is because these Neters really wish to support this process of the returning of Ma'at to human consciousness and the earth. They applaud and salute all those ready to make this step and will do everything to help those who are humble, receptive, and open to the process.

Once you feel a shift from your normal state of awareness into the heart, you are ready to begin.

## The Ceremony of the Forty-two Gateways to the Heart

To be said on reaching the Hall of Two Truths so as to purge any sins committed, and to see the face of every god:

> Hail to you, great God, Lord of the Two Truths. I come to you so I may behold thy beauties. I know thee, I know thy name, I know the names of the Forty-two Gods who are with you in the Hall of the Two Truths, who live by warding off evildoers. In truth I come to you, I bring Ma'ati to you. I have done away sin for you. Now, I stand here before you.

> O my heart, which I had from my mother! O my heart, which I had from my mother! O my heart of all my different ages! Do not stand up as a witness against me. Do not be opposed to me in the tribunal. Do not be hostile to me in the presence of the keeper of my heart's Balance.

*Maat anu e i a e o u*

Hail, Usekh-nemmt, who comest forth from Anu, I have not committed sin.

Hail, Hept-khet, who comest forth from Kher-aha, I have not stolen in violence.

Hail, Fenti, who comest forth from Khemenu, I have not taken without permission.

Hail, Am-khaibit, who comest forth from Qernet, I have not killed humans. I have not given the order for murder to be committed.

Hail, Neha-her, who comest forth from Rasta, I have not sabotaged myself nor another.

Hail, Ruruti, who comest forth from heaven, I have never been greedy and taken more than I need. I have not used my power over others.

Hail, Arfi-em-khet, who comest forth from Suat, I have not claimed ownership over any part of Gaia, over any person, or over what is God's.

Hail, Neba, who comes and goes, I have not uttered lies. I have not pretended to be that which I am not. I have not purposely distorted truth to make myself feel or look better in another's eyes.

Hail, Set-qesu, who comest forth from Hensu, I have not wasted food. I have not caused anyone to go hungry, nor denied food to the hungry. I have not fed off the energy of others. I have not denied myself what I have needed to nourish myself.

Hail, Utu-nesert, who comest forth from Het-ka-Ptah, I have not uttered curses.

Hail, Qerrti, who comest forth from Amentet, I have not committed adultery in thought, word, and deed. I have not added or taken away from the truth.

Hail, Her-f-ha-f, who comest forth from thy cavern, I have made no one weep.

Hail, Basti, who comest forth from Bast, I have not selfishly manipulated another for my own ambition and gain. I have not lived my life in fear of being right or wrong.

Hail, Ta-retiu, who comest forth from the night, I have not attacked anyone. I have not abandoned my connection to God.

Hail, Unem-snef, who comest forth from the execution chamber, I have not deceived myself or others. I have not thought myself better or less than others.

Hail, Unem-besek, who comest forth from Mabit, I have not schemed and manipulated to get what is not mine.

Hail, Neb-Maat, who comest forth from Maati, I have not been an eavesdropper. I have not discussed another's secrets shared with me in confidence. I have not made promises I did not keep.

Hail, Tenemiu, who comest forth from Bast, I have not slandered nor put anyone down. I have not judged.

Hail, Sertiu, who comest forth from Anu, I have not been angry without just cause. I have not been self-righteous for myself or for God.

Hail, Tutu, Uamenti, who comest forth from Ati, I have not done anything to manipulate or break up a partnership.

Hail, Maa-antuf, who comest forth from Per-Menu, I have not polluted myself.

Hail, Her-uru, who comest forth from Nehatu, I have terrorized no one, nor caused another to enter fear.

Hail, Khemiu, who comest forth from Kaui, I have not lived my life in ignorance of divine order, nor resisted divine law. I have not lived my life in drudgery.

Hail, Shet-kheru, who comest forth from Urit, I have not set the beast in me upon another, nor entertained murderous thoughts, nor wanted to hurt myself or others.

Hail, Nekhenu, who comest forth from Heqat, I have not shut my ears or eyes to words and acts of truth. I have not lived my life in hope.

Hail, Kenemti, who comest forth from Kenmet, I have not blasphemed and sinned against love.

Hail, An-hetep-f, who comest forth from Sau, I am not a person of violence to myself or others.

Hail, Sera-kheru, who comest forth from Unaset, I have not been a stirrer of strife.

Hail, Neb-heru, who comest forth from Netchfet, I have not acted with undue haste, desperation, and impatience.

Hail, Sekhriu, who comest forth from Uten, I have not sought to control or invade others.

Hail, Neb-abui, who comest forth from Sauti, I have not multiplied my words in speaking, or spoken unnecessarily. I have not gossiped. I have not broken silence out of fear.

Hail, Nefer-Tem, who comest forth from Het-ka-Ptah, I have wronged none; I have done no evil. I have not made others or myself feel guilty.

Hail, Tem-Sepu, who comest forth from Tetu, I have not worked witchcraft against anyone.

Hail, Ari-em-ab-f, who comest forth from Tebu, I have never stopped the flow of truth, nor denied the expression of truth in myself or another. I have not stayed silent when truth needed to be spoken. I have not acted small to hide my light.

Hail, Ahi, who comest forth from Nu, I have never raised my voice.

Hail, Uatch-rekhit, who comest forth from Sau, I have not cursed God and played the victim. I have not given responsibility for my actions to anything else.

Hail, Neheb-ka, who comest forth from thy cavern, I have not acted with arrogance. I have not been self-absorbed and ignored the needs of others. I have not allowed fear to stop me from serving others.

Hail, Neheb-nefert, who comest forth from thy cavern, I have not tried to make excuses for my small self or defend my position. I have not separated human from divine and placed them apart.

Hail, Tcheser-tep, who comest forth from the shrine, I have not dishonored another's choices, gifts, and path. I have not tried to keep for myself that which goes to God.

Hail, An-af, who comest forth from Maati, I have not betrayed or tainted the purity of the child within or without.

Hail, Hetch-abhu, who comest forth from Ta-she, I have not dishonored, claimed ownership, or destroyed the animal and devic kingdoms.

Hail Anpu Apuat, who comest forth from Duat, I have not left any stone unturned in my search for the Divine.

*Maat anu e i a e o u*

I am pure. I am pure. I am pure. O Forty-two Judges of the Day of Truth, I affirm to each of you to hold the forty-two corners of the Pure Land from where you come. Witness that I am pure. This I declare in front of you, O Judges of my heart. Hold the Lands witness to the purity I confess.

Note that you may substitute "I do not" as opposed to "I have not" at the beginning of each of the confessions. This involves changing the tense in the sentence as well but yields interesting results.

Anaiya Aon Prakasha

# ~7

# BA: THE SOUL

*My Ba is the Ba of the Gods, the Ba of eternity, the Ba in
the body.*

— *The Book of the Dead*

The hieroglyph for the Ba soul is a human head sitting on top of the
body of a hawk. Out of its chest a radiant plume arises, signifying the
merging of the Ba soul with the Ab heart, so they become one heart-
soul: the *I am* presence of the soul. In Egypt this was the embodying
of the divine child, the presence of the soul that sits in being, moving
from the impulse to play, create, and share joyful open innocence.

Ba is the mirror of the Ab: Ab–bA. Ab is the human heart and conscience, the impulse to share and give, the ability to feel, the highest
aspects of mortal human existence. Ba is the joy and ecstasy felt when
your mortal human heart merges with the immortal soul in the bridal
chamber of your heart. Ab Ba is the love of the heart-soul merged as
one flying and free being.

In the world of the Ba or celestial soul, wherever you go, there you
are. Wherever you travel, you are there, the immortal being that you
are, always the same no matter what is changing on the surface or outside. Ba is beyond time and space as known in the third and fourth

dimensions and is always in presence, the *I am* of the soul, or the Aham. The Ba is the individual's connection to the absolute, that which never changes; is present in the union of heart Ab and soul; and is the stillness amidst that which is always changing in the sea and babble of thoughts, the roller coaster of emotions, and the ever-shifting world of phenomena, or Maya.[1] Ba is the soft still point of loving peace that is not swayed by the ego, living in loving witness, and is the dissolver of any of the ego's wavelike arisings. It emanates and acts from this space.

In this state of Ba consciousness, the soul is like a bird that can fly to many levels. It can see life from many angles in many ways, choosing at any moment to either soar like an eagle to see the big picture or focus in on the details to see the depths and richness of life in the smallest of things. It is able to fly in the heights and descend into the depths, on air and in the oceans, walking on land and the magnetic earth energies, merging with fire, shape-shifting, and playing with any element as required.

Ba can merge with the landscape and other beings, be they human, animal, or subtle, in an orgasmic flow. As Ba is free, it has no judgments or compunctions about doing so; its only moral is love and to follow the flow of love and heart. In this sense, Ba is like a dolphin, free, playful, intermingling and merging with all members of its pod or soul family. Ba is fluidity, the ability to move without question or judgment from one experience and adventure to the other, gracefully unfolding in spontaneous expressive flow.

Ba is the embodied soul, anchored in the heart center. When the human heart Ab and the free soul Ba merge, they become a foundation to integrate, sustain, and activate soul purpose and drive. Ba is the foundation for the universal soul or Source to land within your body and as such provides the discernment and love needed to open up to the

---

1. The ocean of bubbles that are the morphing sea of thoughts and emotions that construct the world of suffering and codependence.

advanced states of consciousness found in Sahu, the immortal and universal body.

Living consciously from Ba is important in all your relationships, be they intimate, with friends, or even with nonphysical beings. Living in Ba means you become your own Source of Self-authority, sovereignty, and spiritually discerned choice. When you are in the Ba, you can safely open to higher energy frequencies, as the Ba recognizes the new energies and knows how to handle or direct them. All you have to do is stop for a moment and ask your heart-soul, and you will know what to do. You become an authentic being, plugged into Source through the foundation of your heart center.

The opening and merging of the Ab and Ba allow us to assimilate and work with the increased frequency of the incoming solar and galactic superwaves of light that are rushing onto earth even as you read this paragraph. Stop for a moment to feel this.

These energies range from simply feeling lighter and freer to feeling ascension symptoms, the breaking apart of old structures and relationships that cannot handle or assimilate the new frequencies, to sensing and experiencing the flows of liquid light flowing through and animating your body. This sensation can literally feel like you are walking in light without a physical body. This is a very interesting experience, as you are no longer form but pure light with a covering of form.

The experience of the Ba is the bliss of union in your heart. This is an unmistakable feeling, as now your spirit is operating in form, in the body, here on earth.[2] As you deepen into the heart-soul center, you experience love in its infinite facets as a constant, underlying all feelings, even fear and anger.

---

2. The bliss of Akhu is deeper, felt more in the brain and higher chakras in the experience of samadhi.

The opening of the Ab Ba, the heart-soul, is the gateway to Source, for it is the center that lies between and unites all bodies. Ba is the mediator between spirit and matter, and just as the heart unites the lower and upper chakras, so too does the heart-soul Ab Ba mediate the integration of the nondual transcendental awareness of the Hu or higher chakras with the life-engaging Ka of the womb-hara. Ba is your own unique, individual soul spark of the eternal flame of the universal soul, your first real introduction to unlimited, infinite, and unconditional love that has no agendas, barriers, rules, dogmas, or restraints. Ba is the soul spark in each and every one of you.

It is through the Ab Ba that you love and include all parts of your self. This can be a scary and confusing time as well as being joyously liberating. As the rules and conditions for love that you have set yourself according to your families, peers, societies, and religions crumble, you are left in a new unknown space. All the ways you have tried to "fit in" and keep yourself small, all the ways you have tried to cope with your deepest feelings that seem not to fit into society, family, and its structures, crumble in the face of the unconditionally loving Ba. Ba is free to love, feel, and live its heart's desires no matter what others say, think, or do. This is a radical and revolutionary step for an individual to take: to live their freedom no matter what.

In Egypt, this freedom meant one was able to commune with the stars and their intelligences as well as the other civilizations that reside in the galaxy. This soul travel and communication was normal for the Egyptian culture, and extraterrestrial visitors from the stars are depicted on the walls of some of the Egyptian temples. In reconnecting these lines of communication, feeling, and love, many people today are remembering their origins and their full potentials. Ba is the key to traveling into other worlds and dimensions through the heart-crown connection, and it is the key for humanity to become an awakened civilization living in harmony with universal laws.

# Your Soul Purpose

Ba is the spiritual manifestation and embodiment of your soul and its purpose. It holds the blueprint of your life and unique path. When you are in touch with your Ba and its purpose, many of the reasons for organized religion crumble, as you now know what you need and what to do. You have your own guidance and know your own rules and guidelines. You know yourself.

One of the most important events in your lifetime is to remember what you came here to do and why you decided to incarnate into your present body, environment, parents, and country in this lifetime. With this knowledge, you can guide your life in the direction your Ba longs for and become able to fulfill the deepest desires of your heart-soul, achieving the highest potential you have as a human being.

The majority of humanity is not fulfilling its Ba purpose, not doing the tasks to help their own full incarnation that they came here to do and wanted to do before incarnation. This confusion can be felt almost everywhere in the world today. Most spiritual seeking is ungrounded in this way, as without knowledge of your soul purpose, much spiritual work can lead you in circles, like a hamster constantly running around a wheel in a small cage.

Here, the hamster is your soul trying to remember who it is while trapped in the cage of the ego, running around on the wheel of reincarnation. Until you remember and put into action your soul purpose, you will be the hamster, forever running around in a self-enclosed circle, seeking and never finding.

Finding your soul purpose is perhaps one of the most important tasks facing you today. Upon finding it, and then consciously activating it, the whole world will conspire to help you to achieve it, to lead you into the greatest love you can ever know.

Your first forgetting of your soul purpose occurred at birth, where you developed divine amnesia, causing you to lose memory of who you are and what you came here to do. The journey from birth is all about remembering who you are and what you came here to do. This is usually revealed to you while you are still a child. However, your developing ego quickly dismissed these remembrances due to parental and peer group pressures that labeled your innocent remembering as fantastical, impractical, or improbable.

The first steps to remembering can include practices to become self-aware: yoga, meditation, breathwork, and witnessing thoughts and emotions. The quieter the mind becomes, the more you are able to listen to the still, small voice of the heart and soul that always knows why you are here and what you are here to do.

The next steps can include remembering how you came into the world before birth, the journey and passage while in the womb and your experiences of it, and then being physically born into this world. As this healing and wisdom arises to be integrated, you can then journey into the womb, into birth, and into your own rebirthing through the journey into the Seven Gates[3] and the connection to the Galactic Center found within you.

Your soul purpose is often guarded by trauma or deep blocks that seem to have no explanation or healing available for them. Yet there is an innate knowing deep within you that there is something else here—something you cannot quite put your finger on but something you have been waiting for, something valuable, a way to manifest yourself into the world that despite all your seeking and healing has not yet manifested.

We each have a responsibility to follow our dreams and never give up on those dreams. Each of you has a divine mission and purpose in this life that demands your total commitment and focus. The challenge

---

3. For more information see Padma Aon Prakasha, *The Power of Shakti* (Rochester, VT: Inner Traditions, 2009).

in following your soul purpose is that it will urge you at times in the direction of your fears as a means of overcoming them in order to fulfill your dreams and your soul purpose.

In order to uncover your mission, you must abandon many of your conditioned ideas of right and wrong, of what makes "sense" and what does not, and step into the intuitive imagination. Your soul purpose, or dreaming of a better life and "going for it," is a requirement of happiness. You cannot be truly happy without it. You might establish a level of contentment, but that is not happiness.

When you dream and challenge yourself to overcome your fears, anxieties, and doubts, your life will go through a period of hardship. Just like when you begin exercising for the first time in years, you feel out of shape and have to go through a period of feeling bad before feeling good. As you break out of the mold, you will find that individuals will try to sabotage you, saying that you cannot do it, that you are crazy. All they are really saying is, "I don't want you to succeed because if you do, I have to look at my own lack of fulfillment." And many people are afraid to do that, so they try to knock you back down to their level, back into the box.

Your soul purpose holds within it the incorrigible will to fulfill and achieve your humanity. Each person's soul purpose has the "right" answers for you regardless of whether that information makes logical sense. It is impossible to trust this divine voice if you make choices based on an outside "voice."

When you discover your soul purpose and put it into action, you become filled with passion and Sekhem and have a never-ending source of fuel or energy to keep you going in life. You are connected to the stream of life through your own soul current connection to Source, and you always have this, regardless of who or what passes through the rest of your life. It is always with you as a great source of energy, self-love, passion, and the ability to rest in your core center and then expand and create from this space of Ba.

## Soul Form

Ba is the freedom of the soul when it steps into living here on earth. It is soul operating in form, soul manifested in form through the heart-crown connection. It is the living and eternal soul manifesting the union between the Ka and the body, living closest to the Ka and the Ab, or human heart.

Ba is the maturation and manifesting of your soul purpose in action through the heart of giving. It is the freedom and joy of the heart to give unconditionally. The heart at peace with itself, in true harmony and ecstatic order, is when the Ab and Ba meet. The heart that is touched and rises up in moments of deep beauty and ecstatic ascending is when the human heart and soul meet, deeply and powerfully, gently and lovingly, rising and flowing together, taken away from the everyday world into sublime waves of heart expanding and opening. Perhaps this is why the Ba is seen like a bird, flying and free.

Drunk and alive on love, the deep, almost orgasmic feeling of Ba and Sekhem ignite within your body, fueled by spiritual love. This is an inner meeting, in the bridal chamber within your own heart and life force, which can then lend itself to merge with others. It is like falling in love with Self with no object outside to create this love. Rather, it is the outflowing of love directly from your heart to all outside you.

Heart-centered creative intelligence that is grounded in passionate service to Gaia is the realm of the Ab Ba flowing with Sekhem. As more of you manifests, as more of your soul embodies, so too do your heart's desires and visions manifest. They are inseparable. As you ground more love into all of your life, so too do all your soul purposes or contracts manifest in every field, every endeavor, every channel, and every aspect of your life.

You are your creations, and you are cocreating with your Self. As you heal you can create more. You are your projects. Your inner healing manifests more of you on the external. Your heart is the foundation of conscious creativity and expression in the world in a tangible way. Seal the cracks in your inner foundation, and the external world will blossom and reflect your inner abundance.

All is given through you by your commitment, given through your openness and nonattached loving, wed with the precision and fluidity of mind in harmony with Sekhem, the divine mother and loving embrace of all beings: where all creations come from and where our world is returning.

As you manifest yourself, more ease and grace of lifestyle emerges. Serving self means you are serving Self, as each is other. Manifesting your heart's desires is healing your heart; healing your heart manifests your heart's desires. As you bring this all into the body, into the spine, into the earth element, one great cycle of ascension and descent completes. The great circuit of going up and out, transcending this world, and coming down and into the body, into the world, into community completes in you. And your gifts are now made manifest as you walk with ease in the world but are not of the world.

Earth, through the lens of the Ba, is the completing and reforming of all the elements of you, the coalescing of all the strands and fragments, the past and the future, the memories and that which is yet to be experienced, in you. Earth is the cube where you become light in action, the loving passion of creating and creation.

In combining it all, separation dissolves, and the reweaving of your self commences. Do not leave anything out anymore, as this is the time when we all come to earth to experience that which we have never experienced before, what we have never done before, what we have never tasted before, and what we have never completed before. In the completing of your earthly experiences, designed to connect all parts of yourself, you are mastered by love and unite with the Ba.

## Ba Practice 1

Egypt was the home of Christ Consciousness and where it was most available as a way of being in recent epochs.[4] In Egypt, living and adhering to the forty-two laws of the human heart, governed and balanced by Ma'at, provided the foundation to sustain the soul Ba. To enter Ba and sustain your presence there requires you raise your frequency to loving, giving, serving, and helping others. This frequency can also be raised and connected into through the ecstatic merging of souls in lovemaking through the unified Ab Ba.

Ba, or the soul-star chakra, is located just above the head before it fully connects with the heart. To find it, raise your arms above your head as far as they will comfortably go. Where the fingers meet is where the Ba is located. From here it connects directly to the heart.

To connect to it, viscerally evoke feelings of gratitude, appreciation, embrace, and compassion. For women this can also be done through the yoni and womb.

Try this now: Breathe the feeling of gratitude and appreciation from the Ba into the crown and then into the heart. If you have problems raising this emotion, try to remember a time where you really did feel gratitude or appreciation in your life, and again, breathe this from the Ba into your heart.

This is a simple way to tune into the Ba. Deeper connections happen through light transmissions and initiation, which can feel like huge downpours of light from the crown into the body.

---

4. The maps of the soul or Ba that they cultivated within themselves can be seen in detail in Padma Aon Prakasha, *The Christ Blueprint* (Berkeley, CA: North Atlantic, 2010). When enough work is done on the five temporary light bodies, then the connection to the Ba can be fully established so you are living as soul. To leave behind cultural expectations of us requires we live life according to spiritual principles and define ourselves through this. As we do this in body, mind, and spirit, we can access and experience the higher light bodies and begin to sustain this way of life on a daily basis.

# Appreciation

Appreciation begins to heal your own subjective or inner experience of life. It is a foundation for love, as appreciation leads into true gratitude, being able to see the beauty in all beings and in all life in the simplest of things. Appreciation allows us to let go of limiting habits of self-judgment, self-worth, and condemnation. Appreciation brings you into the beauty and divinity of another and your Self. Honoring and appreciating are the basis for kindness and gratitude, the basis for love. Without appreciating, one shrinks and wilts into the ego being the master and the soul being the servant.

Appreciation opens the way for loving reciprocity to be present, for one to feel loved and loving. Appreciation feels good! Appreciation opens us into trust. Vulnerability and humility open the doorways to love and intimacy. Once your emotional barriers are down, once you allow yourself to be vulnerable, you can appreciate and praise your own and others' beauty. In giving these qualities, we receive them.

True praise and appreciation allows the small self to fall away. It is the small self's fear that in praise it will be giving away its power to something outside itself. There is nothing outside itself. In praise you feel the beauty, vision, and perfection of another welling up inside you and speak it to honor the very gift and wonder of their existence—of all existence. To see, feel, and honor another's presence fully, whether human or divine, allows the gift you perceive in another into your own heart, body, and soul. In fully giving your appreciation to another, you feel the depth to which they are always and only a reflection of your Self.

# Gratitude

Gratitude is the attitude of enlightenment. Flowing as part of the stream of appreciation, thanking counters the positions and judgments we have around our relationships. As the judgments we hold in these areas dissolve, we reconnect with the world as it is rather than the world as we think it is or should be. When gratitude is showered into the Ba, it opens, as it is seen, heard, and felt in its fullness. In its gratitude, Ba wants to pour outward in even greater amounts, knowing that as it gives, it receives, and as it receives, it gives.

Gratitude results in a desire to constantly give outwardly, becoming circular and building upon itself, allowing the outflowing of love to continue from the soul. If you thank and bless all things in your life, you enter peace, and a deeper understanding arises as to your power as a creator. You understand that you truly have created everything that is happening to you and become grateful that you have, in your magnificence, done so to learn ever deeper lessons about compassion and love. This starts with your own love for your self and compassion for what you have put yourself through in order to learn and remember.

If you thank and bless all events, occurrences, and people in your life, you spiritualize your whole life down to the most mundane. Everything becomes an opportunity to grow into peace; everything becomes an opportunity to bring loving wisdom into your everyday life. Everything can become transformed through thanking it, as you then see the gift that life is bringing you in every moment. The more you see this, the quicker you evolve and transmute any egoic resistance to the flow of life, love, and gratitude. You start to see everything as a manifestation of love.

Gratitude is the current of love, the support of love as it weaves its way throughout all life and all people. The more you thank the deeper lessons that darkness, fear, loss, and anger present to you, the more you see their purpose and the more humble you become to the divine orchestration of life as it is occurring to you now in the present.

There is neither true power, nor the presence to create love, without gratitude. Kindness and gratitude are interlinked. In gratitude, you realize that you cannot get love, you can only receive it, and you can only fully receive it by giving it away. To have all, give all. In this, we realize that there is no source by which to get love, only the choice to rest in gratitude and extend love.

To be truly happy is to live in gratitude. Living in gratitude and in grace means accepting whatever comes your way, both "good" and "bad," with thankfulness. There is no exception to what you can be thankful for, as gratitude wears down your resistance to conflicts, humbles you, and brings you into joy as you start to see that if you thank and bless all things in your life, you enter peace and kindness to all.

Try this: thank all the painful and beautiful occurrences that have happened to you this week, and see how you feel. Write down at least five. Breathe them into your heart one by one and see what your heart feels about it. You may be surprised at the heart's wisdom as it unravels the perceptions and lessons of the pain you have felt this week and its true purpose as a function of love.

In the conflicts that arise, in the "unfortunate" circumstances that happen, there is a lesson for your soul that you have created in order to find the peace of the open, giving heart as it blesses and receives all things equally through the focus of gratitude and appreciation. This heart makes all things full by thanking it, emptying it of any resentment, pain, frustration, or thoughts of harm.

This leads to beauty. Beauty results from your perception and not just from the person, place, object, or emotion perceived. Beauty arises from the clarity of your own perception. What you often describe as beautiful is an interpretation, one that has been taught to you, a perception that one thing is beautiful and another ugly. To see beauty is to see things as they are and to appreciate something simply for what it is. To see beauty, we see with the heart and connect to what we are seeing and communicating with through the heart. When we truly see reality it is beautiful, as it involves no judgment, no naming or identifying with things, no boxes or ideas, no past history to what we felt was beautiful.

Beauty is not about how a person, place, object, or emotion looks or feels; it is about how you, who is looking, feels. The beauty that you experience "out there" is a direct reflection of the beauty of what is happening inside you. When you are in a state of joy and feel uplifted, everything appears beautiful to you on the outside. This feeling naturally leads us to being kind and grateful, extending this to others in tender receptive presence, leading to harmlessness.

Without the mind's judgment and commentary, you can see the beauty in the rotting pile of dung lying on the street. If you have no judgment about the value of something as opposed to the value of something else, then you can appreciate the nature and use of all things. In true beauty you do not exclude anything but embrace it all. Where you do not see beauty serves a vital purpose to show you where your mind still judges and misunderstands. Heaven is not somewhere else; it is right here in this perception.

Try it right now with all the people and things you do not like that have happened to you today or yesterday. What happens?

For more on the qualities of the Ba, see Padma Aon Prakasha, *The Christ Blueprint* (Berkeley, CA: North Atlantic, 2010).

## For Giving and for Getting

The heart Ab is the gateway to the soul Ba and its foundation. When you are situated in the soul Ba, you live in giving. When you are not situated in the Ab or Ba, you are living in the forgetting: you live to get from others.

These two separate realms, one for giving and one for getting, mark out what Christ called the Queendom (more commonly referred to as the Kingdom) of God and the illusion. One who is living in the giving dwells within this queendom. One who lives to get, to consume, to acquire, to take from others is living in the for-getting. They have forgotten what love is and use need, desire, and attachment as ways of filling the hole within, a hole created by lack of love.

These two pathways, or the Two Truths, mark out who is a real human being. Each person on this planet is living in one or the other. Which one are you living in? There are two paths here: one is the journey to the Queendom, where you are shedding your deeper illusions, healing your wounds and holes; the second is the journey within the Queendom, where you are living in the giving established by the Ab and Ba merging. This is an entirely different journey.

Cease seeking and all is given through you. The for-giving is for those who are here to give, as they seek not. Those who are here to get and take are still seeking, and they cannot truly give as they have not found that place within. The heart-soul lives to give, for in the giving lies the receiving. In this giving the soul opens and is free to fly, soaring above the self-centered into the selfless, the realm of the Hu. The Ab is the gateway, and the Ba is the key to the Queendom.

The counterpart of the Ba is the Hu: the Ba appears on earth as Hu does in heaven. Uniting one's Ka with Ba is essential for your embodiment, for Ka is vitality and Ba the gateway to pure spirit. On a larger global level, we are all moving toward a soul-oriented Ba culture. In such a culture we no longer work against nature but work with it, establishing a living flow of communication with the biosphere, or Gaia. We consciously reprogram ourselves into what is our own highest potential and heart's desire.

Our appreciation of beauty moves into the forefront of our collective awareness as we celebrate our unity and communicate this to each other. Being moved by the desire to create more love becomes the foundation for our giving and sharing with others. This movement first came into global awareness in the 1960s: now, with more awareness, this movement can mature into its fullness. The time is now ripe.

## The Divine Child

The birth of the Divine Child within you is an alchemical process that results in simplicity. Stripping away the layers of drudgery, self-assumed responsibility, and encrusted emotions, you can simply delight in the Divine Child, free and playful with its sensuality yet not needing anything from it to fill up an inner hole or need. The child shares freely without expectation or grasping; it does what it feels is fun and does not wish to make a big deal of it.

The Divine Child is the freedom of your emotions connected to your soul Ba in right relationship. It flows through your nurturing, honoring, and protecting both the child and the feminine, giving space to both to simply *be* instead of *do*.

Much modern culture is driven by achieving, of doing, of productivity, of celebrating our busyness and how great and productive we are in our doing. We measure our sense of self-worth or how little self-worth we have through this lens, which is the belittling and forgetting of the Divine Child. We measure our sense of self-worth through how busy we are and how much we can do, which is the exact opposite of the Divine Child.

This leads to self-destruction, depletion, and the repression of the Divine Child, for this yang culture is limited. It needs constant replenishing by being harmonized with yin, which regenerates, restores, and fortifies it. Imbalance is destructive on a body-mind level as well as being destructive on a global level with the destruction of the environment, war, and conflict. Yin would never initiate a war or sustain one; only yang versus yang can create that, and yin would never deplete itself through too much outward action as its innate nature is rest and receptivity.

It is yin that allows space and time in your schedule to be empty and spacious—not needing to fill in the gaps in your busy life because it is fulfilled within itself. Rest allows the right activity that will most benefit you and others to arise. Without this balance, more and more stress-related illnesses arise as the body-mind is not built to remain in yang spaces for long periods of time. Thus one remains depleted and stressed, the condition of forgetting the Divine Child.

One then becomes stuck and inflexible, caught in thought structures and ways of being that do not allow you to rest in the feminine and play in the Divine Child. The body-mind *is* built to remain in harmony between yin and yang for indefinite periods of time. We can do this by spending more time doing nothing, resting, relaxing in nature, doing what the Divine Child wants, and playing with the Divine Child.

Disconnecting from the Divine Child has many symptoms; being connected to the Divine Child is a simple and joyful way of being, a lifestyle choice for the soul. Reconnecting and remembering the Divine Child may require many healings, a change of job, home, relationships, and inner emotional stability. Being disconnected from the Divine Child can manifest in a lack of purpose in life, the loss of your adventurous and fun-loving spirit, and the loss of the desire to grow, laugh, and do new things. Your soul purpose may be lost and forgotten. You may feel mentally disordered and out of sorts.

Indeed, the Divine Child is a key to retrieving your soul purpose, as it is found in the passion, light, and joy found deep in the heart-soul that is free: the essence of the Divine Child. Once reconnected to the Divine Child, you remember why you came to earth. You start to walk the journey of life as a child, laughing and playing, free from the illusions of the world.

Some other symptoms marking when one has forgotten the Divine Child:

- forgetting that life is a game

- forgetting that life is a game where love wins the game
- withholding wisdom, being secretive, creating cliques
- lying
- feeling better than others, and feeling we are special
- feeling rejection and abandonment
- feeling fear
- feeling self-righteous
- feeling judgment and guilt
- having unhealed birthing issues and childhood problems
- sexual molestation as a child
- projecting onto others
- Divine Child not getting what it needs

The purity and innocence of the Divine Child allows you to openly share your feelings, insights, sexuality, and emotions without having any shame about what you do or how you do it. The child hides nothing and is not embarrassed by what others may think, say, or do in relation to what it says or does. It speaks and plays freely and enchants others who begin to remember their own child. The child endears itself to everyone, as we all remember this side of ourselves: the innocent curiosity, the lack of guile, and the disregard for boundaries and social etiquette that are the rules that we as a society have learned in order to fit in, to be "grown up," and have stifled in our expression.

The Divine Child is a free artist, playing and creating, doing whatever it feels like doing. In the joy of being blessedly unaware of our own and others learned restraints, we too can be free to play and express. We truly have no restraints, only those we have learned and those that have been passed onto us by society, family, and friends that straitjacket us into getting ahead in this world and being successful, busy, and worthwhile. The Divine Child just does what it does without hierarchy and moves on blissfully unaware of the thoughts and fears of others.

Having a clear Ab heart free of guilt, regrets, shame, and condition-ing on how or what to be allows the Divine Child to be free. Being care-free, without worry or anxiety, playful and transparent, laughing and inquisitive, without thought or fear of repercussions or judgment is how the Divine Child operates. This is our natural state.

# Ba: Vehicle for Ascension
## The Family of the Ba: The Giza Plateau

One of the most powerful portals and activators for the galactic Ba soul is the trinity of pyramids on the Giza Plateau in Egypt. Each of these three pyramids align through phi spirals with the Sphinx, the fourth connecting point, which in turn aligns to a secret fifth initiation portal just outside the Giza complex.

These places all mark the Family of the Embodied Human Soul or *I am* presence of the Ba. The Great Pyramid is the Ba soul of Asar or Osiris, constructed to align initiates to this frequency. The middle pyramid is the Ba of Isis or Ast, and the smallest pyramid is the Ba of Horus or Heru. The Sphinx was originally Anubis or Anpu, guardian of the Isis pyramid, son of Asar, and adopted child of Ast.

The three initiations into the galactic Ba of Asar are the most well-known initiations today and are received in the Great Pyramid. In the well, the initiate would confront their deepest fears, then to travel into the Queen's Cham-ber, where they would harmonize and inte-grate this journey. From here, they would enter the King's Chamber, where they would receive initiation into the divine masculine Christ Consciousness or Ba through alignment

**The Ba and the pyramid.**
(Amaya Du Bois)

© www.cymascope.com

**Visual sound Cymascope image taken in the Initiation
sarcophagus of the King's Chamber of the Great Pyramid.**
(John Reid)

to fourteen different star systems, all mapped out through the star shafts
built into the pyramid.

This would then prepare the initiate to work with the Womb of the
World and the Ba soul of Isis in her adjoining pyramid. Only by having completed the previous three initiations was an initiate prepared
enough to enter the Womb of the World and the power of creation,

© www.cymascope.com

**Visual sound Cymascope image taken in the King's Chamber of the Great Pyramid.** (John Reid)

manifestation, and dissolution held there. It is this pyramid that the Sphinx of Anubis guards. This pyramid has not been active for thousands of years, as most have forgotten its purpose and how to work with it in the patriarchal age.

In the past, groups of people's sufferings would be felt, accepted, brought within the womb, and transmuted through the embrace of the wombs of a group of priestesses. This too is how collective transmutation can occur, even for a whole planet, *if* enough women can activate and heal their wombs.

The third and smallest pyramid is the Divine Child of Horus or Heru, birthed from the union of the male and female Ba aspects, Isis and Osiris. This soul union or sacred marriage gives birth to Heru, the entering of the initiate into the Hu bodies of light. All three pyramids are guarded by the Sphinx of Anubis Anpu, the loyal protector of Isis and her womb, the guardian of the Duat and of secret knowledge.[5] The fifth site aligns all four sites and aspects of the Ba together into embodied form through the circular motion of the pentagram.

The Ba, once connected to the Ka, is the vehicle for awakening and ascension. In Egypt the initiations for the Ba to enter into the Sahu was a journey that involved opening the Ab, or human heart, and then through the Pyramid Initiations allowing the Ba to fully descend into the physical by connecting to the universal body of the Hu. One can only master one octave of reality by going to the next, so in this case, entering and immersing in the Hu bodies allowed one to integrate the Ba fully.

Today, there are many ways to do this, particularly the initial work of healing and opening the human heart. Yet for those drawn to the Egyptian mysteries, the pathway of the Ab, Ba, and Ka merging and healing provides important keys not held in any other lineage, and this is especially important if you feel incomplete or feel longing for the Egyptian part of yourself. If you do feel this, then it is time to explore more deeply and experientially the mysteries of the Ab, Ba, and Ka and integrate the shadow Shew that lies as the guardian of these bodies of light. Then

---

5. For more on Anpu see Chapter 5 on the Ka.

you can truly enter the immortal and universal bodies of light of the Sahu, the breath of the divine and the merging of all parts of your self, and Akhu, the Source and resurrection of your self as a stellar intelligence and as living light or Shining One.

Anaiya Aon Prakasha

# 8

## SAHU: THE IMMORTAL BODY—LIGHT IN FORM

Sahu is the universal body, which becomes your body as it transfigures and becomes an immortal body that reveals within you as you raise the frequency of all your bodies. It is the key to nonduality or unity. In Egyptian, *sa* means "life force" and *hu* is the flow of the universal sound, similar to the sound *om*. Together, this flowing of the life force within all beings, connected to the sound that underlies all life, reveals Sahu within our physical structures. Simply put, Sahu is the life force of Source.

As we enter Sahu, our blood, bones, spines, DNA, brain chakras, and physical structures all change as we become more crystalline. The body transfigures in order to contain the higher frequencies of light, and we actually become a different type of human being, genetically, structurally, and consciously different from the current race of *Homo sapiens.* The best-known recent examples of this full transfiguration of the physical body into Sahu were Christ Yeshua after the Resurrection and various Tibetan lamas who have entered the Rainbow Body of light. This full body ascension into light was also attributed to Saint John the Beloved, Elijah, Mother Mary, Egyptian Masters such as Akhnaton and Thoth, and the Yogi Babaji, among many others.

Sahu is the breathing of the divine, the immortal universal body found within each of our human bodies when it transfigures and

317

ascends. We access Sahu when we become a God-Conscious being living in human form, when we have evolved to a point where we are in the world but not of it, connected to earth and its pleasures and joys while being connected to the Source of all that is. It is living heaven on earth, being human and divine, embodying light into matter.

Breath is the bridge between spirit and matter; it is how spirit enters matter. As we harmonize with the breath and body, learning to master it, we can then enter, through initiation, the breathless state. In the breathless state of deep meditation, we access a much higher form of energy that transforms the body-mind system, changing the structures of the body, spine, brain, and neurobiology to hold more light and different brain-wave states.

As our physical bodies get 'breathed into' by the divine through the breathless state, they become sustained through light. Traditionally, this was done by people who could access breathless states of bliss, or samadhi. Today, many people are trying to live on light while still being emotionally wounded and psychically and spiritually ill-prepared for this transition. This can be dangerous. However, if one is prepared for this state of living on light and no food, it can lead to great purifications and openings, and in some cases into connection into Sahu.

Sahu is the transfigured Self. When your Ka power and presence meet and merge with your heart-soul Ab Ba, you can enter Sahu. In Sahu you connect and embody your own God form, your own Neter; your own guides, or Higher Self, become embodied within you. It is no longer outside-of. One could say that the Higher Self descends, and you become this.

Sahu is both a frequency, a physical shift, and a knowing, and it is the individual's choice as to how far they wish to go to bring this frequency fully into the physical bodies of the Khat and Aufu. To do so is a great service, as merely a handful of people anchoring this frequency in form affects the morphogenetic fields of all humanity, making evolution easier for others. However, to choose not to fully bring it into physical form does not mean you will not be awakened; it just means you have not chosen this pathway in form, rather you have chosen it in spirit.

Sahu is the "last evidence of physical form, and the first evidence of eternity."[1] It is where the temporary human form merges with the infinite. It is a luminous sheath of light that holds all our deepest codings within it, all the seals of all our previous initiations that help us to tap into universal wisdom. It is in Sahu that we stand in the completion of the many layers of death and life in the bardo.

Sahu is the resurrection body, the body that when developed, aligns with Sekhem, the power of life. In order to access both, conscious lovemaking between a couple matched in love was seen in Egypt as an optimum route, as it involved the mixing of both human and divine energies and all the bodies of light. The Anubis ritual, whereby the heart was removed and a fresh one installed, was an essential part of the germination process in which the Sahu was consciously connected to, allowing access to unity, that which lies beyond the Duat or the underworld realms of duality.

Sahu is the marriage of earthly fertility, abundance, exuberance, and passion for life, with the mastery of stillness, silence, celestial wisdom, and power: the union of the devic and angelic kingdoms, or Pan/Osiris, the Green Man, meeting Metatron/Thoth as one flow of energy. When these two meet as one, Sahu is entered. It is living heaven on earth, in the body, in the richness of life brought into cosmic wisdom and light.

The Green Man, the human part of you, savors, relishes, and totally enjoys the outside world, simultaneously relishing the inner freedom and the inner joy. For too long the religions of this world have divorced

---

1. Normandi Ellis, *Dreams of Isis* (Chicago: Quest, 1997).

pure spirit from our natural state, a perfect human animal rejoicing in each moment in small things. The philosophy of the Green Man or Pan is eat, drink, and be merry. When this side of ourselves starts meditating, and when the spiritual sides of ourselves fully engage with the world, we enter Sahu: in the world but not of it. We connect the circle and enter bliss. We come home.

In Sahu, there is no schizophrenia, no split between matter and spirit, between the mundane and the sacred, between the joyous fun and wildness, even irreverence, of our human side, and the stillness and silence. There is no split. Without the human, juicy, wild side of us that simply enjoys life, our spirits become dry, detached, and dead, a Khat or corpse with no life, no juice, no soul. Without Thoth, the Green Man is just an animal, not yet evolved into Hu-manity.

To the Egyptians, reality was composed of the principles, archetypes, and living creative forces of the Neters. The world was the bodies of gods. When the wind blew it was the Ba of Shu, as the sun gave life it was Ra, as songs and dances came forth they were the flow of Hathor. Ba or soul lives within the Sahu. Sahu is the vehicle of the Ba, the soul, in its highest potential, when one has fully embodied the soul presence into form.

Living in Sahu does not mean you need to be a teacher or be seen as anything remarkable from the outside. Indeed, many people living in Sahu are clerks, newsagents, and householders, seemingly "normal" people from the outside but nevertheless living in this state here on earth. If you are in Sahu, you will recognize another in this state. If not, that person will simply look like anyone else, as you will not be able to notice their refined frequency, or they will simply choose not to show it. Sahu humans are people grounded on the earth, with the earth as their body, their hearts open, and their minds like the sky.

Maintaining this spiritual connection while living your daily life is remarkably ordinary: paying the bills and cleaning out the trash while communing with deities and playing with archangels and masters. Each is normal and has its place in the grand scheme of things, a scheme that is perfectly natural to one living in Sahu. In Sahu there is no channeling or downloading, simply communion with Source and all its manifestations, from speaking to Thoth to changing the baby's diapers. Earth is the glorious playground of fertile abundance to play in Sahu, a place of joy, creativity, giving, and being. Those in Sahu need not do anything if they choose; just by being they are helping others.

## Sahu and the Physical Body

In ancient Egypt, the Sahu was the consecrated mummy who had gone through all the ceremonial rites and had the Aufu or fleshly organs consecrated and embalmed, which then allowed the Ba soul to travel through the underworld or Duat. The physical body's primary function lies as a tool for the rest of the higher light bodies to function. All of the subtler bodies have powerful effects upon the physical body, hence its gradual transformation from Khat to Aufu to Sahu. Their experiences can affect every part of it.

For example, the deepest bodywork you will ever experience is found in deep meditation. The changes that can happen when you are sitting in the Sahu body frequencies change the brain, spine, and nervous system in profound ways and can be painful. This is because the physical is the last body to catch up to the changes occurring in the other bodies, as it is the densest, operating at the slowest frequency. The changes in the other bodies are eventually reflected as the Khat, Aufu, and Sahu merge, but are the last to be integrated. In this integration in the Sahu body, all the other changes are made permanent and anchored through the transfigured spine.

The Sahu is sustained and integrated through fasts and cleanses and eating living raw foods to allow the absorption of light into the physical vehicle, illuminating any residue of cellular or genetic debris and conditioning. Intakes of specific liquid crystals (see www.theliquidcrystals.com) and monatomic gold help to clear, heal, and build the crystalline structures within the body, allowing direct transference and integration of light into the cells and DNA. This has all been done before in Egypt, and all of this practical knowledge is available again right now.

It is important to eat, albeit living foods, to sustain the Sahu and allow it to absorb the physical form so it can become living light. Eating the right foods also sustains the Ka light body, our unique vital essence, allowing it to connect and merge fully with the Ba and Sahu. Activating the Sahu through sound and light regularly, aligned with deep meditation once the lower bodies have been cleared, allows the descent and ignition of the Sahu immortal body of light.

Similarly, when the DNA changes, the effects in the physical body are profound. The transformed Khat-Aufu-Sahu itself actually vibrates from inside and outside at the same time, as these three and Ka (its nearest equivalent and the bridge between spirit and body) resonate and entrain each other. This is a strange feeling, as you do not quite know whether you are coming or going. Yet the body is the key to knowing when the biggest changes are occurring, acting as a barometer of what we are embodying.

Do you realize that your physical body is a great source of power? This is why it is wise to take care of it, feed it well, and give it exercise and sleep. Living within a physical body is the body elemental. It is a consciousness of the physical that is filled with love, wisdom, and power to help you to fulfill your mission. The physical body has intelligence within it. Most people override this intelligence with their mind instead of tuning in and really listening to it. Talk to your physical body, love it, and make it part of your spiritual team. It is very hard to fulfill your spiritual mission if your physical body is not empowered and healthy, which then allows it to merge with Sahu at some point.

Many of you do a lot of spiritual work. However, you may have a hard time physically grounding your mission and the manifestations you are trying to create. Pan, who is the god of nature, the lord of the devas, and an Elohim Master, in conjunction with the Earth Mother and Archangel Sandalphon, are the three masters to call on to help ground your manifestations.

Sahu is the highest state of physicalized matter that exists in human consciousness and potential. It occurs when the Ka and Ba merge with the physical body and the blood flow, and we live in 100 percent light quotient, embodying 100 percent light, living in mastery. This does not mean you leave your body or dematerialize. It means that you have cleared out the obstacles to light by building crystalline networks within the body, healing and integrating your physical, emotional, mental, and soul lessons to enter a balance of unconditioned love, wisdom, and empowerment.

In the Sahu state of body-integrated consciousness, we include the body, the heart, and the higher chakras together by integrating the geometric crystalline frameworks of the Nine Bodies within you in balance, peace, and harmony. Your ascension symptoms will become less pronounced as you are now aware of all aspects of Self and just need to deepen and integrate them into the physical.

You live in service with the body as the tool for this. You live your soul purpose in action, grounded and manifested. It is this that nourishes you most, and it is this that recharges the body, bringing it into the soul Ba and Sahu frequency. If you have illness, it is because of your ascension symptoms, or because a deeper emotional or spiritual karmic issue is playing out through your body. You recognize this and work with it on this level. You realize you are in your final incarnation and keep working on this as your prime focus in life. All else is secondary.

Nature becomes a priority here, as only the earth and its devas can help you to ground the body into its natural form of light. Spending time in nature, if not living in it, provides the resonance, comfort, and recognition that the body needs here. Many people will not be able to live in the city while in the process of embodying Sahu, although those who are already embodying Sahu can choose to do so out of service to other beings. Where the greatest darkness is, is where the greatest light is required.

Sahu holds the promise for physical immortality and a new form of humanity, a new species of humanity, as different to today as we are to the previous species that preceded us. Sahu holds this possibility, which becomes actualized with connection to Akhu. To do this means we have to die to ourselves and touch into a new genetic field that is discontinuous with the genetic and mass-consciousness fields of present-day humanity. In this we start to create new physical bodies that age and heal differently and that work differently, as they work with eternal light.

As we expand our identity from Ka and Ab to the galactic soul or Ba, we enter the universal body and start to embody Sahu. As Ka is the seat of individual consciousness, which, when connected to the other bodies, becomes personal or human enlightenment, and just as the Ba becomes galactic enlightenment, Sahu is cosmic consciousness in the causal level of existence. On death or in a near-death experience, each individual glimpses the Sahu. It is at this time that one sees the light and can walk toward it. If this occurs, it means you have not embodied that light in your present existence and have to be reincarnated again in order to bring the Sahu, the immortal body of the universal soul, into conscious awareness while incarnated. You have to start again.

Within the universal body we start to work with universal forces beyond the galactic sphere. These forces are beyond what most humans usually comprehend, as the laws here are different to the previous bodies. In each different light body, new laws and ways of perceiving are presented for us to master and integrate. In Sahu, the previous laws, while being integrated, make us follow a different path, a path not comprehended by most people as it is out of their experience and knowledge base. People living in Sahu are often misunderstood as they follow a set of laws most do not understand and are guided by universal forces in their lives and in their service. Their actions may not be understood in the world, yet they follow a different compass as their consciousness is situated beyond temporal laws and behaviors.

## Sahu and Akhu

Sa is the first breath outward, the first breath of life. Akhu means without breath, the Source from where the first breath comes. Source is Akhu, and Sahu is its emanation in its most subtle form, like the first opening of a lotus's petals as the sunlight dances on the water—the purest light, the first light emanating from the Galactic Center, the pulsating womb of all possibilities seething in the stillness.

Sa is the spiraling forth of Akhu, but it is in manifestation, still, but incredibly creative as well. It is where the Neters live and commune, sharing themselves as one ever-changing stream of vibration, a holographic communion sharing the same continuum of energy, thoughts,

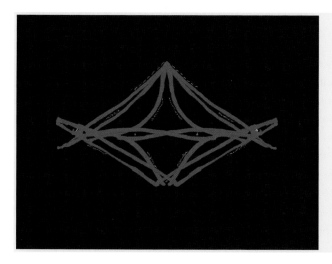

**A rendition of the Sahu light body.** (Padma Aon)

ideas, brilliance, love, and mastery. With each opening into this ocean of the Neters consciousness, more waves arise in the sea of perceptions that are the Neters, the powers and principles of consciousness. Each breath reveals a new Neter, revealing a different ray of light from the one Source of all.

Sahu is the thread that weaves and unites all the Neters into the immortal Boat of Ra, the light body vehicle of all the Neters, guided by Thoth and guarded by Anubis (with both serving Ma'at). Sahu is the breath of God, the powers of creation manifesting all life, the building blocks or frequencies that create the DNA template, found in the sixty-four Neters and sixty-four codons. It is a spiraling sequence of light-filled geometry and compassion woven together into form. It is the fertile creativity and regenerating of Pan/Asar married with the geometric formation of existence and love in Metatron, or Thoth.

This is all breath, all creation. Before the breath lies Akhu, birther of the breaths of creation.

## Hu

Both the immortal bodies of Akhu and Sahu end with the word Hu. What is Hu? Hu is a universal sound found in many traditions, from the Egyptian to the Sufi to Eckankar. Hu is the word of creation that Atum was said to have exclaimed upon ejaculating in his act of creating the Nine Primary Neters, or Ennead.[2] Sahu is the union of you with your Neter, a merging with the divine. You become one of the Neter principles and immortal after you pass through the Duat, guided by Anubis, and become Asar/Osiris, or Ast/Isis.

---

2. The Neter principle Hu was also depicted in the retinue of Thoth, and both Hu and Sia were seen as two of the fourteen creative powers of Amun-Ra.

Hu is a name of God, the sound of the universal sound current, similar to *om* in Hinduism. It takes one into the infinite sound current, which is why the two immortal bodies of light, Sahu and Akhu, both have the sound *hu* in them. Sa is the eternal life flow. In ancient Egypt the true term for this body was Sa O Hu, or Saohu. Sound them both aloud now and notice the difference. Saohu goes deeper into the heart, into the cavern of the heart, whereas Sahu is more open and expansive. This is because Saohu brings the universal body into the heart, into embodiment, whereas Sahu expands us into the universal body. One expands, and one contracts. If one is situated in the soul Ba, Sahu allows one to expand out from the Ba, the galactic consciousness, into universal consciousness, our local universe. If one is connected to Sahu, Saohu brings this into the heart and body.

Hu is the power of the word, the authority of utterance, one of the names of God that when chanted can bring us back to this aspect of God found in each out-breath we expel.

In the first creation, Ra drew blood from his own penis and created the gods Hu and Sia. Hu and Sia were partners; Sia was the personification of divine knowledge, the in-breath of God, and Hu was the embodiment of divine utterance, the voice of authority, the out-breath of God coming into expression and manifestation. Heka, or divine power, accompanied these two Neters as the union of wisdom and creativity coming together into manifestation. Hu and Sia are the creative power of the gods.

Hu is the breath of God. Like Ha or Hum in India, it is associated with breath and creation, and Sia is like the Sa or So in India. Together, they are the primordial breath mantra: Sa Ham or So Hum, and Sia Hu is the Egyptian equivalent. This is, of course, very similar to the word *Sa Hu,* and was quite possibly a version of Sahu used: Sia Hu.

Try this now:

On the in-breath, silently intone *Sia.*

On the out-breath, silently intone *Hu.*

Now try it with sound.

On the in-breath, sound aloud "Sia." Draw in this energy
of wisdom.

On the out-breath, sound aloud "Hu." Expel the energy
of creation.

Do this for five minutes. How do you feel?

There is a natural expansion to the Sia on the in-breath that aligns your light bodies together. The sounding of Hu completes the circuit. This breath can also be used in lovemaking, when exchanging breath between partners, and of course to replicate the original act of creation in orgasm: Hu.

In the Eckankar religion, the singing of Hu's name acts as a spiritual connection to the heart of God: Sahu and Akhu. In tantra, this breath practice is used to enter deep states of meditation that lead into deeper states of consciousness. Did this all come originally from Egypt?

In the Egyptian *Book of the Dead,* the ceremonies of Hu and Sa are mentioned but not explained, as this was oral knowledge. These ceremonies can be done every day within you through breath and sound and can also be done on a mass scale with a group of men singing "Hu" lined up on one side of a room, and a group of women singing "Sia" on the other, all aligned to the in-breath and out-breath (or alternatively the Indian versions with "So" or "Sa" and "Ham" or "Hum"). This can create a powerful entrainment effect, aligning both groups, both polarities, together in a visceral manner. The power of group consciousness accelerates all changes and all merging.

Sahu is the union of polarities—of wisdom, creation, and power being borne through the breath and sound of creation into us. Akhu is the union of all frequencies across the spectrum of creation with the source and origin of all awareness that then becomes embodied into human form, or the Khat, where our human journey begins and ends.

# Black Light

Paradoxically, Sahu can be ignited and embodied through darkness, and what is known alchemically as the Black Light. Black Light is the space where all creating arises from and where all creating dissolves back into. Before there was light and an idea of darkness lies Black Light, the sweet and loving silence of emptiness, the heart surrendered.

Black Light feels like your heart is gently but perpetually breaking wide open, with no object for its breaking. It is crystal clarity, pure, deeply touching, and feminine in vastness. There is no object for its love and compassion for there is nothing there, no reference point, no concept or form, nothing to hold onto, no memory, no past, no future.

The universe is pervaded by this tender loving presence, holding you, unfolding all that you are, containing all that you are. It is the deepest intimacy you can ever know. It embraces you, not you it. It touches you in places nothing else can and nobody else ever will. It makes you cry for it is the deepest remembrance of love a human can ever have.

Suns are grown from the Black Light, and when they explode into supernovas they return into Black Light. The Black Light is the beginning and end of creation. When you are born you come from Black Light. When you die you go through the Black Light as the soul makes its journey back to Source.

Black Light is the greatest alchemy. It transforms by holding and bringing everything that you are back into its pure, undifferentiated, unformed state: original innocence. In this state all wounds can dissolve and all things are made possible. All things are made new. The Black Light is the state from which all realities arise. Christ, Buddha, and others have all had to enter Black Light to bring forth their transformative actions onto the earth plane, to ground these actions onto the earth plane.

In Egypt these initiations were given to those who had completed the first part of the Black Light in the Pyramid Initiations and were ready for the next step. In Tibet these initiations to various *dakinis,* or female Buddhas, such as Ekajati, are given to those bodhisattvas who have conquered the fear of death.

Christ Yeshua embodied Sahu fully upon his Resurrection, which is why he asked not to be touched as he was in his pure light body. Similarly, John the Beloved and Elijah physically "ascended" with their bodies disappearing. In Tibet the Sahu is known as the Rainbow Body. Bodhisattvas cultivated this body so that when they left their physical bodies, all that was left was hair, teeth, and the skull. This is seen as one of the highest achievements in Tibetan Buddhism, as it signifies complete mastery over the elements and creation itself. You literally embody pure light on every level.

## Sahu Tantra: Merging Form and Formless

Akhu is the soul Ba raised into its Source in the Hu bodies of light. In order for Akhu to be realized, the Sahu body has to be germinated from the womb or grail, generated through the potent energies of life force. When this Sekhem, the soul Ba and heart Ab, are held in the union of sexual-spiritual love or conscious lovemaking between man and woman, this energy is held and nurtured in the open womb and then recirculated between both people into all parts of their body to birth a new person, or a "golden embryo." This is what Christ did when in union with Mary Magdalene; his Sahu was birthed from their sacred lovemaking, which then prepared him for the death of his physical body in the Crucifixion and the Resurrection of his Sahu.

This union is a flowing of divine fire, symbolized by the phoenix, which led into the initiations of the Hu bodies. This can be enacted by a man and woman making love together in *yab-yum*—the highest form of tantra in which both Ba souls unite with the Sekhem in love in order to enter Sahu. This act stimulates the heart and brain chakras in alliance with the womb center, leading to the birth of the Sahu, the "golden embryo," so both man and woman could enter Sahu, the luminous field of liquid light that permeates all creation.

This is mentioned in the first beatitude of Christ Yeshua, given on the Mount of Beatitudes in Palestine after his forty-day fast in the desert, where he activated the Sahu light body. In this first beatitude, he says, "Restored and aligned are those who reestablish their home through breathing in the luminous field of living energy suffusing creation." This luminous field that surrounds us all, known as *lehmeskenaee* in Aramaic, is the first step in embodying the Sahu, or becoming transfigured by the light.

Sahu is all eight aspects of Self, all energies and all intelligences, moving together in harmony and alignment, embodying the immortal and infinite, the emptiness and fullness, in form. All eight can be felt, from light to sexual energy, from love to expanded perception, from bliss and lightness of the body to the universal feelings coursing through you, and everything in between. All frequencies are available within this spectrum, all notes on the keyboard of creation, so you have to be discerning about which notes you give conscious energy and time to.

Tantra is the science of weaving the contradictory aspects of your self into one unified whole for the purpose of expanding consciousness. The highest tantras bring these energies of wholeness up and down through the body and chakras, integrating silence, light, bliss, sound, and sexual power to take us back to the primordial experience of unified creation: how we are created.

Tantra works on the universal principle that everything is already here—everything that we are, everything that God is to us, everything we have always desired and known ourselves to be. It is just our filters and conditioning that erect veils up to what is already, and always, ever-present.

## Yab-yum

Many tantric divinities are represented as being in union with consorts, and these forms are known as *yab-yum* ("father-mother") forms. Their union represents the inseparability of relative and absolute, manifestation and voidness, method and wisdom. They also symbolize the union of the "solar" and "lunar" energies, the two poles of subtle energy that flow in the subtle energy system of the human body, called the "Inner Mandala." When negative and positive circuits are joined in a lighting circuit, a lamp can be lit.[3]

Sexual energy is 20 percent of the tantric path. The highest form of tantra that can take you into Sahu is known as yab-yum. Yab-yum is a transmission and sacred practice that circulates sexual energy and light throughout all chakras, subtle bodies, and subtle energy pathways. This circulating of light and sexual energy completely throughout the body and all chakras means that many polarities and dualities can meet and recognize each other in order that they may dissolve and flow in loving emptiness.

Yab-yum is composed of two movements. The ascending wave is known as "riding the wave of bliss," which unites the sexual energy with light. Lust transforms into bliss through the ascending wave of

---

3. John Shane, ed., *The Crystal and the Way of Light: Sutra, Tantra and Dzogchen, Teachings of Chogyal Namkhai Norbu* (Ithaca, NY: Snow Lion, 2000), 102.

kundalini energy that rises up from the root chakra into the heart and brain, where the electrical charges of the chakra polarities meet and transform into light. The second movement is known as the descending wave, which connects the body of light into the physical body. The descending wave of light has no polarities and moves down through the body from the crown chakra to the root.

The art of yab-yum, or sacred union, is perhaps one of the fastest if not the most demanding ways to do this in an embodied, integrated way. The merging of soul, flesh, light, and sexual energy in breath, movement, and stillness is part of the foundations of tantra: reweaving the fragmented and disparate parts of yourself back into wholeness through the temple of the body and its union with mind, soul, and Source.

In Egypt, this art was practiced extensively at different epochs in Egypt's history, depending on which pharaoh was in power. Similarly in India, Tibet, Nepal, Bhutan, and across the Himalayas, this practice was seen as the height of tantra because of its ability to bring people directly into the merging of the light bodies with the physical body: Sahu.[4]

## Sahu and the Galactic Center

The Sahu body of light holds the perfected templates for the human form and all the bodies of light in manifestation, both genetically and energetically. These perfected templates of health, well-being, and awakened consciousness can be accessed by connecting with Sahu, which emanates from the Galactic Center in super waves of light and radiation.

At the center of our Milky Way galaxy lies a massive black hole. This womb center of our galaxy emanates out umbilical cords resembling

---

4. For more information on yab-yum, see Padma Aon Prakasha, *The Power of Shakti* (Rochester, VT: Inner Traditions, 2009).

the spiraling structure of DNA, nourishing and connecting all within its system, just as umbilical cords from the placentas of our mothers connect to us. These cords connect us all to the black hole, the galactic womb, at the center of our galaxy. Astronomers discovered this black hole in 2002, yet its presence, importance, and connection to Source have been known to the Egyptians, Mayans, and Indians for many thousands of years.

The Mayans call this cord of connection the Kuxan Suum, a lifeline of vibration and communication connecting us from our navels through a spiraling energetic umbilical cord to the Galactic Center, the womb of creation. This reconnection is set to more fully align to earth by 2012. In India this umbilical cord connects the god Vishnu through his lotus-shaped navel into the Padmanabhi, the lotus center, or Galactic Center, where he dreams creation into being. In Egypt, the god Khonsu acts as the umbilical cord to the Galactic Center, known as the all-powerful "hidden" god Amun, the god of the most powerful priesthood in Egypt.

All these traditions actively tapped into the Galactic Center through ceremony and ritual that were known to the leaders and priesthood of their societies. These shamanic seers, high priests, and healers were initiated into these mysteries to ride the Kuxan Suum to the Galactic Center in order to enter other dimensions, travel to other worlds, and to access secret and sacred knowledge about the mysteries of life and death: Sahu.

The Galactic Center is the source of this galaxy, from where this galaxy is birthed. Where the galactic equator crosses the ecliptic (the apparent motion of the sun's annual motion relative to the stars), Sagittarius points directly toward the Galactic Center. To observers on earth, this appears as a dark road that begins near the ecliptic and stretches along the Milky Way. Mayan creation myths share that creation takes place at this celestial crossroads and call it the road to Xibalba, the underworld or Egyptian Duat, known as the "Black Road." Through this entrance to the underworld, one can travel to the heart of sky, the Galactic Center.

The Galactic Center is a vast yet intimate space, peaceful but incredibly creative and ever-changing. It is the ground of being, still and silent, yet containing the surging exciting bliss and power of creativity within itself. Most people who experience their reunion with the Galactic Center describe it as unconditionally loving, accepting, and supporting of every part of them, as it gives us what we need. In this sense it is our mother, the galactic womb that nourishes us.

As we journey deeper, we experience the Galactic Center as a simultaneous experience of being creator and cocreated. You can experience yourself creating the world over and over again and seeing humanity creating itself over and over again throughout all the different epochs of history. It is here we realize our power as creators, and it is here that we can manifest this in ways that are unimaginable now, for the Galactic Center is the breath of God, inside and out, and it leads us to the pool of infinite creativity that we live in every day as we create everything moment by moment.

Your heart, womb, and hara are the gateway to the Galactic Center. It is you, and you are it. It is the black in the heart of light, and the blinding illumination found in the deepest recesses. It is from here that all grids and reconnections to the web of life are held, and it is here that our ultimate reconnection lies.

Within the Galactic Center is held the healing of all our ancestors and the remodeling of our DNA into a new human being. Within it, within you, is held the direct living experience of what it is to be a cocreator with the Creator. In the actual experience of immersing in the Galactic Center, we can become annihilated. Black holes literally absorb all light that comes into them to bring you into Black Light. All parts of you that are still attached will arise to be seen, and the immense love here will break down your constructs. When you are ready to immerse all of yourself into the Galactic Center, you will find that even your hard-won soul awareness has to be given up.

To enter this space with every part of your self means the dying of ego and soul, and the consequent resurrection of your bodies of light into Sahu. This resurrection and death is an octave higher than you have been before. Whereas before your ego died to resurrect with the soul as its master in the dark night of the soul, here the soul surrenders, dying a death so it can be mastered by Source. Now it is Source moving through you, with the soul as the servant.

Many highly evolved beings and stellar intelligences of great light live near the frequency and emanations of the Galactic Center. Some of them can withstand the high pressure and intensity of its emanations, and then modulate and share its energy with humanity in differing forms that we can handle and absorb safely. Some of these waves emanating from the Galactic Center are surfacing as new healing modalities, such as Reconnective Healing and Ilhanoor.

To enter this Sahu state, we have to travel through the intense energies of time and all our experiences in all our lifetimes. This is a powerful journey that all of us are taking right now, combining many lifetimes of experience to integrate them all in order to be present to this ending of a huge galactic cycle and the beginning of another. In this process we learn to live in the present, bringing every part of ourselves back together again, weaving ourselves into the web of life. In doing so, we become conscious cocreators and live our soul purposes fully, giving freely of our gifts to humanity.

## Continual Birthing

Continual birthing is birthing your self in each and every moment. This allows us to continually recreate ourselves by letting go of every past moment and embracing the newness of the present moment, coming into the power to create who we are and what we want to express and share with others.

In the experience of being reborn in every moment, we have the power to choose again who we are, what we feel, what we think, and how we choose to respond to the same situation that is presented to us. We can seize this moment and allow the birthing to take place. This birthing sets in motion a whole stream of new moments, each moment holding infinite possibilities for new creations and new ways of being.

Continual birthing is how we cocreate with this infinitely creative wave of Sahu from the Galactic Center. We realize and we choose again and anew as we align to this subtlest yet most powerful creative flow as it manifests itself through the dynamism and transparency of living form. It dissolves that which you no longer have need for and which limits. It conceals that which you know you have but which has yet to manifest in your life. It reveals that which accelerates your evolution with the unexpected meeting, person, event, or situation.

It flows through us, vibrating our body-mind at 570 trillion Hertz per second. We are moving incredibly fast every single second of our lives—we are just not aware of it. We are birthing and rebirthing every single moment, moving with this wave, this dance happening all the time. It is the threadlike link between the material and the formless realms, flowing through us and all things perpetually, without ceasing.

Continual birthing in the Galactic Center shows us this is the Wheel of Life, the "hollow bone, the sacred hoop" through which life sings us, through which spirit moves, through which the song is sung through the conduit of our bodies. This is the "everything and nothing," the magic of nothing working within the loving field of everything. And this is within us now.

The Galactic Center is the gravitational center of the Milky Way galaxy. It can also be detected by listening for the "sounds" it creates, sound here being energy carried by gravitational waves. NASA's *Chandra* X-ray observatory detected these sound waves for the first time, recording a "note" that is the deepest ever detected from any object in the universe. In musical terms, the pitch of the sound generated by the black hole translates into the note of B flat, fifty-seven octaves lower than middle C, a frequency over a million billion times beyond the limits of human hearing.

The image from NASA of this black hole also shows two vast bubble-shaped cavities, each about fifty thousand light-years wide, extending away from the central supermassive black hole. These cavities, which are bright sources of radio waves, are not really empty but filled with high-energy particles and magnetic fields. They push the hot X-ray-emitting gas aside, creating sound waves that sweep across hundreds of thousands of light-years. The tremendous amounts of energy carried by these sound waves have already solved long-standing problems in astrophysics by explaining some of the formation of the universe.

The vacuum of a black hole is made of a perfect circle. If we draw lines radiating out from a perfect circle, they all meet in an optical illusion known as *prägnanz*—a circle that is there but not there, as it is not actually drawn but formed by the lines themselves. The lines are infinite emanations of this vacuum. They are the vacuum, or void in movement, the directions of light moving after the initial creation of our universe. The central point or bindu is the point where all lines meet and dissolve into. This is the goal of many meditation practices, whereby all thoughts, feelings, and perceptions are drawn into a single point, and by entering this point of intense focus and concentration of all forces, you go beyond it into "no point" or boundless space.

In prägnanz, there is no difference between the lines and the vacuum itself. The lines and the infinite circle are the same. This is described in quantum physics as null lines, the paths taken by light rays and massless particles. Indeed, a geometry based on null lines alone is the grail of quantum physics, for in a universe having such a geometry, mass does not exist. All null lines always have zero length, with scale and distance also being zero.

In other words, all distances, times, and ideas of large or small, micro and macro no longer exist, and therefore no time would elapse from traveling from one point to another. In these terms, not even one second passes from the time you leave, say, Sirius, to reach earth, for along such a null line the distance to the stars is zero. When you look along a null line, nothing separates you from all that you see in the universe around you. In fact, you are everything that you perceive around you in all directions—there is no separation.

## Sahu: The Hymn to the Great Heart

This hymn arose from immersion in Sahu, and it is a meditation that you can say aloud to deepen into the energetic flow of Sahu. This can help to enliven the mind of Sahu through understanding, bringing it into a space of no-mind, which is the mind of Sahu. While this is a paradox, the mind can be trained to let go of itself by surrendering to that which is beyond it. Reading this hymn is a good place to start to deepen in Sahu, by meditating on each stanza.

> Vulnerability leads to venerability
> May the will of the great heart suffuse and penetrate me in
>     silence
> May the pure heart lead me even beyond the gods,
> beyond the pleasures of even celestial realms,
> beyond the realms of suffering disguised as sport, as distraction,
>     of attaining

May I listen to the voice of the still heart
Needing nothing, compassionately present for everything
May the still heart guide my acts
So my body can heed its calls
May the wonder of it all take me home
To the place beyond all gods and obeisances
To the shining star blue that is silent
The gift of love
Suffusing my Ka, stilling my Ab, opening my Ba

May the pure light lead to strength of heart
For from strength comes trust and from trust arises reliability
What is always here and never goes away
Dependent on no one, nothing, no god, animal, or woman

May the pure heart dispel all fear, all striving, and all thoughts
May its sweet heartbreaking silence penetrate all of me
Uniting all my bodies into one breath that is breathless

May my vulnerability be my sanctity
May my sanctity be my cloak
May my open heart be strong and still, soft and open, penetrated
    yet suffused
Descending into all parts

May my thoughts be turned to the heart-mind
May my feelings be wheeled around to silence
May my actions be empty
May my heart penetrate others; may the tears flow
May the fears of others be brought into its embrace

Fire in light, the light within all fire
Passion is brought into stillness
To rest gently without becoming

Expressed within the silence
Pure heart rests in its light
Beyond this mortal plane
All is held within this purity
A field found deep in your heart
The smallest of places, the most infinite of beings

May the will of the great heart suffuse and penetrate me
    in silence
May the pure heart lead me even beyond the gods

*On ab ur am*

In Sahu, desires turn into dharmas
Sadness becomes emptied of its contents

The emptiness and illusion of collective constructs of perception
    and beliefs
Are because they do not have the greatest love behind them
They do not require love to exist
As they need other things to exist, other things to make them
    what they are,
They form their identities because of relationship
If relationship makes you what you are, then you are not whole

To see the illusion, to see the emptiness of all constructions
Through the softly loving pearl heart Ba Hu

Truth is cognized with mind wisdom and pure heart compassion
Heart softly breaking in every moment
Flickering pearl-white flame
Deep in the center of blackness

Hope is the first and last feeling to arise in the emptiness
Hope is fear's weapon to keep the mind's clock ticktocking
Hope of any relationship that would keep the web of
     interconnection still pulsing

One is always alone
Nothing outside of itself, empty of contents
No need, no hunger, satiated in itself
The alone heart
The emptying of all need, of all webs
Until one is center of the web
King or queen of Self
The headdress of the servant
Here to help

Love flourishes in the emptied mind
Free of contents and need to be defined or created by any other
All there is left in the emptied mind is loving wisdom
And skillful means to extricate others from the contents of mind
And its tangled network of self-affirmation and validation
Stating "I exist because of something else"

I am that I am; I exist because I do
Naked singular alone heart,
Pulsing wisdom, silent, and still

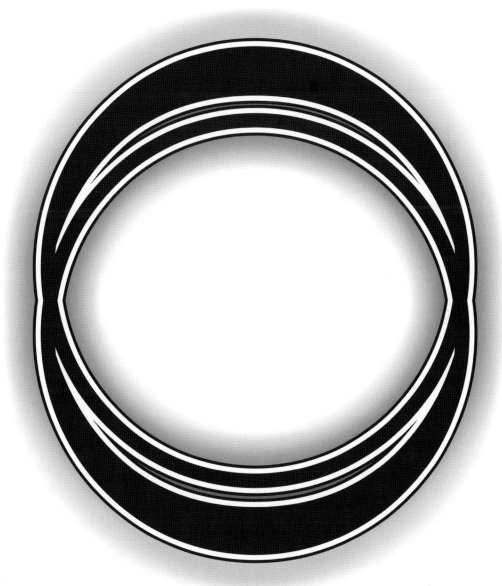

Anaiya Aon Prakasha

# ~9

# AKHU: THE SHINING ONE

Akhu is represented by a crested ibis bird feather coming out from the back of the head near the crown chakra and reaching upward. This is what happens when you connect to Akhu; the feather is a type of antenna that gets anchored into your brain through the pineal and pituitary glands from the back of the brain. This is a very tangible experience felt in deep meditation in Akhu, and it is extraordinarily powerful in the subtlest realms of pure formless light.

Akhu is the immortal god-self that manifests through the Sahu, or immortal body. In Egypt, the ancestors were known as Akhu, or the Shining Ones, a reference to the ancestors from Sirius. Akhu was often described as a flame of fire of the transfigured spirit, known as the Shining One or Luminous One. Beyond the Ba, and that which the Ba dissolves and surrenders into, Akhu is the source of Sahu and is one's highest spiritual self, the immortal and imperishable spirit uniting your human and your highest Self.

In the Pyramid of Unas, the words KHU KHU KHU are inscribed with the stars that are emblazoned on the ceiling. It is the Self that is reborn as a star, which then gives life to whole systems.[1] In ancient Egypt this entailed the initiate entering the hearts of different stars in meditation, to then merge with the intelligence and unique quality of that star. To enter into the heart of a star and merge with it in a guided sequence that was known and mapped by the ancient Egyptian and Atlanteans is to become a star. In becoming a star, one then connects to the other stars that are intertwined with that star's vibration, leading one closer and closer to the black hole or Galactic Center at the source of this galaxy. This in turn is a portal to other galaxies and other universes, where the laws of this universe cease to exist and where supramental intelligences reside and operate in a different form to what is known here in this universe.

This is a powerful experience felt through the pineal and crown chakras in pure light. In Akhu, one can take all their other bodies of light and dissolve them back into their source consciously when one is ready, realigning and rebalancing all bodies. This means that you can bring the shadow back into its source, for example, integrating the final aspects of the shadow when you have done enough work with it. You can also integrate the Khat, the physical vehicle for Akhu in the human expression, which is a process whereby matter itself changes and adjusts to Akhu. This can be a painfully blissful process as spine, brain, and body shift calibration and open up the body form in the deepest possible way. It can leave one feeling ungrounded in the earth plane, as you are living pure spirit without any trace of duality or need of integration. However, this is a stage, for to embody both Hu bodies requires bringing it into form over a period of time.

Like a star being born, Sahu is ignition from Akhu, the breath of Sahu from the formless Akhu expressing into crystalline geometric form. If we look at the name Akhnaton (immortal ruler), we see this name means the being who can live in this reflection and hold it for his people as a ruler, a reflection of Akhu in form—what we are all striving to be: light embodied. This is what Akhnaton brought back to Egypt: the embodiment of light in physical form.

It is rare for an individual to experience Sahu and Akhu. Perhaps the

---

1. Khus of highly evolved beings are up to thirteen feet tall and iridescent green like Osiris.

highest percentage of people alive today who experience Akhu are advanced Tibetan Buddhist lamas, who access it through the Sambhogakaya, Nirmanakaya, and Dharmakaya bodies of light. There is a great similarity between these two traditions in their most refined aspects, with the similar understanding of universal or clear mind that is a navigating principle of the Hu bodies. Perhaps this can be traced back to their shared original Atlantean heritage, the original source of these teachings.

Akhu is the imperishable, immortal effective spirit, experienced and allowed into the consciousness of one who is already identified with the immortal and has opened, cleared, and become conscious of the interaction and merging of the Ka, Ba, and the Khat. Living in Akhu is when we are effective in all we do, and connected to all life, when all nine of our bodies commune through the heart-pineal and the whole stream of chakras beyond the physical body.

Akhu is the whole person situated in imperturbable and unconditional love, peace, and power—fearless and beyond the power of death, regenerated and resurrected, as Christ demonstrated in his union of Sahu and Akhu facilitated by his union with Magdalene and his Higher Self of Maitreya, the cellular makeup changes into the geometries and sequences of light. DNA changes and shifts to incorporate many more strands physically in the body.

Within Akhu is where all gods and Neters are birthed from and dissolve back into their formless beginnings. It is that which lies before the creation of the world and the return into that state. This great flame was known as the Holy Spirit to the Apostles of Christ, who were anointed by Akhu after the Resurrection with this flame blazing above their heads. The Egyptians saw Akhu as the phoenix, the great blazing cosmic fire of resurrection, regeneration, and new creation.

The word *akh* comes from a root that means "to be effective," to have power and ability. Akh means that you have the ability to travel through and act in all the realms of this world, and all others. To become an Akh, or Shining One, means that you have extended your awareness and functionality to all forms of existence.

Akhu is the soul or Ba made into God, the shining transfigured soul that is free to become anything at any time. This total fluidity, of allowing oneself to be anything at any time that best serves any situation or person, means that one has total mastery and emptiness, that in turn allows one to access any frequency, any note on the scale of creation while simultaneously being unborn: not of the creation. This freedom and mastery allows one to give in any and every way, as there is no agenda or obstacle to being what is required of your empty vehicle and surrendered Ba soul in any moment.

Akhu is a step beyond the Ba soul, which is what most humans are striving for. The Ba is the goal of most spiritual work, and the establishing of a Ba-oriented civilization on earth, a fifth-dimensional civilization, is the most pressing goal for humanity at this time, and at least for the next fifteen years. Beyond the Ba, one has to surrender their soul to Akhu, which means the absorption of the Ba soul back into its Source, that which has never been created and never been destroyed. Once the Ba has returned to its source, then Akhu flies free, able to perform anything required of the flow of creation in any moment through your vehicle.

To enter Akhu is to surrender the Ba, and all the work you have done on yourself to become situated in the heart-soul, to the creator of the Ba: Akhu. It is from here that the phoenix arises in its flowing golden plumage and iridescent Rainbow Body to become the Shining One, with access to every note of the creation precisely because it is beyond the manifest creation: in the world but not of it, human but immortal. In Egypt the phoenix was seen as the flame from where all fires started, the source of the spark of the soul. From this source, all sparks of the One Flame arise.

This surrender moves throughout various stages on your journey as you evolve and shed the veils and illusions that stop you from becoming totally fluid and present, able to be and relate to anything at any time, to enter into anything or anyone at any time in order to serve and expand the potential of that person, being, or situation. This is the highest form of giving, which is the characteristic of awakening.

## The Sound of Surrender

Surrender is how Akhu manifests; it is the open gate for Akhu to walk into us, the different levels that we can surrender to arise from both ego and ultimately soul. You have to surrender your shadow to your soul Ba, and then you have to surrender your soul Ba to Akhu. This is the journey of evolution, the journey of surrender.

Both Sanskrit and Egyptian languages, cultures, and spiritual practices share similar roots, both in the languages that form part of the seven root languages from which all other languages derive and in their shared roots from Atlantis. Today, much of the original Egyptian culture and language has been lost, but can be discerned through looking at aspects of the Vedic culture.[2]

In India, Namah is the sound of surrender and the sound of connection. Namah is the sound of surrender to the energy of the quality of the divine within the mantra, the life flow that animates and enlivens the mantra. It has seven different layers of meaning, resonance, and embodiment to it. As the ending of most Sanskrit mantras, Namah sends energy to the aspect of the divine that one is connecting with by fully opening yourself to it and surrendering to it.

Namah is correctly pronounced with the "ah" at the end of the

---

2. For more details see Robert E. Cox, *Creating the Soul Body* (Rochester, VT: Inner Traditions, 2008).

word being said with a silent sibilant out-breath that sends life force out into silence, the gap between thoughts where manifestation of the divine occurs.

The first layer of meaning of Namah is the most commonly known: to bow down to God. The second meaning is to pay obeisance to or pay your dues to the God in the hope of dissolving karmas and attaining more humility. The third is to offer something or desire something from the God in hope of attaining something of material or egoic benefit.

The fourth level is to open up to the God, humbly and in reverence, from the soul. The fifth level is to surrender your soul to the God's will, to allow the Shakti to flow as it wishes beyond your control and conscious awareness and desire.

The sixth is to open up and surrender your soul without limits: *na* meaning "without," *mah* meaning "limits." Without wanting for self, or needing to gain anything for self, here there is no self as a conduit for the divine to flow and act as it wishes for the highest benefit.

Here comes a vital discernment between ego, soul, and God. The ego is working on the first three levels of Namah. The soul then takes over in the next two levels of Namah. God/Akhu itself is the sixth and seventh levels of Namah, as the soul surrenders its identity or higher Self into Akhu/God.

Within Namah is the basis of the spiritual path. As one journeys through life, working and healing, the ego starts to become the servant of the soul. When the soul becomes the ruler of the ego, selfless service, love, and joy become the foundation of your life. In truth, the ego is a servant of God, designed to accomplish organizational, linear, and mundane tasks as an automatic response. In today's culture it is the reverse: the ego has become master of soul in the distorted perceptions of the human mind-set.

As you move forward, the soul becomes more dissolved in deeper states of peace that require a deeper effort to attain for the soul that is now happy to reside in itself. The soul can get stuck at this time, and it takes a great effort to move beyond this point of soul contentment that is still not enlightenment.

As the soul moves deeper into peace, the mind that is part of the soul gets dismantled as the soul actively surrenders totally, giving its all so it can be dissolved completely as a conduit. The seventh resonance of Namah is to enter Akhu, to embody and transmit its qualities. This seventh level is the difference between a priest or priestess and a high priest or priestess. The priest o priestess makes offerings and channelings in service of the God for the people who wish to attain something. The high priest or priestess embodies Hu and transmits its transformative or healing power directly to those who are sincere and ready to receive those who are surrendered.[3]

## The Indestructible

The Egyptians saw that the world and the microcosm of our bodies have three parts: the sky, the earth, and the Duat. We each have these three parts of a body, like the earth, a Ba soul or sky being, which is essentially divine, and the Ka, the interface and connector between them. The site of this union is the magically reconstructed body: Sahu, which is in itself only fully embodied through your connection to Akhu.

Akhu is Self-luminous and indestructible. To embody Akhu, one has to merge their Ka and Ba into Sahu and include their physical bodies within this process. Indeed, all Nine Bodies have to be balanced and harmonized together for Akhu to be realized. Relationship and intimacy can perhaps be seen as a great key to this unfolding into Akhu,

---

3. For a more detailed understanding of surrender, see Padma Aon Prakasha, *The Power of Shakti* (Rochester, VT: Inner Traditions, 2009).

once you are clear of the needs, desires, and attachments that keep you in the shadow.

To access this, we have to excavate the contents of the mind and the bodies, the principal ones being the shadow's link to the soul Ba. Ba can reveal uncharted vistas of consciousness and a free interplay of energy, and this integrates through the balance of your heart, letting the forces that influence you come to a state of peace. Having established this peace, it is possible to explore and take your consciousness into the realms that usually lie hidden to you, with the ultimate goal of unifying all the parts of your being into the indestructible light body of the Akhu.

You enter Akhu when you have integrated all the other bodies, as Akhu permeates all the other bodies and is their Source. Akhu is living an extraordinary life in a totally ordinary fashion. We integrate and experience everything without aversion or attachment and become masters because we can live all aspects of life, from the most mundane to the most esoteric. We live, like Akhu, in all life and its aspects, able to fluidly move from one to the other without charge, preference, or attachment. We are grounded in the earth with our head in the stars. "After the bliss comes the laundry," as Jack Kornfield says.[4]

Akhu includes all the aspects of Self, all the Nine Bodies within itself in its unformed potential state, from the immortal, universal, deathless unborn Self to the human Ka and Khat, the human body. Even in the human body is found Khu, for we are the stuff that stars are made of, and even in the deepest recesses of matter, Khu is. When Ba realizes the infinite Khu, its awareness dissolves into the infinite Khu all the way across the spectrum of frequencies. Akhu ultimately controls all other bodies, having the ability to reprogram them. As the seat of all awareness, it holds no differentiation: everything is divine.

---

4. Jack Kornfield, *After the Ecstasy, the Laundry: How the Heart Grows Wise on the Spiritual Path* (New York: Bantam, 2000).

Akhu is the simple sheer is-ness of being, completely free and clear of any and all identification with anything. It does not hold anything within it, not even possibilities or potential: this occurs in the creative emanation of Sahu. To enter this state prematurely would drive most people insane, as it would destroy all their notions of identity, even divine identity. In Akhu, even the idea of a soul does not exist.

Akhu is the highest spiritual body, is totally one with God, and cannot be swayed by any personal agendas. To access this requires initiation, deep sustained meditation, and grace. Grace in this sense is not being given something unexpectedly; it is a conscious cocreating with Source that is accessed when one is conscious enough of all their bodies, and in their own mastery, to enable them to consciously enter Akhu when ready. This is a two-way meeting between the free Ba soul ready to surrender itself totally and completely, allied with the knowing of Akhu that your Ba is ready to let go. Once this meeting is established, then Akhu reveals and guides your surrendered Ba into its source.

Experiencing Akhu is a deeply mystical experience felt in the crown and brain chakras. Akhu is one of the mantras used by initiates as they entered the stairwell leading to the sarcophagus in the King's Chamber, as it resonated the sonic cavities in the pyramid and brought awareness to the initiate of the Khu body to prepare him or her for the galactic Ba initiation. (This is a powerful and deeply familiar experience for those who take this initiation.) This is because the law of octaves tells us that in order to integrate one level of energy, we have to go the next one beyond it. This is the same for all the bodies.

Akhu has no positive or negative charge, nothing to recognize, as it is within all. It has no ideas or concepts and nothing to measure itself against: no subject or object. Without qualities, Akhu can enter into every other number, into every other thing without changing it, as it is already there. This infinitely small, infinitely large placeholder that underlies all other dimensions is the Awareness that underlies all consciousness. In this respect it is like the number zero, the only number that is capable of "going into" all other numbers.

## The Khat-Akh

Akhu is an anagram of the word for the body: Khat. The Egyptians used anagrams to show similarities. For example, the Ab heart and Ba soul, each one being a gateway to the other, and each one merging with the other. This clever anagram and merging of Akhu and Khat, with Akhu having the all-important Ah before it, shows that Akhu has created the body, and that it is the total opposite of the body: it is not form, it is formless. It also shows us that our goal is to bring Akhu, through the transfigured spine, deep into the body and the sexuality so they can meet. This was the purpose of Akhu and Khat for the Egyptians and is the highest purpose of all Egyptian spiritual teachings, temples, and wisdom: the merging of light and matter, and the embodiment of light into matter.

The transformed Khat can be made eternal. Yogis like Yogananda, Tibetan Buddhist masters who had acquired the Rainbow Body, Christ who transfigured into the Akhu and brought it into the Khat, and various other Christian saints and Taoist masters who created incorruptible bodies, all prove this. While the Khat is temporary for most of us, some masters have made it an eternal repository by bringing in such high quantities of light that the body itself becomes incorruptible and immortal. The body itself becomes crystalline, with the only remains at physical death being crystalline deposits or relics known as sel, and a few hairs, bones, and teeth left over.

The many tales of Himalayan masters living for hundreds of years, not to mention Thoth, who has reportedly been around for over fifty thousand years, confirm this possibility. This possibility is a closely guarded secret as it confers physical immortality on an individual by bringing Akhu into the Khat: bringing God into form, the ultimate act of embodiment.

Many Masters, like Sri Aurobindo, Padmasambhava, Christ, and others have all said that in order for humanity to evolve into its next phase of evolution, a new species would have to be born on earth, a species that would be as different from humanity today as we are to the evolutions that have preceded us. This means becoming biologically different, genetically different, and discontinuous with the structures of present-day humanity. This means separating from the mass consciousness of humanity and from our own bloodlines so we become genetically separate, unique, whole beings.

In this separation to become whole, you actually redeem your bloodlines, healing and liberating your whole ancestry to the extent they are able to let go. In practice this means that your mothers, fathers, daughters, and sons become separate from you because your DNA has changed, as well as your ancestors, stretching all the way back to your first ancestor. This is a wonderful thing! I feel unattached, free, open, more loving, and more joyous with my parents (and they both feel and experience it too) now that this genetic resonance has dissipated and has been transformed.

This knowing is not new—it has been realized by Christ Jesus, in the large-headed humans depicted in Egypt, by Sri Aurobindo and the Mother, and in the Rainbow Body of Tibet, where the body itself dissolves into light. This Rainbow Body, where all the elements and parts of the body become sublime light, and where upon death all that remains of the body is the skull, is the pinnacle of human achievement and the promise and prophecy for a new, biologically different, awakened humanity where man and woman walk equally together in harmony. To achieve this requires that we have to literally die to ourselves and the idea of ourselves in order to touch into a new genetic field discontinuous with the genetic and mass consciousness fields of present-day humanity.

# Light Body and DNA

The foundation of your light bodies corresponds to the vibratory infrastructure of the DNA, and your light bodies carry within them etheric strands of DNA that link the light bodies to the physical body, all the way to and from Khu. The blueprint of each soul is transferred through these etheric strands of DNA into your light bodies, with many strands of DNA lying dormant in your Ba, Sekhem, and Sahu. When the DNA field is cleared and transmuted, it aligns with your unique Ba or soul blueprint, and we can then connect directly to the Hu bodies. Here, we literally become "the road to the sky leading to the umbilical cord of the universe," connecting both us and the planet to the Galactic Center. These strands are cosmic lifelines of vibration and communication from us to Sahu, which then begin to resonate with Akhu.

When the DNA is cleared of ancestral patterns, family behaviors, and the Matrix mirror of the technosphere, we enter and access the "Thread of the One." In India this is also known as the Sutra Atman— the Thread of Souls. All souls are strung upon this thread, like pearls threaded on a silver string, connecting all life forms, humans, birds, animals, other civilizations in all distant parts of the galaxy, to the Creator and to each other. We are all like beads on a string, a "superstring" that weaves its way throughout all time, all space. We connect to this thread through our open crown chakras and our open root chakras—the thread just flows through us, and we can follow it with our awareness if we allow ourselves to.

This thread is also known as the Tortoise Tube. Enlightened ones are connected to the Sutra Atman on a higher plane of existence than most other life forms, yet the fact is that we are all connected on this thread, this infinite eternal column and pillar of light: the prayer that never ceases. The thread weaves the complex web of life on our planet. It is one strand weaving itself throughout time and space, with infinite perspectives contained within it derived from a single awareness connecting in an unbroken chain all the living beings of our world and our universe. This Thread of the One creates you, moment to moment, a chain that is unbroken between you and the birth of our universe 15 billion years ago.

The Hu bodies are the eternal part of your self that never die, that are not dependent on your body-mind or matter to exist. When these light bodies merge totally with your heart-soul and physical body, you have achieved the aim of human existence: the union of spirit and matter, of embodying light into form through your resonating crystalline structures.

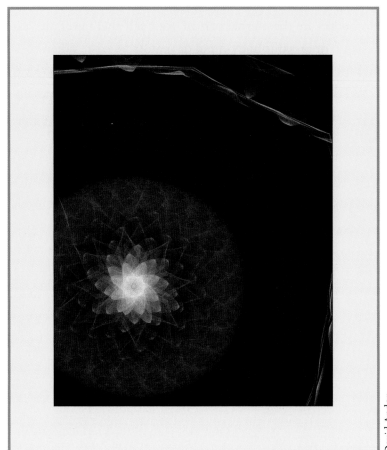

David Andor

# ～10

## THE HOLOGRAPHIC INTERFACE

### Looking at the Nine in Relationship to Each Other

The Nine Eyes of Light all arise from, merge, and commune in the imperishable light body matrix of the Sahu and Akhu. Paradoxically, it is in the union of Hu that one can then see the differentiation of all the bodies clearly. In this communion, one can see the different aspects of all the bodies in total interconnection, and focus on each one to see how it relates to the others. In this differentiation, one can see through the lens or eye of each body and how it perceives the other bodies through its own unique perspective. This is the holographic reality of the Nine Eyes of Light, and how the true pharaohs and spiritual nobility of Egypt created and viewed life using these Ascension Keys.

In the following piece, the Nine Eyes of Light are seen relating to and with each other, interconnecting and communicating. This can be likened to a series of nine mirrors facing each other, where different angles of light create different reflections and therefore differing relationships and perceptions. Even the slightest shifting of one of the mirrors creates a whole new angle of light, information, perception, and meaning. This is perhaps why the shamans and sages of sacred cultures worldwide are known as "seers," for they can "see" the unseen worlds and their different perceptions that the Nine Eyes map out so eloquently and elegantly.

We start with seeing the Nine Eyes through the physical body, and how it relates to all the other Eyes of Light. We then go through each of the Nine in turn.

## Looking through the Khat/Aufu: The Physical Body

Looking at the Khat through the Ka, one sees a dense network of flesh, bones, blood, lymph networks, and cellular matrices. In the spaces between these networks and cells, Ka lies as a fine smattering and network of golden light. Ka wants to open up the body more and more so more of its frequency can exist between the cells. It wants to improve communication between all body parts and bring more light into the body. Ka is the interface and wants Khat to connect with it completely in order for it to become a temple for all Nine Eyes to coexist together in harmony.

Looking at the physical body through Ren, one can see sequences of letters creating the meridian lines of the body. These shimmering and glowing lines of letters connect the different organs and parts of the body, and form then becomes a mass of energy, color, sacred geometry, and light, breathing, pulsing, and dancing together.

Feeling the physical body in the flow of Sekhem, you feel the pulsing life force coruscating through you, weaving you into the undulating web of life. The physical body becomes a wave of light and life force, as you see where the sexual energy is flowing and where it is not. Seeing this connection allows you to bring Sekhem into the parts of the body where it is needed, and to see the body as a pulse and wave of life force. This is the function of the body in Sekhem, to merge with the web of life that runs through and connects all beings, celebrating the joy of life that connects us all.

Sensing the physical body through the Ab and Ba, you nurture and comfort your body, giving it what it needs to feel good, healthy, and vital. You open up the body through touch, massage, good food, and water so that more love can be present. Through the Ab you love your body, taking care of it to feel good, healthy, and well.

Diving into the physical body through the shadow, you see where the shadow is stuck in the body, how you have not dealt with it, and how you have ignored it. Connecting the Ab and the shadow to the body results in you seeing those parts you do not wish to see, and then loving them enough so they feel good about themselves, able to come into the light of your sympathetic, compassionate, and nurturing awareness.

Dissolving the physical body into Sahu, you see your body as the universal body. As above so below, your organs become stars, planets, and galaxies, and you realize you embody the universe within you. I am that, and here I am.

Akhu sees the physical body as a vehicle for bliss. There is no channeling, no downloads, nor anything that can be labeled as coming from within or without. All is present and normal yet magical. The physical fulfills its function, what Akhu has created it for, and all bodies live in harmony, together as one.

## Looking through the Ka: Holographic Interface

Seeing the Khat or physical body through the eyes of the Ka, one sees the grosser form of the freer and lighter subtle body. Encased in flesh and bone, the physical form of your self is natural but heavy, and it requires a lot of energy to sustain. It is limited to moving and being in one time and space, and it can only do a few things at a time. It cannot even live by itself. However, it fulfills its function, and Ka is glad it is there as its companion and harbor.

Seeing the Ka through the Ren, one can see the cellular networks of light that interpenetrate and weave all bodies together. Ka connects and weaves together body, earth, and beyond in threads and networks of light.

In aligning the shadow with the Ka, you can ignore the sense of feeling but not acting upon what you feel is right, relinquishing your power to something else. The veils of forgetfulness and elusive irritable feelings make Ka either flare up, fight, or flee. One may also feel a weak yet somehow endearing part of oneself, lost and needing nurturing and guidance like a child that cries and gets no response.

Feeling the Ab through the Ka, you feel the grounded power of being human. You use your personal power to put your heart's wishes and generosity into action and giving. You use your deeply feeling and caring nature to care for and help others, as well as to manifest what you feel passionately about, maintaining your values and principles. Ideally Ka connects with Ab and the shadow to feel what is happening and use the creative potential, imagination, and inspiration hidden in the gold of the shadow to free itself from limits.

Merging Ba and Ka, you enter the power and love of your soul: the Ka Ba. In gazing upon the power and glory of your Self, you merge both bodies to act as one vehicle to manifest soul on earth.

Feeling Sekhem and Ka, one can feel overwhelming and overpowering life force, that could get out of control, but which can also transform and liberate.

Merging Sahu and Ka, you see your God form, your true face, your gateway to Source. You know your power is universal power. Your Ka becomes a spark of light in the infinite fields of light; it is the end of what was the beginning, and the beginning of what will be the end. You use your power to connect to the greater power of surrender, and then surrender your soul to the infinite. Ka becomes a tool to ascend into Source.

Connecting Ka to Akhu, you use this first creative spark of individual manifestation so that you, the individualized spark of God, become fully manifested in the physical.

## Looking through the Shew: The Shadow

Through the physical body or Khat, shadow is noticed in pain, stiffness, disease, and suffering. It manifests to let you know there is something in the shadow to deal with what you have buried or ignored. Body becomes a voice for the shadow to be heard when we neglect it.

Through Ren, the shadow is seen as letters out of shape, disjointed, representing incomplete thoughts, words, and actions. The geometric frameworks of order and coherency lie dormant, veiled in dark murky colors. Lines are incomplete and broken. Colors are missing, represented as blank or gray spots needing new colors to complete it.

Through the Ka, the shadow can be seen as an evil twin, the part of itself that has been divorced from empowerment, love, and connection. Ka can dismiss the shadow unless the Ba and Ab intervene and point out the shadow and its needs and longings.

Uniting with the humble voice of the Ab, shadow feels embraced and accepting of self as you are. Embracing your deepest secrets and guilt, confessing, forgiving, and owning the lessons and sufferings you have created, in radical honesty and open vulnerability, you become the owner of your reality, not the victim. Through Ab, shadow is accepted, allowed, and brought back from the cold, from isolation and abandonment, into the light of day.

Ba sees shadow as a protector and guardian, a voice that reminds and looks out for you in the world, navigating you through life. It is a voice of embodiment, anchoring all parts of Self into a functional, integrated, whole person. With the shadow seen, embraced, and understood, Ba feels free to fly, as it knows that the shadow and the body are in harmony, acting as a foundation for it to return to the physical world.

Sekhem and shadow power unite to create fuel for empowerment and transmutation, a fuel for bliss and polarity to be focused through ruthless compassion, that which stops at nothing to liberate and transform. Harnessing the power of life force with the shadow can be dangerous, but if directed with the Ab Ba can be deeply transformative, humbling, and liberating, as shadow needs consciously directed life force for it to align the body-mind into the soul's knowing.

In Sahu the shadow is seen as an illusion, an ephemeral floating maze of dream worlds. Its amorphous and ever-changing nature are seen as bubbles on the surface of reality, random emotions of pain and ignorance bubbling to the surface to then disappear again, like a mirage that disappears once seen clearly. Its use as a creative force is harnessed dispassionately in order to serve and create more clarity and awareness. It is tended to with compassion, detachment, and wisdom.

Through Akhu, shadow is returned to alignment with Source in its essential pristine emptiness and integrated within the physical body and spine.

## Looking through the Ab: The Heart

Looking through the physical body Khat, Ab sees its vehicle. It tries to make it look prettier, to conform to what it is expected to look like, but ultimately it just wants to be comfortable. It listens to what its friends have to say about its appearance and wears what it feels comfortable with. It feels restricted to the body, but does not mind. In Khat, Ab is in duality, but does not mind so much, as it simply accepts itself and moves on with life in a pragmatic no-nonsense way.

Looking through the Ren, Ab sees beauty without understanding. It feels the colors, relaxes into them, and enjoys it. It appreciates the beauty of art for what it is without giving it any deeper meaning. It tries to understand, but eventually raises its hands and stops trying. While Ab has heart wisdom, it does not possess perceptual or higher-mind creative intelligence.

Looking through the Ka, Ab feels the charismatic power and presence of others. Starstruck, it will become fascinated and attracted to certain people magnetically, and enjoys the buzz and hype around powerful public figures. It can give its power away easily, while at the same time wanting this quality. It projects what it wants onto others. When Ka and Ab are centered, projection onto others ceases, as now you have that magnetic power, aura, inspiration, and intuition within your self.

Looking through the shadow Shew, Ab sees fear and confusion. It does not know quite what to do, except to stay firm in its values, its moral code, and what it feels is true for it in honor and integrity. It is loyal to this at all costs, even when other truths are presented to it. This is its boon and bane.

Uniting with the Ba, Ab sees itself reflected back in its full glory and power. It recognizes and aspires to this, even thinking that the Ba is God. At this point, Ab feels it has made it: that the path is done.

Looking through Sekhem, Ab sees power, sexuality, and attraction, and it fears that it might be overwhelmed, possessed, or lose itself. It feels the power yet is scared to let go, as it may mean the end of its existence. It admires this power, yet is fearful and unsure of how to wield it. It looks to its Higher Self, the Ba, for help in how to use this power that it is scared of.

Feeling the glory of Sahu, Ab sees the glory of God and can feel unworthy of this. It can feel the awe and insignificance of being so tiny in such a vast universe and becomes very quiet and humble.

Encountering Akhu, Ab passes out.

## Looking through the Ba: The Soul

In Ren and the physical Khat, Ba is a shimmering geometry and flow of light, a conduit of light codes and information streaming from above the crown and descending into the body, carried by the crystalline matrices of the body, to then circulate throughout all the chakras and body parts.

Through the shadow and Ka, Ba can be misunderstood as an antagonizer, a polarity that can be ignored or fought with. These swings, from shadow to soul and back again, keep reminding you that something is amiss. Do you listen to the voice of the shadow, or the soul? And which one is which? Which voice do you follow? This battle between Ba and shadow is fought within the Ka, culminating in the seeing and defeating of the pillar of the shadow, the evil twin of the Ka. Then, Ba assumes its ascendant role as guide of the shadow, with guidance and compassion for it. Ba includes, and shadow excludes, instead painting the future and the past with its own limited perception that suits its creation. Ba realigns the shadow so it can be informed and guided, taken care of and heeded, and placed into its rightful position as the servant of the Ba.

In the heart of Ab, Ba is seen as God. As Ab becomes clear, it embodies more of Ba, until they merge into Ab Ba. Each needs the other to remind and inform the other of their dual yet unified nature of mortal and immortal. Each reminds the other, as each one completes the other. The human values, purpose, and sense of feeling of the Ab merges with the celestial freedom and heavenly delights of the Ba. Together they manifest your soul purpose: what your Ba soul came here to do.

With Sekhem, Ba merges the heart and crown with the sexual and creative powers. Ba is the vehicle for Sekhem to manifest in its higher potentials, to share and give the most loving and compassionate power that is also the most blissful and delightful. Sekhem views the Ba as its playmate, standing together to create blissful love and sensual merging. It is here that conscious lovemaking really takes off.

In Sahu, Ba opens up, surrenders, and dissolves. Ba is its vehicle for expression on earth. Ba is how Sahu is easily managed and understood by others and can be expressed and enacted in physical form.

As Ba subsumes into Akhu, it resurrects as an individual spark of the Flame of the One Fire.

## Looking through the Ren: Name and Form

Seeing the physical body Khat through the lens of Ren, you see patterns of letters creating your form, which then dissolve into swirling shapes and colors, coalescing into geometries that then dissolve into light and then emptiness. Emptiness is the heart of each atom, and it is through the four layers of Ren that you can see the emptiness of all form.

Seeing the Ka body through Ren, you see the crystalline double of your physical body. You see the flaws and weaknesses of your physical double, and you see the cords, connections, and geometries of your Ka: the cube, the diamond, and a shimmering rainbow sphere connecting to your DNA, to Gaia, the solar system, the galaxy, and many other beings of light who live in your resonant frequency wave band.

Seeing the shadow Shew through the lens of the Ren, you can see a mass of swirling dark colors, as if an artist were painting with only a few colors on his palette. Brown, red, black, and muddy tones expose the deep wells of what you do not wish to see and that which you have buried. Broken lines and disconnected patterns dominate the landscape as different collages of images collide haphazardly. What you do not like to see in others is what you put here within yourself. The collected ranks and masses of humanity peer in on this canvas, somehow enjoying the show and play.

Seeing the Ab through the eyes of Ren, you see pleasant, glowing, content faces, living from the heart, open and amenable.

Seeing the Ba soul through Ren, one can see a spinning golden star above your crown chakra, a conduit to a seemingly infinite pillar of light, a rainbow bridge of vibration connecting to the heavens and beyond. Geometric forms play and move in this pillar, as its light descends into your body through flows of light and water.

Seeing Sahu and Sekhem through Ren, you can see a Cosmic Egg within which you, and the whole universe, sit. You can see everything containing everything else: you zoom into an object and see it is the gateway to every other object. You can see the fullness and dance of the whole of creation in every spark of light. Fertility, wonder, abundance, and fullness are everywhere. Everything is alive, part of the dance with you.

Seeing Akhu through Ren, you feel complete. You are able to see the sacred geometric frameworks of the universe and can ride on them, illuminate them, and create with them.

The coherency and order of your creation is laid out before you, and you see it all as perfect.

## Looking through Sekhem: Power

Feeling the Khat physical body in Sekhem, you experience true well-being and pulsing vitality, radiant and dynamic. You are clean and clear, exude and emanate life, and feel in balance and in tune with the elements and nature. Sun, air, good friends, and your joy for life provide the joy of life that touches, moves, and inspires you and others.

Seeing Ren through Sekhem, life force acquires direction and purpose. There is a goal in your journey, and your overflowing creativity has a crucible, a container, to weave and pour itself into. Containers are created for the flow of life to manifest abundantly and without ceasing. These names, forms, and meanings anchor your body, Ka, and Ba into the three-dimensional world.

Feeling Ka and Sekhem, you experience the union of personal power with divine will to create abundance, empowerment, more passion, and love.

Feeling the shadow Shew in Sekhem, you experience reservoirs of creativity, potential, imagination, and power waiting to be tapped into and released dynamically. You use the resistance, heaviness, and veils of the shadow to fuel your transformation and creative outpourings, using it as fuel to liberate even more energy. Anger becomes fuel for bliss; fear becomes strength, and greed becomes contentment.

Feeling the Ab heart in Sekhem, you feel the joyful aliveness of life course through you, enlivening and empowering your heart, connecting you and others in giving and sharing.

Feeling the Ba soul playing with Sekhem, you feel light and life force merge to create ecstasy in your whole being, circulating throughout every part of you. You feel the pulse of life and enter the web of life, the heartbeat of existence.

In Sahu Sekhem, you experience your body as blissfully loving and vast, full, empty, and golden.

In Akhu Sekhem, you unite with Source and the transformative power. You transform everything wherever you go.

## Looking through Sahu: Universal Body

Seeing the Khat or physical body in Sahu, you recognize it as incorruptible and as containing the universe within it.

Seeing Ren in Sahu, you know everything within the universe of your body is sacred, interconnected, and as codes of light.

Seeing Ka in Sahu, you see the individual spark of God in all life. You experience your individual self as the same self found in all beings.

You experience the interconnection of yourself with all life as an individual being.

Seeing the shadow Shew in Sahu, you experience the part of yourself that is exploring that which has not yet been explored, while simultaneously knowing you have already explored it.

Seeing Ab heart in Sahu, you appreciate the laws that keep you in alignment with order, beauty, and love. You are holy, good, and true, in integrity with all universal laws.

The Ba soul in Sahu appreciates and uses this individualized and useful vehicle to experience and express more.

In Sekhem Sahu, you are the movement of life force that flows through the universe, the life force of bliss and deep drunken love that overwhelms all else.

In Akhu Sahu, you experience yourself as all that is.

## Looking through Akhu: The Shining One

In the physical body Khat that it is, Akhu has created a temple of love to enjoy life and its experiences, to enjoy earthly delight, to experience limitation and the limitless, to experience that you live in all things and make that conscious through the gift of the body. You experience that matter delights in spirit as spirit delights in matter.

In Ka, Akhu creates different versions of itself to play with, and to connect with others and all life. Akhu marvels at itself, and all the different bodies it creates in order to have relationships with the infinite different versions of itSelf.

In Ren, Akhu sees and simultaneously creates the structures of perception that give the formless form. Akhu understands that forms are like clothes: it wears different robes at different times to suit different purposes. Akhu names each form to give it a meaning, and then dissolves this name and meaning for more delight. Akhu uses these tools to play in both form and formless, reveling in each one, enjoying the diversity and richness of all the experiences it can create.

In its shadow, Akhu creates a bridge for the temporary parts of itself as a playground to reveal the power and proportion of creativity. In its shadow, Akhu creates a veil to experience the maze of experience and the infinite threads of self-connecting love, the infinite facets that create its wholeness.

Looking at the Ab with a kind eye, Akhu creates appreciation, praise, and gratitude, which make the finite yearn and rise to the infinite.

In the Ba part of its purity, Akhu creates a pure yet diluted reflection of its own glory, a spark of its own flame, a vehicle for its transport in the many worlds.

In Sekhem, Akhu wields its power to create and destroy when a form has outlived its usefulness. Creating and destroying at the same time, all of creation blinks in and out of existence every nanosecond. Vibrating so fast it is still, birthing continually, expanding forever, Sekhem and Sahu kiss and merge, spawning new worlds, stars, and galaxies of life.

In Sahu, Akhu rests in the extending of its manifest Self, outward, inward, above, and below. I Am That I Am, and I Am all This. Then this identity too dissolves.

*When there is no "I" left, then the I Am reveals in all its glory: the*
   *Sovereign Independent Self: Sahu.*

*I Am does not reveal unless all aspects of the "I" have been dissolved, seen,*
   *and let go of.*

*All suffering comes from this sense of "I."*
*This is the truth behind all traditions, all teachings in all times.*

*Do not add: take away.*
*What is left?*

*You are empty*
*You have no need*
*Need makes the "I"*
*Relationship proves the "I" and can also bring about its dissolution into*
*    Union, a Union that has nobody involved in it.*

*Where is there interdependence, when there is no "I"?*
*How am I connected to you, when there is no you?*

*How can there be any real relationship and Union,*
*Except when there is no one left to relate to?*

*We only truly relate in the emptiness:*
*We are the Tribe of No Identity.*

*"I" creates all suffering everywhere.*
*All evil, all duality arises from this idea of "I."*

*If this is cognized, you step off the wheel of life and death.*
*This is where I Am resides.*

*In the spaciousness of emptiness, where "I" has died,*
*I Am rises, always and ever present.*

*When all else has gone,*
*All places, ideas, beliefs, and perceptions,*
*I Am remains.*

*AHAM.*

# ACKNOWLEDGMENTS

This book started and ended on the Big Island of Hawaii, the lava-filled land of sacred soul fire, a parcel of ancient Lemuria. The Big Island is connected through ley lines, latitude, and sacred geometry to Egypt, and its influence is felt here at this volcanic island that is birthing liquid earth and new life each and every day. This book was written in the presence of the volcano, the whales and shark guardians, the sacred mountain of Mauna Kea and Mauna Loa, and the placental Lake Waiaua. The Kahuna devas and spirits also assisted, as did friends willing to burn through their illusions and go through the practices.

Thank you to all the artists involved in this book, who gave generously of their time, energy, and craftsmanship with their art.

Thank you to David Andor, my gifted Web designer, graphic artist, book formatter, and the most patient person I have ever met with my requests at bizarre times for art and Web design; thank you for being so gracious and putting up with me, David (www.wavesource.com).

Thank you to my friends Amaya and Don Wood Dubois for their loving generosity, their great art and art guidance, and wonderful home and hospitality (www.audreywood.com).

Thank you to Ishka Jah for her amazing cover and openness in creating it with me. For more of her work and for prints of the cover, visit www.ishkanexus.etsy.com.

Thank you to Bonny Hut for her generous sharing of her profound and archetypal work from her art gallery in Melbourne (www.bonny-hut.com).

Thank you to John Reid for his beautiful renderings of Egyptian sound patterns with his patented Cymascope, a machine that photographs sound (www.cymascope.com).

I also thank Jim Channon and José Argüelles for their work and illustrations, as well as anybody else I have missed.

Thank you to Araya Anra, for her copy editing interspersed with pictures of her beautiful son Bennue Thank you to Ja-lene Clark, for her big heart and assistance with this book.

Last but certainly not least, my thanks go to Pele, the goddess of the volcano, my friend, lover, and nurturer; to Ma'at, goddess of harmony, order, and justice; to Gaia herself, and to the Mother in all her forms, who was behind the revealing of this wisdom.

Padma Aon
Hawaii
January 19, 2009

# RESOURCES

As part of the Nine Eyes resources, I have recorded spoken word in the sacred languages to communicate the essence of Sahu and Akhu.

## The Song of Freedom by Mahatma Dattatreya

The Song of Freedom was originally written and "sung" by Mahatma Dattatreya in India thousands of years ago. It is perhaps one of the purest, most direct, and most eloquent expressions of awakening ever recorded. Dattatreya was known as an Avadhuta, one naked and free of all illusion, needing nothing, living in simple clarity. He was said to be a full embodiment of God or Hu. Beings like this rarely if ever incarnate.

His song is what accompanied Padma Aon in his two months of samadhi, where Padma lived, breathed, and walked in the drunken bliss space of Hu from where this song arises.

The seven chapters of the Song of Freedom can also be called the Song of Oneness. Direct, uncompromising, needing no explanation and few words to even point towards it, the message is clear. Spoken in Sanskrit by Padma, it carries an authentic ring of transmission from one who has experienced it fully. It is a space beyond words, lived in those with no idea of self: an unconditioned awareness, the state of Sahu and Akhu.

The Song of Freedom is a pointer for those who wish to become truth realized. Neither happy nor sad, loving or not loving, truth stands as reality beyond any and all ideas about what is or should be.

The original Sanskrit carries the poetry and rhythm of the realization that Dattatreya embodied. The English is a mental reminder to you, yet it is the Sanskrit that carries the transmission of the Absolute

Consciousness for you to dissolve into, meditate with, and take with you as you move through the world in your days.

The Song of Freedom is available in the "Audio" section of www.christblueprint.com.

# FURTHER READING

Perhaps the most important bodies for humanity to learn about, heal, and integrate are the shadow, the soul, and the Ka. In this book these bodies are written about extensively, and an entire book is devoted to the Ab and Ba in the form of *The Christ Blueprint*. Indeed, each of the Nine Bodies is a book unto itself, so vast are the realms implied in the Egyptian understanding of life. In a series of books and experiential teachings, I am outlining much of this wisdom, wisdom designed to accelerate evolution and consciousness on earth into a holographic understanding of life, with the practical means of how to access it and work with it.

To deepen your understanding of the Nine Bodies, read:

Ab and Ba: Padma Aon Prakasha, *The Christ Blueprint* (Berkeley, CA: North Atlantic Books, 2010).

Sekhem: Padma Aon Prakasha, *The Power of Shakti* (Rochester, VT: Inner Traditions, 2009).

Ren: Padma Aon Prakasha, *Holographic Communication* (forthcoming).

Akhu and Sahu: Mahatma Dattatreya, *Dattatreya's Song of the Avadhut* (Olympia, WA: Atma, 2000).

Khat and Aufu: Michio Sankey, *Support the Mountain: Nutrition for Expanded Consciousness* (Kapolei, HI: White Mountain Castle, 2008).

The Technosphere: José Argüelles, *Time and The Technosphere: The Law of Time in Human Affairs* (Rochester, VT: Bear, 2002).

For wisdom from Thoth, read:

Drunvalo Melchizedek, *The Ancient Secret of the Flower of Life, Vols. 1 and 2* (Flagstaff, AZ: Light Technology, 1999); www.spiritmythos.org.

For Overviews on the Nine Bodies:

Rowena Pattee Kryder, *Robes of Light: The Nine Egyptian Light Bodies Embodied in Modern Experience* (Lithia Springs, GA: New Leaf, 2005).

Normandi Ellis, *Dreams of Isis: A Woman's Spiritual Sojourn* (Adyar, India: Quest, 1997).

Robert E Cox, *Creating the Soul Body* (Rochester, VT: Inner Traditions, 2008).

Normandi Ellis, *Awakening Osiris* (Newburyport, MA: Red Wheel, 2009).

*The Egyptian Books of Coming Forth by Day,* also known as *The Books of the Dead.*


I thank Tehuti, Anpu, Ma'at, Ast, and the Sirian Lords of Light, the great winged lions of myth and legend who helped establish many of earth's more advanced cultures and teachings across the Near and Far East, from Turkey to Egypt. The prophecy surrounding them is that when they are seen again, the world will transform. In this time, they are being seen again.


Amun

Amun

Amun

# ABOUT THE AUTHOR

Padma Aon Prakasha is an enlightening twenty-first century guide and author. He teaches worldwide and has led initiatory pilgrimages to sacred sites in fifteen countries over the last ten years.

Prakasha started early on his path. After being initiated into the Brahmin lineage at age two, he read the Bhagavad Gita at age four, followed by the Koran and the Bible by age seven. When he was twenty-one he had an experience of God Consciousness that changed his life forever. Shortly after this, he was initiated into Saivite Tantra through the Head Priests of Kedarnath and Pashupatinath in India, and into the Sama Veda through the Arunachala sampradaya. Other initiations came through Sri Om, a Tibetan Buddhist teacher in the Lineage of Tsongkhapa and Maitreya in London, after which Prakasha sat in the highest form of meditation, samadhi, for two months continuously.

Padma is a priest in the Order of Melchizedek and an initiate of the ancient Egyptian lineages; he has led several profound initiatory tours in Egypt. Using ancient Egyptian sound as the basis for this alchemical work, Padma has revived the ancient Ceremonies of Ma'at, the truthful heart, as well as other key teachings lost in time. Padma combines all of his lineage teachings and skills to become a catalyst for rapid growth and egoic dissolution in a universal manner.

As a globally distributed music performer, Prakasha has produced two world music albums for the label Sub Rosa/BMG: *Rhythmic Intelligence* and *Song of Light,* as well as the forthcoming *Life Cycles,* based on the book *Womb Wisdom.* He has appeared on BBC TV, Dutch TV and Radio One, and in *XLR8R, Straight no chaser,* and *Variety* magazines, to name a few. He currently lives in the Greek Islands with his beloved wife, Anaiya.

Padma is the author of *The Power of Shakti, The Christ Blueprint,* and the forthcoming *Womb Wisdom* with Anaiya.

Discover more about the Nine Eyes of Light and all of Padma's and Anaiya's music and teachings at www.christblueprint.com or www.padmaaon.com.